D0777390

# SCALING PROCEDURES

To Susan and Claire
Rick Netemeyer
To Patti, Anna, Wallace, and their families
Bill Bearden
To my parents
Subhash Sharma

# SCALING PROCEDURES

*Issues and Applications*

**Richard G. Netemeyer**
*University of Virginia*

**William O. Bearden**
*University of South Carolina*

**Subhash Sharma**
*University of South Carolina*

**SAGE** Publications
*International Educational and Professional Publisher*
Thousand Oaks ▪ London ▪ New Delhi

Copyright © 2003 by Sage Publications, Inc.

All rights reserved. No part of this book may be reproduced or utilized in any form or by any means, electronic or mechanical, including photocopying, recording, or by any information storage and retrieval system, without permission in writing from the publisher.

*For information:*

Sage Publications, Inc.
2455 Teller Road
Thousand Oaks, California 91320
E-mail: order@sagepub.com

Sage Publications Ltd.
6 Bonhill Street
London EC2A 4PU
United Kingdom

Sage Publications India Pvt. Ltd.
B-42 Panchsheel Enclave
New Delhi 110 017 India

Printed in the United States of America

**Library of Congress Cataloging-in-Publication Data**

Netemeyer, Richard G., 1956-
Scaling procedures: Issues and applications /
Richard G. Netemeyer, William O. Bearden, Subhash Sharma.
    p. cm.
Includes bibliographical references and index.
ISBN 0-7619-2026–9 (c)—ISBN 0-7619-2027-7 (p)
    1. Scaling (Social sciences) I. Bearden, William O., 1945-
II. Sharma, Subhash. III. Title.
H61.27 .N48 2003
300.′7′2—dc21                    2002014928

This book is printed on acid-free paper.

03   04   05   06   07   10   9   8   7   6   5   4   3   2   1

| | |
|---|---|
| *Acquisitions Editor:* | Al Bruckner |
| *Editorial Assistant:* | MaryAnn Vail |
| *Copy Editor:* | A. J. Sobczak |
| *Production Editor:* | Diane S. Foster |
| *Typesetter:* | C&M Digitals (P) Ltd. |
| *Proofreader:* | Scott Oney |
| *Indexer:* | Molly Hall |
| *Cover Designer:* | Sandy Sauvajot |

# CONTENTS

# ACKNOWLEDGMENTS

The authors would like to thank the following people for their helpful comments on earlier drafts of this text: David Hardesty, Ajith Kumar, Ken Manning, Susan Netemeyer, Ed Rigdon, Eric Spangenberg, and Kelley Tepper Tian. We would also like to express our sincere appreciation to A. J. Sobczak for his assistance in editing and improving this text.

# FOREWORD

—•◦•—

Effective measurement is a cornerstone of scientific research. There are several strategies for developing and refining measures, and the relevance of a given strategy will depend on what type of scientific phenomenon is being measured. In this book, we focus on developing and validating measures of latent social-psychological constructs. Given their latent nature, these constructs represent abstractions that can be assessed only indirectly. The indirect assessment of these constructs is accomplished via self-report/paper-and-pencil measures on which multiple items or indicators are used to measure the construct, that is, "scaling" a construct. The purpose of our book is to discuss issues involved in developing and validating multi-item scales of self-report/ paper-and-pencil measures.

In Chapter 1, we emphasize the importance of theory in scale development and briefly overview the concepts of dimensionality, reliability, and validity. We also offer a four-step approach for scale development that encompasses these three concepts. The book then proceeds with individual chapters regarding scale dimensionality (Chapter 2), reliability (Chapter 3), and validity (Chapter 4). Chapters 5, 6, and 7 elaborate on the four-step approach and offer empirical examples relevant to each step. The four-step approach is consistent with much of the extant scale development literature (Churchill, 1979; Clark & Watson, 1995; DeVellis, 1991; Haynes, Nelson, & Blaine, 1999; Nunnally & Bernstein, 1994; Spector, 1992). We are certainly indebted to the many authors who have proposed appropriate scale development procedures and/or described quality scale development endeavors. As the readers of this book undoubtedly will realize, the recommended steps, as well as the overlapping activities assumed to constitute each step, are offered as a logical, sequential process; however, the process of scale development may well be an iterative and ongoing procedure in which restarts are required as researchers learn from their efforts/mistakes and revisions are needed in such steps as conceptual definition, item generation, and defining construct dimensionality.

# ONE

# INTRODUCTION
# AND OVERVIEW

———•••———

## PURPOSE OF THE BOOK

Measurement is at the heart of virtually all scientific endeavors. Measures, and the psychometric properties used to evaluate them, will vary by the type of measurement undertaken and the context and goals of the scientific endeavor. There are several strategies for developing and refining measurement/assessment instruments, and the relevance of a given strategy will depend on what type of scientific phenomenon is being assessed and its underlying measurement model. In this book, we focus on developing and validating paper-and-pencil measures of latent social-psychological constructs. Furthermore, the constructs focused upon are perceptual; a respondent rates himself or herself or others on constructs that are subjective or opinion-based. Mental/ability testing and classification measurement for clinical diagnosis are not an emphasis of this text. Although several of the principles of mental/ability testing and measurement for clinical diagnosis are applied in developing and validating social-psychological measures, such as classical test theory and generalizability theory, other principles more akin to ability/mental testing and clinical diagnosis are not emphasized. (The interested reader is referred to Anastasi and Urbina [1998], Crocker and Algina [1986], Hambleton, Swaminathin, and Rogers [1991], Haynes, Nelson, and Blaine [1999], and Kaplan and Saccuzzo [1997] for a discussion of mental/ability testing and clinical diagnosis.)

Given their latent nature, the constructs we focus on represent abstractions that can be assessed only indirectly. The indirect assessment of these constructs is accomplished via self-report/paper-and-pencil measures on which multiple items or indicators are used to measure the construct, that is, "scaling" a construct. Although measurement of psychological constructs also involves "classification," that is, defining whether objects fall in the same or different categories with respect to a given attribute, this text is on scaling. As such, the purpose of this book is to discuss the issues involved in developing and validating multi-item scales of self-report/paper-and-pencil measures.

## PERSPECTIVES ON MEASUREMENT
## IN THE SOCIAL SCIENCES

### What Is Measurement?

At its core, measurement consists of rules for assigning symbols to objects to numerically represent quantities of attributes. Measurement includes evaluating numbers such that they reflect the differing degrees of the attribute being assessed (DeVellis, 1991; Haynes et al., 1999; Nunnally & Bernstein, 1994). In the social sciences, most of the time the "objects" are people, "rules" involve the explicitly stated assignment of numbers, and "attributes" are particular features of the objects being measured. As such, it is important to note that objects (e.g., people) are not measured; their attributes are measured (e.g., self-esteem).

Rules of measurement require a bit more explanation. Some rules are obvious and universal, such as measuring weight in pounds or kilograms. Rules for measuring social-psychological constructs are not so obvious. For example, what are appropriate rules for measuring constructs such as self-esteem, job satisfaction, and consumer self-confidence? Although there are no "universal" rules for measuring such constructs, developing rules that are eventually accepted is important for standardization and establishing norms. A measure is standardized when (a) rules of measurement are clear, (b) it is practical to apply, (c) it is not demanding of the administrator or respondent, and (d) results do not depend on the administrator (Nunnally & Bernstein, 1994). Such a measure yields similar results across applications (i.e., the measure is reliable) and offers scores that can be easily interpreted as low, medium, and high.

The focus on measuring attributes also requires clarification. As stated, we are not measuring a person per se; we are measuring his or her attributes. This distinction is important because it emphasizes the abstract nature of social-psychological measurement. That is, we must "abstract" the attribute from the person. Many studies in the social sciences attempt to determine the relationship between two attributes (e.g., self-esteem and need for achievement). To avoid confounding among related attributes, the exact nature of the attribute must be carefully determined and specified. Furthermore, an assessment must be made if the attribute can be measured at all. As noted by Nunnally and Bernstein (1994), some attributes are so abstract that they may not be amenable to measurement (e.g., clairvoyance).

## Usefulness of Social Science Measures

What properties constitute a measure's usefulness? As previously stated, there are multiple criteria (psychometric properties) that are used to evaluate measures. The criteria that are most relevant depend on the goals of the assessment and the scientific endeavor undertaken. Given that our text focuses on scaling latent social-psychological constructs, we focus on those psychometric properties most applicable to such constructs.

Although differing opinions exist, one view that seems to be shared by most social scientists is that results based on a measure should be repeatable and that the measure itself is standardized. *Repeatability* and *standardization* are related concepts. Under similar circumstances, a research finding based on the same measure should replicate. This is the basic tenet of repeatability—that the measure performs reliably under similar testing conditions.

Sound psychometric procedures for scale development include establishing norms. When these norms can be interpreted as describing a person as low, medium, or high on an attribute, the measure is felt to be standardized. Standardization has several advantages.

First, although we measure perceptions that by their very nature are subjective, a standardized measure enhances social science objectivity. When one researcher can independently verify a relation between two constructs that was found by another researcher, objectivity is enhanced—given the measures used are the same and are standardized. If disagreement exists as to the appropriateness of the measures used in obtaining the finding, objectivity is compromised. In the social sciences, we often test theories, but a theory can be tested adequately only to the extent that the attributes of the theory (constructs) are adequately measured. When agreed upon procedures exist for measuring the attributes of interest, the objectivity of theory tests is enhanced.

Second, standardization produces quantifiable numerical results. Again, though this text does not address classification per se, such quantification does allow for the creation of categories (e.g., low, medium, high) for mathematical and statistical analyses (ANOVA), or for use as factor levels in experimental designs. Quantification also enhances communication and generalizability of results. Knowledge accumulates in the social sciences when researchers compare their results with the results of previous studies. When the same, standardized measures are used across scientific applications, results termed as "low" in self-esteem or "high" in self-esteem have common meaning across researchers. This enhances both the communication of results and generalizability of findings.

Third, measure/scale development is a time-consuming endeavor. If a measure has been well developed, however, the time spent is also time "well spent." Once standardization occurs, the measure is available for use with little or no time invested because of its agreed upon standards. At the very heart of repeatability and standardization are the measurement properties of *reliability* and *validity*. These two concepts are elaborated upon later in this chapter and extensively discussed and examined in Chapters 3 through 7.

## Scaling of Latent Psychological Constructs With Multiple Items

As we have previously stated, social scientists focus on measuring attributes of objects that tend to be abstract. Such abstractions are latent by nature. Latent constructs are not directly observable or quantifiable. A latent construct is also variable; that is, the strength and magnitude for the ratings on a latent construct may change over time. For example, need for achievement represents a latent construct (i.e., a personal attribute). It cannot be observed directly by a researcher and thus requires a scale to estimate its actual magnitude at a given point in time. Furthermore, an individual's level of need for achievement may change over time.

Our text also focuses on latent social-psychological constructs that are theoretical in nature. That is, the construct being measured is embedded in a theoretical framework and/or has theoretical underpinnings. For example, the construct of job satisfaction is at the center of theories of employee turnover (e.g., Tett & Meyer, 1993) and is concerned with its own theoretical content domain, for example, satisfaction with pay, satisfaction with supervisors, and satisfaction with coworkers. Conversely, some constructs are either empirical or atheoretical in nature. Opinion polls oftentimes assess purely empirical constructs. We are not suggesting that such constructs and measurement approaches have little value in the social sciences. In fact, they may prove useful for theory development. For example, an opinion poll (empirical and likely atheoretical) assessing political liberalism-conservatism and favoring or not favoring gun control could reveal that those who are politically liberal favor gun control more than those who are politically conservative, leading to the theoretical proposition that liberals favor gun control. We are merely stating that constructs based in theory are the focus of this text.

It is generally agreed that measures of latent theoretical constructs require multiple items or statements to more accurately reveal the varying levels of the constructs; that is, are scaled (Clark & Watson, 1995; DeVellis, 1991; Haynes, Richard, & Kubany, 1995; Nunnally & Bernstein, 1994). Again, given that an object's (person's) level on an attribute that is latent and psychologically abstract cannot be directly measured, a scale must be constructed. Although sometimes it may be possible to infer a level of a latent psychological construct via behavior (e.g., from repeated brand purchase, one infers that an individual believes the brand is a good value for the money [latent construct]), many times a behavior may not be indicative of a latent construct. In such cases, a well-constructed and validated multi-item paper-and-pencil scale of the construct is needed.

Finally, we would like to reiterate that scaling, and not indexing, is our focus. In scaling, scores on items in the scale are theoretically driven by the latent construct; that is, they are "reflected" by the latent construct. With an index, scores on items (indicators) drive the total score of the index; that is, the items/indicators "form" the constructed index score. Although still latent in many respects, formative items/indicators are not considered scales because their scores are not necessarily reflected by the latent construct. An often-used example of formative items/indicators that result in an index is socioeconomic status (SES). Items or indicators might include income, education level, occupation, and dwelling type. Although some of these indicators have the latent property of not being directly observable, their scores are considered "forming" the index of SES and not vice versa (reflective). For a more detailed discussion of "formative" vs. "reflective" measures, the interested reader is referred to Bollen and Lennox (1991), Diamantopoulus and Winklhofer (2001), MacCallum and Browne (1993), and Smith and McCarthy (1995).

## Recent Trends in Scaling Latent Psychological Constructs

As succinctly stated by Clark and Watson (1995), "Scale development remains a growth industry within psychology" (p. 309). This statement applies to all related fields in the social sciences, including business functional areas such as marketing, accounting, management information systems, strategic management, and organizational behavior. In fact, several recent texts that have compiled scales often used in marketing and organizational behavior are now available (e.g., Bearden & Netemeyer, 1998; Bruner & Hensel, 1997; Price & Mueller, 1986; Robinson, Shaver, & Wrightsman, 1991). Two primary factors account for the recent interest in scale development.

First, as theories in the social sciences develop and evolve, so does the need to test them objectively. These theories require operationalizations of the constructs of interest. When the constructs are measured well (reliably and validly), theory testing is enhanced. Furthermore, it is often found that a once-used scale needs to be updated or refined to better reflect a construct of interest. Many measurement articles in the social sciences represent new scales, derived from existing measures, that are felt to more accurately or more efficiently reflect constructs of interest. Second, the advancement of computer and software technology has greatly helped our ability to develop measures. Statistical packages such as SPSS, SAS, BMDP, LISREL, EQS, CALIS, and AMOS, as well as their increased "user friendliness," have made it easier and quicker to perform most of the basic and many of the more advanced analyses recommended in scale development. It should be noted that there is a caveat here. Computer technology and statistical packages may allow for quicker scale development, but not necessarily better scale development. The recommended procedures advocated in this text and other books and articles should be adhered to in developing psychometrically sound scales (Clark & Watson, 1995; DeVellis, 1991; Haynes et al., 1999; Haynes et al., 1995; Nunnally & Bernstein, 1994; Spector, 1992).

Not only has there been a trend toward more scales, but the procedures used to develop and validate scales also have been evolving. Aided by the advances in the previously listed statistical packages, comprehensive and elaborate tests of scale dimensionality, method effects, and variance partitioning have become apparent (cf. Bearden & Netemeyer, 1998). A more pronounced concern for content and face validity of items early in the development stage, as well as scale length considerations, are evident as well (Clark & Watson, 1995; Haynes et al., 1995). Although around for some time, generalizability theory (G-Theory) is now being more frequently applied in scale development and validation (Marcoulides, 1998; Shavelson & Webb, 1991). All these issues (i.e., dimensionality, face and content validity, scale length, and G-Theory) are addressed in this text.

## LATENT CONSTRUCTS

As previously stated, latent constructs are not directly observable or quantifiable, and scores on measures of latent constructs may be variable. That is, the strength and magnitude for the scores may change over time. There is a seemingly endless array of latent constructs in the social sciences, ranging from those that are very broad, such as "extraversion" of the Big Five personality traits, to more narrow constructs that may be considered subcomponents of broader constructs, such as "talkativeness" as a subcomponent of extraversion (Clark & Watson, 1995). As such, latent constructs require a thoughtful elaboration regarding the level of abstraction and specificity.

### Theory and Validity

The importance of theory in developing measures of latent constructs cannot be overstated. In their classic works on measurement and validity, Cronbach and Meehl (1955) and Loevinger (1957) eloquently stated the importance of theory in measurement. For measures of a latent construct to have relevance in the social sciences, the latent construct should be grounded in a theoretical framework. Even narrowly abstracted constructs based in theory are more useful as antecedents or consequences of other latent constructs or behaviors when embedded in theory. As such, a latent construct's relevance to the social sciences depends greatly on the theories in which it is couched. In other words, what does the latent construct of interest predict, and/or what predicts the latent construct? These relationships have been referred to as a latent construct's "nomological net" (Cronbach & Meehl, 1955).

Theory is concerned not only with the latent construct of interest but with the validity of the measurement of the construct as well. The two, theory and validity, are intertwined: The relevance of a latent construct largely depends on its "construct validity." Simply stated, construct validity is an assessment of the degree to which a measure actually measures the latent construct it is intended to measure. Cronbach and Meehl (1955) stated that demonstrating construct validity involves at least three steps: (a) specifying a set of theoretical constructs and their relations (a theory), (b) developing methods to measure the constructs of the theory, and (c) empirically testing how well manifest (observable) indicators (items) measure the constructs in the theory and testing the hypothesized relations among the constructs of theory as well (i.e., the nomological net). Furthermore, assessing construct validity is an ongoing process. One study supporting a construct's validity is not enough to conclude that the measure has been validated. Multiple tests and applications over time are required, and some of these may require a refinement of the construct itself, as well as its measure. As stated by Clark and Watson (1995), "The most precise and efficient measures are those with established construct validity; they are manifestations of constructs in an articulated theory that is well supported by empirical data" (p. 310).

### Importance of the Literature Review

A well-grounded theory begins with conceptualizations based on a thorough review of the literature. Such literature reviews serve two important purposes. (We will elaborate upon the importance of the literature review later in this text, as it is considered a key issue in scale development. For now, only two broad points are mentioned.) First, a literature review should alert the researcher to previous attempts to conceptualize the construct of interest and theories in which the construct may prove useful as an independent or dependent variable. As such, a more precise conceptualization of the construct, its boundaries and content domain, and potential antecedents and consequences can be uncovered. A rigorous literature review also will indicate past attempts at measuring the construct and the strengths and weaknesses of such attempts.

Second, given that scale development and validation is a time-consuming and sometimes costly endeavor, a thorough literature review should help answer the following question: Is a scale needed at all? If good measures of a construct already exist, the value of a new measure may be small relative to the costs involved in development. A new measure should show some theoretical or empirical advantage over existing measures of the same construct to be useful. In fact, some authors refer to this as an aspect of "incremental validity." Given the objectives of this text, for a new scale to have incremental validity over existing measures, it should either capture the targeted construct more accurately or be more efficient (e.g., shorter, cheaper, more user friendly, easier to respond to) than existing measures. In sum, a thorough literature review can help avoid the redundancy of developing another scale to assess an already well measured construct.

## OVERVIEW OF DIMENSIONALITY, RELIABILITY, AND VALIDITY

Dimensionality, reliability, and validity are all interrelated measurement properties. What follows is a brief overview of these properties and how they are related. As emphasized above, the process of scale development starts with a thorough review of the literature in which a solid theoretical definition of the construct and its domain is delineated and outlined. This definition, and attendant description, should entail what is included in the domain of the construct, what is excluded from the construct's domain, and the a priori dimensionality of the construct's domain. The theoretical definition, the domain of the construct, and dimensionality should be derived from a thorough review of the existing literature and, ideally, expert opinion. In essence, the construct's definition and content domain determine theoretical dimensionality.

### Dimensionality

A measure's dimensionality is concerned with the homogeneity of items. Basically, a measure that is considered unidimensional has statistical properties demonstrating that its items underlie a single construct or factor. When the measure is multidimensional, items tap more than one dimension or factor. A construct's domain can be hypothesized as unidimensional, as multidimensional, and/or as a higher-order factor. Thus, the scale (or subscales/factors) used to operationalize the construct should reflect the hypothesized dimensionality. Given that scale (factor) unidimensionality is considered prerequisite to reliability and validity, assessment of unidimensionality should be paramount (Cortina, 1993; Gerbing & Anderson, 1988; Hattie, 1985; Schmitt, 1996).

A number of procedures have been employed to check the dimensionality of a scale (e.g., item analysis and exploratory factor analysis). One somewhat agreed upon technique is confirmatory factor analysis, in which several multi-item factors (and relations among the factors) can be specified and evaluated on criteria used to assess dimensionality (e.g., fit indices, presence of correlated measurement errors, and degree of cross-loading) (Anderson & Gerbing, 1988; Clark & Watson, 1995; Floyd & Widaman, 1995; Gerbing & Anderson, 1988; Hattie, 1985; Kumar & Dillon, 1987). Chapter 2 of this text discusses the concept of dimensionality, and later chapters offer empirical examples.

## Reliability

Reliability is concerned with that portion of measurement that is due to permanent effects that persist from sample to sample. There are two broad types of reliability referred to in the psychometric literature: (a) test-retest (temporal stability)—the correlation between the same person's score on the same set of items at two points in time; and (b) internal consistency—the inter-relatedness among items or sets of items in the scale.

*Test-retest reliability* is concerned with the stability of a respondent's item responses over time. A test-retest or "stability" coefficient usually is estimated by the magnitude of the correlation between the same measures (and sample) on different assessment occasions. If the stability coefficient is low in magnitude, with no change in the construct over time, the reliability of the measure is in doubt. Thus, test-retest reliability is useful because it offers information regarding the degree of confidence one has that the measure reflects the construct and is generalizable to other assessment occasions (Haynes et al., 1999). Interestingly, test-retest reliability has not been assessed in scale use or development as frequently as internal consistency (Robinson et al., 1991). It is unfortunate that test-retest estimates are available for so few of the scales in the social sciences, and those planning scale development work should give stronger consideration to assessing test-retest reliability in addition to using other procedures of evaluating reliability and validity.

*Internal consistency* assesses item interrelatedness. Items composing a scale (or subscale) should show high levels of internal consistency. Some commonly used criteria for assessing internal consistency are individual corrected item-to-total correlations, the average interitem correlation among scale items, and a number of reliability coefficients (Churchill, 1979; Cortina, 1993;

DeVellis, 1991; Nunnally & Bernstein, 1994; Robinson et al., 1991). The most widely used internal consistency reliability coefficient is Cronbach's (1951) coefficient alpha. (Others are briefly discussed later in this text. For now, we limit our discussion to coefficient alpha.) Although a number of rules of thumb also exist concerning what constitutes an acceptable level of coefficient alpha, scale length must be considered. As the number of items increases, alpha will tend to increase. Because parsimony is also a concern in measurement (Clark & Watson, 1995; Cortina, 1993), an important question is "How many items does it take to measure a construct?" The answer to this question depends partially on the domain and dimensions of the construct. Naturally, a construct with a wide domain and multiple dimensions will require more items to adequately tap the domain/dimensions than a construct with a narrow domain and few dimensions. Given that most scales are self-administered and that respondent fatigue and/or noncooperation need to be considered, scale brevity is often advantageous (Churchill & Peter, 1984; Cortina, 1993; DeVellis, 1991; Nunnally & Bernstein, 1994).

With the advent of structural equation modeling, other tests of internal consistency or internal structure/stability became available. Composite reliability (construct reliability), which is similar to coefficient alpha, can be calculated directly from the LISREL, CALIS, EQS, or AMOS output (cf. Fornell & Larcker, 1981). A more stringent test of internal structure/stability involves assessing the amount of variance captured by a construct's measure in relation to the amount of variance due to measurement error—the average variance extracted (AVE). By using a combination of the criteria above (i.e., corrected item-to-total correlations, examining the average interitem correlation, coefficient alpha, composite reliability, and AVE), scales can be developed in an efficient manner without sacrificing internal consistency.

## Construct Validity

Construct validity refers to how well a measure actually measures the construct it is intended to measure. Construct validity is the ultimate goal in the development of an assessment instrument and encompasses all evidence bearing on a measure (Haynes et al., 1999). Some disagreement exists as to the classification of and types of validity that fall under the rubric of construct validity. Still, many researchers believe that translation (content and face), convergent, discriminant, criterion-related (or predictive), nomological, and known-group validity collectively represent the most frequently employed sources of construct validity. Given that all evidence bearing on a measure contributes to establishing construct validity, a measure must also a priori exhibit its theoretical dimensionality and show evidence of reliability to be considered valid. As such, dimensionality and reliability are necessary but insufficient conditions for construct validity. Again, a number of procedures exist for establishing construct validity. Although these are expanded upon throughout the remainder of the text, we offer a brief discussion of each validity type.

*Translation validity* is concerned with the content of items; two subtypes have been delineated—content and face validity. The term *content validity* has been defined in many ways, with most definitions stressing that a measure's items are a proper sample of the theoretical domain of the construct (Messick, 1993; Nunnally & Bernstein, 1994). Most definitions are consistent with the following: Content validity reflects "the degree to which elements of an assessment instrument are relevant to and representative of the targeted construct for a particular assessment purpose" (Haynes et al., 1995, p. 238). "Elements" refer to the content of individual items, response formats, and instructions to respondents, and "representativeness" refers to the degree to which the elements are proportional to the facets (domains) of the targeted construct and to the degree that the entire domain of the targeted construct has been sampled. That is, the items should appear consistent with the theoretical domain of the construct in all respects, including response formats and instructions. In developing scales that are content valid, it is generally recommended that a number of items be generated that "tap the domain of the construct," that the items be screened by judges with expertise in the literature, and that pilot tests on samples from relevant populations be conducted to trim and refine the pool of items (DeVellis, 1991; Robinson et al., 1991). Haynes et al. (1995) offer an excellent description of procedures for establishing content validity that are elaborated upon in Chapters 3 through 7.

*Face validity* has been referred to as the "mere appearance that a measure has validity" (Kaplan & Saccuzzo, 1997, p. 132). Although the terms "face validity" and "content validity" have been used interchangeably, some argue that face validity should be separate from content validity (Anastasi & Urbina, 1998; Nevo, 1985). Others go a bit further and delineate face from content validity in terms of researcher and respondent. A highly face valid instrument enhances its use in practical situations by (among other things) inducing cooperation of respondents via ease of use, proper reading level, clarity, easily read instructions, and easy-to-use response formats. A somewhat accepted definition of face validity implies that an instrument or test, when used "in a practical situation should, in addition to having pragmatic or statistical validity, appear practical, pertinent and related to the purposes of the instrument [test] as well; i.e., it should not only *be* valid, but it should *also appear* valid to respondents" (Nevo, 1985, p. 287). Thus, face validity may be more concerned with what respondents from relevant populations infer with respect to what is being measured.

*Convergent* validity refers to the degree to which two measures designed to measure the same construct are related. Convergence is found if the two different measures of the same construct are highly correlated. *Discriminant* validity assesses the degree to which two measures designed to measure similar, but conceptually different, constructs are related. A low to moderate correlation is often considered evidence of discriminant validity. Multitrait-multimethod matrices (MTMM) have often been used to assess convergent and discriminant validity where maximally different measurement methods (i.e., self-report vs. observational) are required (Campbell & Fiske, 1959; Churchill, 1979; Peter, 1979, 1981). Later in this text, we offer an MTMM example and a structural equation modeling approach to examine discriminant validity (e.g., Anderson & Gerbing, 1988; Fornell & Larcker, 1981).

*Nomological* validity has been defined as the degree to which predictions from a formal theoretical network containing the concept under scrutiny are confirmed (Campbell, 1960). It assesses the degree to which constructs that are theoretically related are empirically related (i.e., their measures correlate significantly in the predicted direction). Guidelines for establishing nomological validity also exist but have been criticized as well (Peter, 1981). As with internal consistency and convergent and discriminant validation, structural equation packages recently have been used to assess nomological validity of scale measures. Several books (e.g., Bollen, 1989; Byrne, 2001; Hayduk, 1996; Hoyle, 1995; Schumacker & Lomax, 1996) and articles (e.g., Anderson & Gerbing, 1988; Bagozzi, Yi, & Phillips, 1991; Bentler & Chou, 1987) illustrate modeling techniques, evaluative criteria, and guidelines for what constitutes nomological validity.

Definitions of *criterion-related validity* vary, and some definitions are similar to the definitions of other validity types. For example, criterion-related validity has been referred to as the degree to which a measure covaries with previously validated or "gold-standard" measures of the same constructs (Haynes et al., 1999). This definition is similar to that of convergent validity.

Criterion-related validity also has been referred to as the extent to which a measure corresponds to another measure of interest (Kaplan & Saccuzzo, 1997). Some contend that criterion-related validity is the same as *predictive validity*—the functional form or relation between a predictor and a criterion before, during, or after a predictor is applied (Nunnally & Bernstein, 1994). Such an approach is based on the temporal relation of the predictor and its criterion, that is, "post-dictive," "concurrent," and "predictive" validity. What most definitions have in common is that criterion-related validity is assessed by a theoretically specified pattern of relations between a measure and a criterion often referred to as a validity coefficient. Chapter 4 further explores criterion-related validity.

*Known-group validity* involves the measure's ability to distinguish reliably between groups of people that should score high on the trait and low on the trait. As examples, a person who is truly conservative should score significantly higher on a conservatism scale than a person who is liberal, and salespeople in the retail car business and large computer business should differ in their levels of customer orientation (Saxe & Weitz, 1982). Thus, mean score differences between groups for a given construct can be used as evidence of known-group validity. An excellent application of known-group validity testing can be found in Jarvis and Petty (1996).

## OVERVIEW OF RECOMMENDED PROCEDURES AND STEPS IN SCALE DEVELOPMENT

As is clearly evidenced from the preceding pages, numerous articles and books advocate "how" to develop a scale (e.g., Churchill, 1979; Clark & Watson, 1995; DeVellis, 1991; Haynes et al., 1999; Nunnally & Bernstein, 1994; Spector, 1992). Steps and procedures vary from author to author based on the goals and purposes of the measurement. Still, most writings do share a common set of guidelines for scale development. Given our focus, the steps and procedures used to guide this text are based on scaling self-report paper-and-pencil measures of latent social-psychological constructs. Figure 1.1 offers a diagram of the steps we recommend in scale development. Each of these steps is elaborated upon in upcoming chapters. For now, we offer a brief overview of what each step entails.

**Step 1:** **Construct Definition and Content Domain**
　　　　**Issues to Consider:**
　　　　(a) The importance of clear construct definition, content domain, and the role of theory
　　　　(b) The focus on "effect" items/indicators vs. "formative" items/indicators
　　　　(c) Construct dimensionality: unidimensional, multidimensional, or a higher-order construct?

**Step 2:** **Generating and Judging Measurement Items**
　　　　**Issues to Consider:**
　　　　(a) Theoretical assumptions about items (e.g., domain sampling)
　　　　(b) Generating potential items and determining the response format
　　　　　　(1) How many items as an initial pool
　　　　　　(2) Dichotomous vs. multichotomous response formats
　　　　　　(3) Item wording issues
　　　　(c) The focus on "content" validity in relation to theoretical dimensionality
　　　　(d) Item judging (expert and layperson)—the focus on "content" and "face" validity

**Step 3:** **Designing and Conducting Studies to Develop and Refine the Scale**
　　　　**Issues to Consider:**
　　　　(a) Pilot testing as an item-trimming procedure
　　　　(b) The use of several samples from relevant populations for scale development
　　　　(c) Designing the studies to test psychometric properties
　　　　(d) Initial item analyses via exploratory factor analyses (EFAs)
　　　　(e) Initial item analyses and internal consistency estimates
　　　　(f) Initial estimates of validity
　　　　(g) Retaining items for the next set of studies

**Step 4:** **Finalizing the Scale**
　　　　**Issues to Consider:**
　　　　(a) The importance of several samples from relevant populations
　　　　(b) Designing the studies to test the various types of validity
　　　　(c) Item analyses via EFA
　　　　　　(1) The importance of EFA consistency from Step 3 to Step 4
　　　　　　(2) Deriving an initial factor structure—dimensionality and theory
　　　　(d) Item analyses and confirmatory factor analyses (CFAs)
　　　　　　(1) Testing the theoretical factor structure and model specification
　　　　　　(2) Evaluating CFA measurement models
　　　　　　(3) Factor model invariance across studies (i.e., multiple-group analyses)
　　　　(e) Additional item analyses via internal consistency estimates
　　　　(f) Additional estimates of validity
　　　　(g) Establishing norms across studies
　　　　(h Applying G-Theory

---

**Figure 1.1**     Steps in Scale Development

## Step 1: Construct Definition and Content Domain

As we have stated throughout this introductory chapter, the importance of theory in scale development cannot be overstated, and developing and refining a theory requires a thorough literature review. During the literature review and theory development processes, several issues should be stressed: (a) the importance of clear construct definition, content domain, and the role of theory; (b) a focus on "effect" or "reflective" items rather than "formative" indicators; and (c) construct dimensionality—unidimensional, multidimensional, or a higher-order construct.

## Step 2: Generating and Judging Measurement Items

This second step involves generating and judging a pool of items from which the scale will be derived. Several issues must be considered, including the following: (a) theoretical assumptions about items (e.g., domain sampling), (b) generating potential items and determining the response format (i.e., how many items as an initial pool, dichotomous vs. multichotomous response formats, and item wording issues), (c) the focus on "content" validity and its relation to theoretical dimensionality, and (d) item judging (both expert and layperson)—the focus on "content" and "face" validity.

## Step 3: Designing and Conducting
## Studies to Develop and Refine the Scale

Once a suitable pool of items has been generated and judged, empirical testing of the items on relevant samples is the next step. Issues and procedures to be considered include (a) pilot testing as an item-trimming procedure, (b) the use of several samples from relevant populations for scale development, (c) designing studies to test psychometric properties, (d) initial item analyses via exploratory factor analyses (EFAs), (e) initial item analyses and internal consistency estimates, (f) initial estimates of validity, and (g) retaining items for the next set of studies.

## Step 4: Finalizing the Scale

Several studies should be used to help finalize the scale. Many of the procedures used and issues involved in refining the scale will also be applicable to deriving the final form of the scale. These include (a) the importance of several samples from relevant populations, (b) designing the studies to test the various types of validity, (c) item analyses via EFA with a focus on the consistency of EFA results across samples from Step 3 to Step 4 in testing an initial factor structure, (d) item analyses and confirmatory factor analyses (CFAs), (e) additional item analyses via internal consistency estimates, (f) additional estimates of validity, (g) establishing norms across studies, and (h) given that numerous studies have been done across various settings, applying generalizability theory to the final form of the scale.

## SUMMARY AND PREVIEW OF THE TEXT

In this opening chapter, we have tried to provide the reader with an overview of the purpose of our text. To reiterate, our purpose is to focus on measuring latent perceptual social-psychological constructs via paper-and-pencil self-reports. For a construct to be valuable, it must have theoretical and/or practical relevance to the social scientist. Thus, a careful consideration must be made of what the construct of interest predicts and/or what predicts the construct of interest. Here, the notion of theory and "knowing" the literature is all-important. Furthermore, given the importance of measurement in the social sciences, any measure must be valid to allow for constructing confident inferences from empirical studies. Such validity rests on how well the latent construct being measured is based in theory.

Also in this opening chapter, we have overviewed the concepts of dimensionality, reliability, and validity, as well as summarized a series of steps for deriving measures with adequate psychometric properties. The remainder of our text elaborates on dimensionality, reliability, and validity, and the four steps in scale construction. Specifically, Chapter 2 discusses dimensionality, its relation to reliability and validity, and procedures for establishing dimensionality. Chapter 3 discusses reliability, its relation to validity, and procedures for establishing reliability, including G-Theory. Chapter 4 discusses validity and procedures for providing evidence of validity. Chapters 5, 6, and 7 provide detailed examples of the four steps in scale development, and Chapter 8 offers concluding remarks, with a focus on the need to constantly reevaluate constructs, their measures, and the validity of the measures.

# ⊰ TWO ⊱

# DIMENSIONALITY

————•◦•————

## INTRODUCTION

Establishing dimensionality of constructs is an important part of the scale development process. It is almost impossible to develop good measures of a construct without knowledge of the construct's dimensionality. For example, consider the task of developing a scale to measure intelligence. Does intelligence have a single facet or dimension (i.e., is it unidimensional), or does it have multiple facets or dimensions (i.e., is it multidimensional)? If intelligence is a unidimensional construct, then a single number is required to measure one's intelligence. If, however, one subscribes to Howard Gardner's theory (Gardner, 1993) that intelligence comprises the following eight dimensions—linguistic, logical, musical, spatial, kinesthetic, intrapersonal, interpersonal, and naturalistic—then measures for each of the eight dimensions are required to measure one's intelligence. Unfortunately, dimensionality has come to mean very different things to substantive researchers. The purpose of this chapter is to discuss the meaning of dimensionality of constructs and its relationship to reliability. Specifically, we will address the following two questions: (a) What is unidimensionality? and (b) Is there a distinction between the dimensionality of a construct, the dimensionality of a set of manifest items used to measure the construct, and dimensionality of manifest items used to measure the construct?

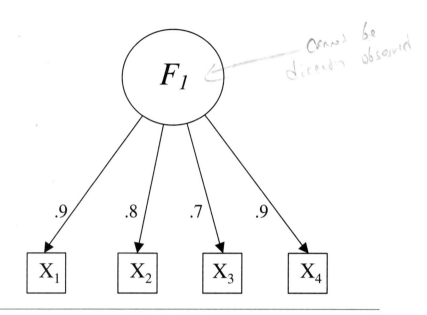

*cannbe directly observed*

**Figure 2.1** One-Factor Model

## DIMENSIONALITY OF A CONSTRUCT, ITEMS, AND A SET OF ITEMS

### Unidimensionality

Table 2.1 offers a correlation matrix for the factor (or measurement) model given in Figure 2.1. Consistent with our focus on "reflective" or "effect" measures, Figure 2.1 shows that $F_1$ affects $x_1$, $x_2$, $x_3$, and $x_4$. It is also assumed that the x variables can be measured or observed, whereas $F_1$ cannot be measured or observed. That is, $F_1$ typically is referred to as an unobservable or latent construct, and the x variables are referred to as indicators, items, or manifest variables of the latent construct. The partial correlation, $r_{12\cdot3}$, between any pair of variables (i.e., variables 1 and 2) after *removing* or *partialing* the effect of a third variable (i.e., variable 3) is given by

$$r_{12\cdot3} = \frac{r_{12} - r_{13}r_{23}}{\sqrt{1 - r_{13}^2}\ \sqrt{1 - r_{23}^2}}.$$

(2.1)

**Table 2.1**        Correlation Matrix for the Model in Figure 2.1

|        | $F_1$ | $x_1$ | $x_2$ | $x_3$ | $x_4$ |
|--------|-------|-------|-------|-------|-------|
| $F_1$  | 1.00  |       |       |       |       |
| $x_1$  | 0.90  | 1.00  |       |       |       |
| $x_2$  | 0.80  | 0.72  | 1.00  |       |       |
| $x_3$  | 0.70  | 0.63  | 0.56  | 1.00  |       |
| $x_4$  | 0.90  | 0.81  | 0.72  | 0.63  | 1.00  |

Using the values in Table 2.1 and the above formula, the partial correlation between $x_1$ and $x_2$ after partialing the effect of $F_1$ is equal to

$$\frac{0.72 - 0.9 \times 0.8}{\sqrt{1 - .9^2}\sqrt{1 - .8^2}} = 0.$$

Using Equation 2.1, it can be shown easily that the partial correlations among all pairs of x variables given in Table 2.1 are equal to zero. That is, once the effect of $F_1$ has been *removed* or *partialed* out, the partial correlations or the relationships among the x variables disappear. In other words, $F_1$ is responsible for all the relationships among the x variables; therefore, $F_1$ is referred to as the common factor. The $x_1$-$x_4$ set of items is unidimensional because the correlations among them, after they have been partialed out for the effect of a single common factor (i.e., $F_1$), are equal to zero. Thus, a set of items is considered to be unidimensional if the correlations among them can be accounted for by a single common factor. This conceptualization of unidimensionality is consistent with that proposed by McDonald (1981) and Hattie (1985).

Notice that each of the four items in Figure 2.1 is a measure of *one and only one* construct and therefore each item is unidimensional. That is, an item is considered to be unidimensional if it is a measure of only a single construct or latent factor. Now, if multiple sets of *n* items from the domain of the construct are taken and the partial correlations among each set are equal to zero, then the construct is said to be unidimensional. It is possible, however, that a set of items may be unidimensional, yet the construct or the individual indicators may not be unidimensional. This interesting issue will be elaborated on further later in the chapter.

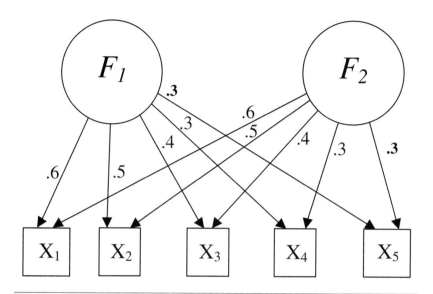

**Figure 2.2**

## Multidimensionality

Table 2.2 shows the correlation matrix for the two-factor model given in Figure 2.2, in which the x variables are affected by common factors $F_1$ and $F_2$. The partial correlation between $x_1$ and $x_2$ after the effect of $F_1$ is partialed out is equal to

$$\frac{0.60 - 0.6 \times 0.5}{\sqrt{1 - 0.6^2} \ \sqrt{1 - 0.5^2}} = 0.43.$$

Similarly, the partial correlation between $x_1$ and $x_2$ after partialing out the effect of $F_2$ is equal to

$$\frac{0.6 - 0.6 \times 0.5}{\sqrt{1 - .6^2} \ \sqrt{1 - .5^2}} = 0.43.$$

Thus, both partial correlations are *not* equal to zero. This suggests that the correlations among the variables cannot be accounted for by a single factor and, therefore, the set of items is not unidimensional. The partial correlation

**Table 2.2**     Correlation Matrix for the Model in Figure 2.2

|        | $F_1$ | $F_2$ | $x_1$ | $x_2$ | $x_3$ | $x_4$ | $x_5$ |
|--------|-------|-------|-------|-------|-------|-------|-------|
| $F_1$  | 1.00  |       |       |       |       |       |       |
| $F_2$  | 0.00  | 1.00  |       |       |       |       |       |
| $x_1$  | 0.60  | 0.60  | 1.00  |       |       |       |       |
| $x_2$  | 0.50  | 0.50  | 0.60  | 1.00  |       |       |       |
| $x_3$  | 0.40  | 0.40  | 0.48  | 0.40  | 1.00  |       |       |
| $x_4$  | 0.30  | 0.30  | 0.36  | 0.30  | 0.24  | 1.00  |       |
| $x_5$  | 0.30  | 0.30  | 0.36  | 0.30  | 0.24  | 0.18  | 1.00  |

between any two variables 1 and 2 after partialing the effect of variables 3 and 4 is given by Equation 2.2.

$$r_{12 \cdot 34} = \frac{r_{12 \cdot 4} - r_{13 \cdot 4} \times r_{23 \cdot 4}}{\sqrt{1 - r_{13 \cdot 4}^2}\ \sqrt{1 - r_{23 \cdot 4}^2}} \tag{2.2}$$

Using Equation 2.2, the partial correlation between $x_1$ and $x_2$ after partialing the effects of $F_1$ and $F_2$ is equal to zero (see Appendix 2A for the computations). Using the computational steps shown in Appendix 2A, it can be shown easily that the partial correlations among the $x_1$-$x_5$ set of variables after controlling for $F_1$ and $F_2$ are all equal to zero. That is, two factors or latent constructs are needed to account for the correlations among the x variables and, therefore, two dimensions account for the $x_1$-$x_5$ set of variables. The dimensionality of a given set of variables is equal to the number of latent constructs needed to account for the correlations among the variables. Notice further that each of the five items represents two constructs. That is, the dimensionality of each item or construct is equal to two because each of these items is a measure of two constructs. Once again, if multiple sets of items are taken from the domain of the two constructs and the partial correlations among variables of each set after removing the effect of $F_1$ and $F_2$ are equal to zero, then the construct is said to be multidimensional (two-dimensional in this case).

The above rationale can be extended to more than two constructs. If two factors do not reduce the partial correlations to zero, then the construct has more than two dimensions. In general, the dimensionality of a set of items is equal to the number of constructs or factors needed to reduce the partial correlations to zero. Furthermore, if multiple sets of items are drawn from the domain of the construct and *p* factors are needed to account for the correlations among the items, then the dimensionality of the construct is said to be *p*.

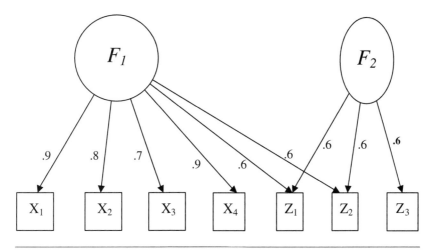

**Figure 2.3**

## DOES UNIDIMENSIONALITY OF A SET
## OF ITEMS IMPLY UNIDIMENSIONALITY
## OF THE ITEMS OR THE CONSTRUCT?

Table 2.3 shows the correlation matrix for the factor model given in Figure 2.3. In Figure 2.3, $F_1$ affects $x_1$, $x_2$, $x_3$, $x_4$, $z_1$, and $z_2$. $F_2$ affects $z_1$, $z_2$, and $z_3$. Notice that $x_1$-$x_4$ are manifest items only for $F_1$, $z_1$ and $z_2$ are manifest items for both $F_1$ and $F_2$, and $z_3$ is a manifest item only for $F_2$. Table 2.4 gives partial correlations among various sets of variables pertaining to Figure 2.3. Following are some of the observations that can be drawn from the results presented in Tables 2.4a-2.4e.

**Table 2.3**    Correlation Matrix for the Model in Figure 2.3

|  | $F_1$ | $F_2$ | $x_1$ | $x_2$ | $x_3$ | $x_4$ | $z_1$ | $z_2$ | $z_3$ |
|---|---|---|---|---|---|---|---|---|---|
| $F_1$ | 1.00 | | | | | | | | |
| $F_2$ | 0.00 | 1.00 | | | | | | | |
| $x_1$ | 0.90 | 0.00 | 1.00 | | | | | | |
| $x_2$ | 0.80 | 0.00 | 0.72 | 1.00 | | | | | |
| $x_3$ | 0.70 | 0.00 | 0.63 | 0.56 | 1.00 | | | | |
| $x_4$ | 0.90 | 0.00 | 0.81 | 0.72 | 0.63 | 1.00 | | | |
| $z_1$ | 0.60 | 0.60 | 0.54 | 0.48 | 0.42 | 0.54 | 1.00 | | |
| $z_2$ | 0.60 | 0.60 | 0.54 | 0.48 | 0.42 | 0.54 | 0.72 | 1.00 | |
| $z_3$ | 0.00 | 0.60 | 0.00 | 0.00 | 0.00 | 0.00 | 0.36 | 0.36 | 1.00 |

**Table 2.4a**     Partial Correlations for the Model in Figure 2.3:
Case 1—Partialing the Effect of $F_1$ From $x_1$–$x_4$

|          | $x_1$ | $x_2$ | $x_3$ | $x_4$ |
|----------|-------|-------|-------|-------|
| $x_1$    | 1.00  |       |       |       |
| $x_2$    | 0.00  | 1.00  |       |       |
| $x_3$    | 0.00  | 0.00  | 1.00  |       |
| $x_4$    | 0.00  | 0.00  | 0.00  | 1.00  |

**Table 2.4b**     Partial Correlations for the Model in Figure 2.3: Case 2—Partialing
the Effect of $F_1$ From $x_1$–$x_4$ and $z_1$

|          | $x_1$ | $x_2$ | $x_3$ | $x_4$ | $z_1$ |
|----------|-------|-------|-------|-------|-------|
| $x_1$    | 1.00  |       |       |       |       |
| $x_2$    | 0.00  | 1.00  |       |       |       |
| $x_3$    | 0.00  | 0.00  | 1.00  |       |       |
| $x_4$    | 0.00  | 0.00  | 0.00  | 1.00  |       |
| $z_1$    | 0.00  | 0.00  | 0.00  | 0.00  | 1.00  |

**Table 2.4c**     Partial Correlations for the Model in Figure 2.3: Case 2—Partialing
the Effect of $F_1$ From $x_1$–$x_4$ and $z_2$

|          | $x_1$ | $x_2$ | $x_3$ | $x_4$ | $z_2$ |
|----------|-------|-------|-------|-------|-------|
| $x_1$    | 1.00  |       |       |       |       |
| $x_2$    | 0.00  | 1.00  |       |       |       |
| $x_3$    | 0.00  | 0.00  | 1.00  |       |       |
| $x_4$    | 0.00  | 0.00  | 0.00  | 1.00  |       |
| $z_2$    | 0.00  | 0.00  | 0.00  | 0.00  | 1.00  |

**Table 2.4d**     Partial Correlations for the Model in Figure 2.3: Case 3—Partialing
the Effect of $F_1$ From $x_1$–$x_4$, $z_1$, and $z_2$

|          | $x_1$ | $x_2$ | $x_3$ | $x_4$ | $z_1$ | $z_2$ |
|----------|-------|-------|-------|-------|-------|-------|
| $x_1$    | 1.00  |       |       |       |       |       |
| $x_2$    | 0.00  | 1.00  |       |       |       |       |
| $x_3$    | 0.00  | 0.00  | 1.00  |       |       |       |
| $x_4$    | 0.00  | 0.00  | 0.00  | 1.00  |       |       |
| $z_1$    | 0.00  | 0.00  | 0.00  | 0.00  | 1.00  |       |
| $z_2$    | 0.00  | 0.00  | 0.00  | 0.00  | 0.225 | 1.00  |

**Table 2.4e**   Partial Correlations for the Model in Figure 2.3: Case 3—Partialing the Effect of $F_1$ and $F_2$ From $x_1$–$x_4$, $z_1$, and $z_2$

|       | $x_1$ | $x_2$ | $x_3$ | $x_4$ | $z_1$ | $z_2$ |
|-------|-------|-------|-------|-------|-------|-------|
| $x_1$ | 1.00  |       |       |       |       |       |
| $x_2$ | 0.00  | 1.00  |       |       |       |       |
| $x_3$ | 0.00  | 0.00  | 1.00  |       |       |       |
| $x_4$ | 0.00  | 0.00  | 0.00  | 1.00  |       |       |
| $z_1$ | 0.00  | 0.00  | 0.00  | 0.00  | 1.00  |       |
| $z_2$ | 0.00  | 0.00  | 0.00  | 0.00  | 0.00  | 1.00  |

Case 1: In the case shown in Table 2.4a, the $x_1$-$x_4$ set of items is unidimensional, as one common factor accounts for the correlations among the items, and each item is unidimensional, as it measures one and only one construct.

Case 2: In the case shown in Tables 2.4b and 2.4c, the $x_1$-$x_4$ and $z_1$ set of items is unidimensional, as the correlations among the items can be accounted for by a single factor. Item $z_1$ is not unidimensional, however, as it is a measure of two factors. That is, it is possible for a set of items to be unidimensional, yet each item in the set may or may not be unidimensional. Similarly, the set of items $x_1$-$x_4$ and $z_2$ is unidimensional; however, item $z_2$ is not unidimensional.

Case 3: In the case shown in Tables 2.4d and 2.4e, the $x_1$-$x_4$, $z_1$, and $z_2$ set of items is not unidimensional, as the correlation between $z_1$ and $z_2$ cannot be accounted for by one factor. The correlations among this set of items can be accounted for by two factors. Therefore, this set of items is multidimensional (i.e., two dimensions). Furthermore, items $z_1$ and $z_2$ are multidimensional and not unidimensional. The reader can easily see that items $x_1$-$x_4$ and $z_1$-$z_3$ are not unidimensional, as the partial correlations among them cannot be accounted for by a single factor.

Based on the above observations, it can be concluded that if the conceptual definition of the construct remains the same, then the $F_1$ construct is not unidimensional, as all sets of items from the domain of the construct are not unidimensional. Typically, when this happens, the construct is usually said to be context dependent, as its dimensionality and maybe the construct's conceptual meaning might change depending upon which set of items is used to measure the construct.

## RELEVANCE OF UNIDIMENSIONALITY

A review of the extant literature using confirmatory factor analysis (CFA), covariance structure modeling, or structural equation modeling (SEM) strongly suggests the preference for use of items that are unidimensional and, in the context of a specific research study, load strongly on one and only one factor (Gerbing & Anderson, 1988; Neuberg, West, Thompson, & Judice, 1997). Although there has been no systematic inquiry into why such items should be preferred, prima facie, the strong preference for such items appears historically grounded in the practice of using a summed score of the items on specific scales in ANOVA and regression-based analysis instead of individual items. In fact, even when individual items are used in covariance structure models (e.g., SEM), the tendency is to report statistics such as corrected item-to-total correlations and coefficient alpha, which are characteristics of, or involve, summed scores.

If the researcher uses composite scores in a covariance structure model, then, from a conceptual viewpoint, it is desirable that the items that form the summed score should be unidimensional (Floyd & Widaman, 1995; Neuberg et al., 1997). This is the most compelling argument in favor of using items that are unidimensional. If, on the other hand, the set of items are unidimensional but the individual items are not unidimensional, then the use of summed scores is not appropriate, as the summed scores would also contain the effect of other factors on which the items load. Under these situations, researchers might use factor scores instead of summed scores as input for further analysis, despite the known problems with factor score indeterminacy and estimation (Sharma, 1996). Factor scores are formed as linear combinations of each factor's manifest items using factor score regression coefficients as weights. This approach has the advantage that items need not have non-zero loadings only on one latent factor. It should be noted, however, that structural relationships based on factor scores may still be attenuated, because factor scores contain error. Nonetheless, this approach may be less problematic than using composites based on summed scores.

## HOW TO ASSESS
## DIMENSIONALITY OF CONSTRUCTS

Coefficient alpha (Cronbach, 1951) is the most popular measure that is reported for assessing the internal consistency of scales, and in many cases, a high coefficient alpha is considered evidence of the unidimensionality of the construct. Unfortunately, this is not true. For example, the coefficient alpha estimate for the $x_1$-$x_4$ and $z_1$-$z_3$ set of items of Figure 2.3 is equal to .852, and one might conclude that the set of items is unidimensional. It is now well accepted that coefficient alpha is meaningful only for a unidimensional set of items (Clark & Watson, 1995; Cortina, 1993). For a set of items that are not unidimensional, confusion exists as to what exactly is assessed by coefficient alpha. In Chapter 3, we expand the discussion of the relationship between internal consistency and dimensionality. For now, the following section provides a brief discussion of some of the available procedures for assessing dimensionality of constructs.

As mentioned earlier, dimensionality is defined as the number of common factors or latent constructs needed to account for the correlation among the variables. Therefore, factor analysis is an appropriate and popular method for assessing dimensionality of constructs. One could use either exploratory factor analysis (EFA) or confirmatory factor analysis (CFA) or both to assess the dimensionality of constructs. Following is a brief discussion of the use of each one of these techniques for assessing dimensionality.[1]

### Exploratory Factor Analysis (EFA)

The implicit assumption underlying the use of EFA is that the researcher generally has a limited idea with respect to the dimensionality of constructs and which items belong or load on which factor. Furthermore, EFA typically is conducted during the initial stage of scale development. Still, EFA can be used to gain insights as to the potential dimensionality of items and scales. Table 2.5 gives the SPSS syntax commands for reading the

---

[1]A detailed discussion of exploratory and confirmatory factor analysis is beyond the scope of this textbook. For further details on these techniques, the interested reader is referred to Sharma (1996).

**Table 2.5**      SPSS Commands for Exploratory Factor Analysis

```
Title Exploratory Factor Analysis for Data in Table 2-3.
MATRIX DATA VARIABLES=x1 to x4 z1 z2 z3/
  CONTENTS=MEAN STDDEV
CORR/N=200/FORMAT=LOWER.
BEGIN DATA
0 0 0 0 0 0 0
1 1 1 1 1 1 1
1.00
0.72   1.00
0.63   0.56   1.00
0.81   0.72   0.63   1.00
0.54   0.48   0.42   0.54   1.00
0.54   0.48   0.42   0.54   0.72   1.00
0.00   0.00   0.00   0.00   0.36   0.36   1.00
END DATA.
FACTOR
 /MATRIX=IN(COR=*)
 /ANALYSIS=x1 to x4 z1 to z3
 /EXTRACTION=PAF
 /PRINT=All
 /PLOT=Eigen.
```

correlation matrix given in Table 2.3 for performing EFA, and Exhibit 2.1 depicts a portion of the output. Following is a brief discussion of the resulting output.

The number of factors accounting for the correlations among the variables represents the dimensionality of a set of variables. A number of rules of thumb or heuristics are used to determine the number of factors. They include (a) the eigenvalue-greater-than-one rule, (b) the scree plot, and (c) the scree plot with parallel analysis.[2] According to the eigenvalue-greater-than-one rule, the number of factors is equal to the number of eigenvalues greater than one. The rationale is that a given factor must account for at least as much variance as can be accounted for by a single item or variable. In the present case, the eigenvalue-greater-than-one rule suggests the presence of two factors, and therefore it might be concluded that the set of items is not unidimensional. The eigenvalue-greater-than-one rule has come under considerable criticism. Cliff

---

[2]The eigenvalue-greater-than-one rule and the scree plot with parallel analysis can be used only when the correlation matrix is used in factor analysis.

**Exhibit 2.1**     Partial SPSS Output for Data in Table 2.3

## Total Variance Explained

*Initial Eigenvalues*

| Factor | Total | % of Variance | Cumulative % |
|---|---|---|---|
| 1 | 3.961 | 56.580 | 56.580 |
| 2 | 1.337 | 19.094 | 75.674 |
| 3 | .500 | 7.141 | 82.815 |
| 4 | .437 | 6.249 | 89.064 |
| 5 | .296 | 4.222 | 93.286 |
| 6 | .280 | 4.000 | 97.286 |
| 7 | .190 | 2.714 | 100.000 |

Extraction Method: Principal Axis Factoring.

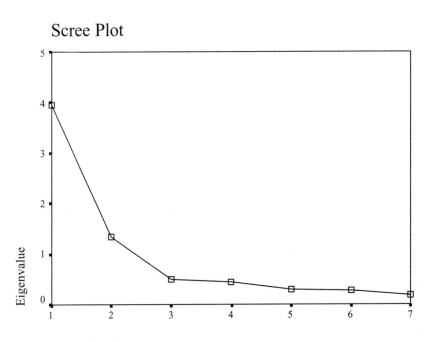

Scree Plot

(1988) specifically provides strong arguments against its use in identifying the number of factors.

The scree plot proposed by Cattell (1966) is another popular technique. The scree plot is a plot of the eigenvalues against the number of factors, and one looks for an "elbow" signifying a sharp drop in variance accounted for by a given factor. It is assumed that factors at or beyond the elbow are nuisance factors and merely represent error or unique components. As can be seen from the scree plot given in Exhibit 2.2, the elbow suggests the presence of two factors. That is, the set of items is multidimensional. In many instances, however, it is not possible to completely identify the elbow. In such cases, one can use the parallel plot procedure suggested by Horn (1965). With this procedure, the parallel plot represents the eigenvalues that would result if the data set were to contain no common factors. That is, the correlations among the variables are completely due to sampling error. Extensive simulations are required to estimate the eigenvalues for the parallel plot; however, based on empirically derived equations, Allen and Hubbard (1986) have developed the following equation to estimate the eigenvalues for obtaining the parallel plot:

**Exhibit 2.2**     Scree and Parallel Plots

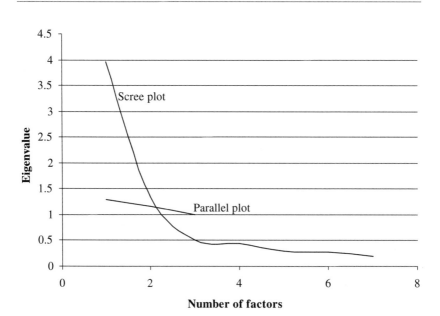

$$\ln \lambda_k = a_k + b_k \ln (n - 1) + c_k \ln \{(p - k - 1)$$
$$(p - k + 2)/2\} + d_k \ln \lambda_{k-1} \qquad (2.3)$$

where $\lambda_k$ is the estimate of the $k$th eigenvalue, $p$ is the number of variables or items, $n$ is the number of observations, $a_k$, $b_k$, $c_k$, and $d_k$ are regression coefficients, and $\ln \lambda_0$ is assumed to be 1. Exhibit 2.3 gives the empirically derived coefficients for the above equation. Using Equation 2.3, the first eigenvalue is equal to

$$\ln \lambda_1 = .9794 - .2059 \ln (200 - 1) + .1226 \ln \{(7 - 1 - 1)$$
$$(7 - 1 + 2)/2\} + 0.00 \times 1$$
$$= .257$$

$$\lambda_1 = e^{.257} = 1.293$$

and the second eigenvalue is equal to

$$\ln \lambda_2 = -.3781 + .0461 \ln (200 - 1) + .004 \ln \{(7 - 2 - 1)$$
$$(7 - 2 + 2)/2\} + 1.0578 \times .257$$
$$= .148$$

$$\lambda_1 = e^{.148} = 1.160.$$

The above procedure is repeated to compute the remaining eigenvalues.[3] Exhibit 2.2 gives the parallel plot. As can be seen, the plot suggests two factors; that is, the dimensionality of the set of items is two.

The number of factors identified by the above procedures needs to be confirmed further by ensuring that the number of factors is sufficient to account for all the correlations among the variables as this is a key objective of factor analysis. That is, the researcher is normally interested in determining the "fit" of the factor model to data. Two commonly used measures are the root-mean-square residual (RMSR) and the root-mean-square of partial correlations among the variables (RMSP). These are computed from the residual correlation matrix and the partial correlation matrix. The residual correlation matrix is the difference between the sample correlation matrix and the computed or estimated correlation matrix using estimated factor loadings. The partial correlation matrix has been defined earlier. RMSR and RMSP can be computed as

---

[3] If the computed eigenvalues are negative, they are assumed to be zero.

**Exhibit 2.3**　　　Regression Coefficients for the Principal Components

| Root (k) | Number of Points[a] | a | b | c | d | $R^2$ |
|---|---|---|---|---|---|---|
| 1 | 62 | .9794 | −.2059 | .1226 | 0.0000 | .931 |
| 2 | 62 | −.3781 | .0461 | .0040 | 1.0578 | .998 |
| 3 | 62 | −.3306 | .0424 | .0003 | 1.0805 | .998 |
| 4 | 55 | −.2795 | .0364 | −.0003 | 1.0714 | .998 |
| 5 | 55 | −.2670 | .0360 | −.0024 | 1.0899 | .998 |
| 6 | 55 | −.2632 | .0368 | −.0040 | 1.1039 | .998 |
| 7 | 55 | −.2580 | .0360 | −.0039 | 1.1173 | .998 |
| 8 | 55 | −.2544 | .0373 | −.0064 | 1.1421 | .998 |
| 9 | 48 | −.2111 | .0329 | −.0079 | 1.1229 | .998 |
| 10 | 48 | −.1964 | .0310 | −.0083 | 1.1320 | .998 |
| 11 | 48 | −.1858 | .0288 | −.0073 | 1.1284 | .999 |
| 12 | 48 | −.1701 | .0276 | −.0090 | 1.1534 | .998 |
| 13 | 48 | −.1697 | .0266 | −.0075 | 1.1632 | .998 |
| 14 | 41 | −.1226 | .0229 | −.0113 | 1.1462 | .999 |
| 15 | 41 | −.1005 | .0212 | −.0133 | 1.1668 | .999 |
| 16 | 41 | −.1079 | .0193 | −.0088 | 1.1374 | .999 |
| 17 | 41 | −.0866 | .0177 | −.0110 | 1.1718 | .999 |
| 18 | 41 | −.0743 | .0139 | −.0081 | 1.1571 | .999 |
| 19 | 34 | −.0910 | .0152 | −.0056 | 1.0934 | .999 |
| 20 | 34 | −.0879 | .0145 | −.0051 | 1.1005 | .999 |
| 21 | 34 | −.0666 | .0118 | −.0056 | 1.1111 | .999+ |
| 22 | 34 | −.0865 | .0124 | −.0022 | 1.0990 | .999+ |
| 23 | 34 | −.0919 | .0123 | −.0009 | 1.0831 | .999+ |
| 24 | 29 | −.0838 | .0116 | −.0016 | 1.0835 | .999+ |
| 25 | 28 | −.0392 | .0083 | −.0053 | 1.1109 | .999+ |
| 26 | 28 | −.0338 | .0065 | −.0039 | 1.1091 | .999+ |
| 27 | 28 | .0057 | .0015 | −.0049 | 1.1276 | .999+ |
| 28 | 28 | .0017 | .0011 | −.0034 | 1.1185 | .999+ |
| 29 | 22 | −.0214 | .0048 | −.0041 | 1.0915 | .999+ |
| 30 | 22 | −.0364 | .0063 | −.0030 | 1.0875 | .999+ |
| 31 | 22 | −.0041 | .0022 | −.0033 | 1.0991 | .999+ |
| 32 | 22 | .0598 | −.0067 | −.0032 | 1.1307 | .999+ |
| 33 | 21 | .0534 | −.0062 | −.0023 | 1.1238 | .999+ |
| 34 | 16 | .0301 | −.0032 | −.0027 | 1.0978 | .999+ |
| 35 | 16 | .0071 | .0009 | −.0038 | 1.0895 | .999+ |
| 36 | 16 | .0521 | −.0052 | −.0030 | 1.1095 | .999+ |
| 37 | 16 | .0824 | −.0105 | −.0014 | 1.1209 | .999+ |
| 38 | 16 | .1865 | −.0235 | −.0033 | 1.1567 | .999+ |
| 39 | 10 | .0075 | .0009 | −.0039 | 1.0773 | .999+ |
| 40 | 10 | .0050 | −.0021 | .0025 | 1.0802 | .999+ |
| 41 | 10 | .0695 | −.0087 | −.0016 | 1.0978 | .999+ |

| Root (k) | Number of Points[a] | a | b | c | d | $R^2$ |
|---|---|---|---|---|---|---|
| 42 | 10 | .0686 | −.0086 | −.0003 | 1.1004 | .999+ |
| 43 | 10 | .1370 | −.0181 | .0012 | 1.1291 | .999+ |
| 44 | 10 | .1936 | −.0264 | .0000 | 1.1315 | .999+ |
| 45 | 10 | .3493 | −.0470 | .0000 | 1.1814 | .999+ |
| 46 | 5 | .1444 | −.0185 | .0000 | 1.1188 | .999+ |
| 47 | 5 | .0550 | −.0067 | .0000 | 1.0902 | .999+ |
| 48 | 5 | .1417 | −.0189 | .0000 | 1.1079 | .999+ |

SOURCE: From Table 1 of "Regression Equations for the Latent Roots of Random Data Correlation Matrices With Unities on the Diagonal," *Multivariate Behavioral Research, 21,* pp. 393-398, Allen and Hubbard, copyright 1986 by Lawrence Erlbaum Associates. Reprinted with permission.
a. The number of points used in the regression.

$$RMSR = \sqrt{\frac{2\sum_{i=1}^{k}\sum_{j=i}^{k} res_{ij}^2}{k(k-1)}}$$

$$RMSP = \sqrt{\frac{2\sum_{i=1}^{k}\sum_{j=i}^{k} pc_{ij}^2}{k(k-1)}} \tag{2.4}$$

where $res_{ij}$ and $pc_{ij}$ are, respectively, the residual correlation and the partial correlation between variables $i$ and $j$. Exhibit 2.4 gives the residual correlation matrix provided by SPSS for one- and two-factor models. Using Equation 2.4, the RMSR for a two-factor model is .00021, and for the one-factor model it is .215. Although there are no guidelines as to how low is "low," there is a *substantial* difference between the RMSR for the one- and two-factor models; therefore, the two-factor model provides the better account of correlations among the variables.[4]

---

[4] SPSS does not provide the RMSP. SAS, on the other hand, provides both of the matrices and also computes the two indices.

**Exhibit 2.4**   Partial SPSS Output for Two-Factor and One-Factor Solutions

## Two-Factor Solution

**Reproduced Correlation**

| | X1 | X2 | X3 | X4 | Z1 | Z2 | Z3 |
|---|---|---|---|---|---|---|---|
| **Reproduced Correlation** | | | | | | | |
| X1 | .810[b] | .720 | .630 | .810 | .540 | .540 | 1.893E-04 |
| X2 | .720 | .640[b] | .560 | .720 | .480 | .480 | 3.751E-05 |
| X3 | .630 | .560 | .490[b] | .630 | .420 | .420 | 5.103E-05 |
| X4 | .810 | .720 | .630 | .810[b] | .540 | .540 | 1.893E-04 |
| Z1 | .540 | .480 | .420 | .540 | .720[b] | .720 | .360 |
| Z2 | .540 | .480 | .420 | .540 | .720 | .720[b] | .360 |
| Z3 | 1.893E-04 | 3.751E-05 | 5.103E-05 | 1.893E-04 | .360 | .360 | .359[b] |
| **Residual[a]** | | | | | | | |
| X1 | | -5.284E-05 | -5.296E-06 | 2.717E-04 | 9.458E-05 | 9.458E-05 | -1.893E-04 |
| X2 | -5.284E-05 | | -2.337E-04 | -5.284E-05 | 1.876E-05 | 1.876E-05 | -3.751E-05 |
| X3 | -5.296E-06 | -2.337E-04 | | -5.296E-06 | 2.548E-05 | 2.548E-05 | -5.103E-05 |
| X4 | 2.717E-04 | -5.284E-05 | -5.296E-06 | | 9.458E-05 | 9.458E-05 | -1.893E-04 |
| Z1 | 9.458E-05 | 1.876E-05 | 2.548E-05 | 9.458E-05 | | 2.049E-04 | 3.388E-04 |
| Z2 | 9.458E-05 | 1.876E-05 | 2.548E-05 | 9.458E-05 | 2.049E-04 | | 3.388E-04 |
| Z3 | -1.893E.04 | -3.751E-05 | -5.103E-05 | -1.893E-04 | 3.388E-04 | 3.388E-04 | |

Extraction Method: Principal Axis Factoring.

a. Residuals are computed between observed and reproduced correlations. There are 0 (.0%) nonredundant residuals with absolute values greater than 0.05.

b. Reproduced communalities

## One-Factor Solution

### Reproduced Correlations

| | | X1 | X2 | X3 | X4 | Z1 | Z2 | Z3 |
|---|---|---|---|---|---|---|---|---|
| Reproduced Correlation | X1 | .754[b] | .674 | .592 | .754 | .606 | .606 | .123 |
| | X2 | .674 | .602[b] | .529 | .674 | .541 | .541 | .110 |
| | X3 | .592 | .529 | .464[b] | .592 | .475 | .475 | 9.646E-02 |
| | X4 | .754 | .674 | .592 | .754[b] | .606 | .606 | .123 |
| | Z1 | .606 | .541 | .475 | .606 | .487[b] | .487 | 9.880E-02 |
| | Z2 | .606 | .541 | .475 | .606 | .487 | .487[b] | 9.880E-02 |
| | Z3 | .123 | .110 | 9.646E-02 | .123 | 9.880E-02 | 9.880E-02 | 2.005E-02[b] |
| Residual[a] | X1 | | 4.613E-02 | 3.836E-02 | 5.574E-02 | -6.605E-02 | -6.605E-02 | -.123 |
| | X2 | 4.613E-02 | | 3.142E-02 | 4.613E-02 | -6.145E-02 | -6.145E-02 | -.110 |
| | X3 | 3.836E-02 | 3.142E-02 | | 3.836E-02 | -5.538E-02 | -5.538E-02 | -9.646E-02 |
| | X4 | 5.574E-02 | 4.613E-02 | 3.836E-02 | | -6.605E-02 | -6.605E-02 | -.123 |
| | Z1 | -6.605E-02 | -6.145E-02 | -5.538E-02 | -6.605E-02 | | .233 | .261 |
| | Z2 | -6.605E-02 | -6.145E-02 | -5.538E-02 | -6.605E-02 | .233 | | .261 |
| | Z3 | -.123 | -.110 | -9.646E-02 | -.123 | .261 | .261 | |

Extraction Method: Principal Axis Factoring.

a. Residuals are computed between observed and reproduced correlations. There are 16 (76.0%) nonredundant residuals with absolute values greater that 0.05.

b. Reproduced communalities

## Confirmatory Factor Analysis (CFA)

Although EFA gives an idea of dimensionality, CFA, as the name implies, essentially focuses on whether a hypothesized factor model does or does not fit the data. Thus, CFA is now a commonly accepted method to test/confirm dimensionality. The number of factors, the factor structure (i.e., which items load on which factors), and the relationship among factors (i.e., whether the factors are correlated) are specified a priori. For example, consider the factor model given in Figure 2.3. This model hypothesizes that the set of items measures two factors and that these factors are not correlated. Furthermore, it is assumed that items $x_1$-$x_4$ are measures of the first factor $F_1$, items $z_1$ and $z_2$ measure factors $F_1$ and $F_2$, and $z_3$ measures $F_2$. The objective then is to determine whether the data support the hypothesized model or not. Essentially, the null and alternate hypotheses are

$H_o$: The model fits the data.

$H_a$: The model does not fit the data.

Obviously, nonrejection of the null hypothesis is desired. The above hypotheses can be tested by estimating the model parameters using maximum likelihood estimation (MLE) or a related technique via CFA, and employing the resulting chi-square goodness-of-fit statistic.[5]

A number of software packages, such as SAS, LISREL, EQS, and AMOS, can be used to conduct CFA. Table 2.6 gives the commands for the PROC CALIS procedure in SAS, and Exhibit 2.5 gives the output. The chi-square test statistic is zero with 12 degrees of freedom and is not significant at $p < .05$, implying that the null hypothesis cannot be rejected. That is, the model is supported by the data.[6] In contrast, the chi-square test statistic for a one-factor model in which all the indicators load on the single factor is 126.25 with 14 degrees of freedom, and is statistically significant at $p < .05$. That is, the one-factor model is not supported by the data. The estimated factor loadings of the

---

[5] For detailed discussion of confirmatory factor analysis, see Sharma (1996).

[6] It should be noted that the model fit is perfect, as hypothetical data were used for the model in Figure 2.3. Normally, for actual data and large sample sizes, the fit will not be perfect and the chi-square statistic test will be large and significant.

**Table 2.6**    CALIS Commands for Confirmatory Factor Analysis

```
Title Confirmatory Factor Analysis for Model in Figure
  2-3;
Data table23(Type=corr);
Input _type_ $ _name_ $ x1 x2 x3 x4 z1 z2 z3;
cards;
```

| corr | x1 | 1.00 | . | . | . | . | . | . |
|------|----|------|------|------|------|------|------|------|
| corr | x2 | 0.72 | 1.00 | . | . | . | . | . |
| corr | x3 | 0.63 | 0.56 | 1.00 | . | . | . | . |
| corr | x4 | 0.81 | 0.72 | 0.63 | 1.00 | . | . | . |
| corr | z1 | 0.54 | 0.48 | 0.42 | 0.54 | 1.00 | . | . |
| corr | z2 | 0.54 | 0.48 | 0.42 | 0.54 | 0.72 | 1.00 | . |
| corr | z3 | 0.00 | 0.00 | 0.00 | 0.00 | 0.36 | 0.36 | 1.00 |
| std | . | 1 | 1 | 1 | 1 | 1 | 1 | 1 |
| N | . | 200 | 200 | 200 | 200 | 200 | 200 | 200 |

```
;
run;
Proc Calis;
Lineqs
  x1 = 11f1 f1 + e1,
  x2 = 12f1 f1 + e2,
  x3 = 13f1 f1 + e3,
  x4 = 14f1 f1 + e4,
  z1 = 15f1 f1 + lz1f2 f2 + e5,
  z2 = 16f1 f1 + lz2f1 f2 + e6,
  z3 = 17f2 f2 + e7;
  std
  e1 e2 e3 e4 e5 e6 e7 = vare1 vare2 vare3 vare4 vare5
  vare6 vare7,
  f1 f2 = 2*1.0;
run;
```

two-factor model are, within rounding error, the same as those reported in Figure 2.3.

There are a number of issues pertaining to the use of the chi-square test statistic for hypothesis testing, the most important being its sensitivity to sample size (Bearden, Sharma, & Teel, 1982; Hoyle, 1995; McDonald & Marsh, 1990). A number of other alternate goodness-of-fit statistics have been proposed that supposedly are not sensitive to sample size and other model parameters. These will be discussed in Chapter 7.

**Exhibit 2.5**     Partial SAS Output for Data in Table 2.3

## Goodness-of-Fit Results

```
Fit Function                                          0.0000
Goodness of Fit Index (GFI)                           1.0000
GFI Adjusted for Degrees of Freedom (AGFI)            1.0000
Root Mean Square Residual (RMR)                       0.0000
Parsimonious GFI (Mulaik, 1989)                       0.5714
Chi-Square                                            0.0000
Chi-Square DF                                         12
Pr > Chi-Square                                       1.0000
Independence Model Chi-Square                       797.28
Independence Model Chi-Square DF                     21
RMSEA Estimate                                        0.0000
RMSEA 90% Lower Confidence Limit                         .
RMSEA 90% Upper Confidence Limit                         .
ECVI Estimate                                         0.1675
ECVI 90% Lower Confidence Limit                          .
ECVI 90% Upper Confidence Limit                          .
Probability of Close Fit                              1.0000
Bentler's Comparative Fit Index                       1.0000
Normal Theory Reweighted LS Chi-Square               0.0000
Akaike's Information Criterion                      -24.0000
Bozdogan's (1987) CAIC                             -75.5798
Schwarz's Bayesian Criterion                       -63.5798
McDonald's (1989) Centrality                          1.0305
Bentler & Bonett's (1980) Non-normed Index           1.0271
Bentler & Bonett's (1980) NFI                         1.0000
James, Mulaik, & Brett (1982) Parsimonious NFI        0.5714
Z-Test of Wilson & Hilferty (1931)                   -7.2124
Bollen (1986) Normed Index Rho1                       1.0000
Bollen (1988) Non-normed Index Delta2                 1.0153
Hoelter's (1983) Critical N                              .
```

## Parameter Estimates

```
Manifest Variable Equations with Standardized Estimates
   x1  = 0.9000*f1 + 0.4359 e1
             l1f1
   x2  = 0.8000*f1 + 0.6000 e2
             l2f1
```

```
x3  = 0.7000*f1 + 0.7141 e3
           13f1
x4  = 0.9000*f1 + 0.4359 e4
           14f1
z1  = 0.6000*f1 + 0.6000*f2   + 0.5292 e5
           15f1          1z1f2
z2  = 0.6000*f1 + 0.6000*f2   + 0.5292 e6
           16f1          1z2f1
z3  = 0.6000*f2 + 0.8000 e7
```

## SUMMARY

The concept of unidimensionality was discussed in this chapter. The following points summarize the concepts presented.

1. A set of items is unidimensional if the correlations among the items after the effect of a single factor are partialed out are zero. That is, a set of items is unidimensional if a single factor model fits the data.

2. The dimensionality of a set of items is the number of common factors needed to reduce the partial correlations among the items to zero.

3. A given item is unidimensional if it measures one and only one construct. The dimensionality of an item is equal to the number of factors it measures.

4. It is possible that a set of items is unidimensional even though some of the items in the set are not unidimensional.

5. A construct is unidimensional if every set of $p$ items taken randomly from the domain of the construct is unidimensional.

6. Exploratory and confirmatory factor analyses are two methods for assessing dimensionality of constructs.

# Appendix 2A

---

## COMPUTING PARTIAL CORRELATIONS

$$r_{12 \cdot F_1} = \frac{.60 - .6 \times .50}{\sqrt{1 - .6^2} \; \sqrt{1 - .5^2}} = .43$$

$$r_{12 \cdot F_2} = \frac{.60 - .6 \times .50}{\sqrt{1 - .6^2} \; \sqrt{1 - .5^2}} = .43$$

$$r_{12 \cdot F_1, F_2} = \frac{r_{12 \cdot F_2} - r_{1F_1 \cdot F_2} \times r_{2F_1 \cdot F_2}}{\sqrt{1 - r_{1F_1 \cdot F_2}^2} \; \sqrt{1 - r_{2F_1 \cdot F_2}^2}}$$

$$r_{1F_1 \cdot F_2} = \frac{r_{1F_1} - r_{1F_2} \times r_{F_1 F_2}}{\sqrt{1 - r_{1F_2}^2} \; \sqrt{1 - r_{F_1 F_2}^2}} = \frac{.6 - .6 \times 0}{\sqrt{1 - .6^2} \; \sqrt{1 - 0}} = .75$$

$$r_{2F_1 \cdot F_2} = \frac{r_{2F_1} - r_{2F_2} \times r_{F_1 F_2}}{\sqrt{1 - r_{2F_2}^2} \; \sqrt{1 - r_{F_1 F_2}^2}} = \frac{.5 - .5 \times 0}{\sqrt{1 - .5^2} \; \sqrt{1 - 0}} = .58$$

$$r_{12 \cdot F, F_{21}} = \frac{.43 - .75 \times .58}{\sqrt{1 - .75^2} \; \sqrt{1 - .58^2}} \approx 0$$

# THREE

# RELIABILITY

---◆◆◆---

## INTRODUCTION

In the previous chapter, we discussed issues related to the dimensionality of latent constructs and their measurement items. We concluded that knowledge of the dimensionality of a construct is critical for developing items to measure that construct. After the items have been developed and trimmed, the next important step is to examine the reliability and validity of the scale. The purpose of this chapter is to discuss the concept of reliability and provide suggested procedures to assess it. In addition, we will discuss generalizability theory. The validity of a scale and procedures to assess validity will be addressed in the next chapter.

## THE TRUE-SCORE MODEL

Reliability of measurements is closely associated with the concept of the true-score model of classical test theory. Consider Figure 3.1a, which depicts "x" as the observed measure of a latent construct. As per the true-score model, the observed score, x, can be divided into true score and error (i.e., measurement error).[1] That is,

$$x = T + e \tag{3.1}$$

---

[1] See Crocker and Algina (1986) for a detailed discussion of the true-score model and the related theory.

(a)                                                          (b)

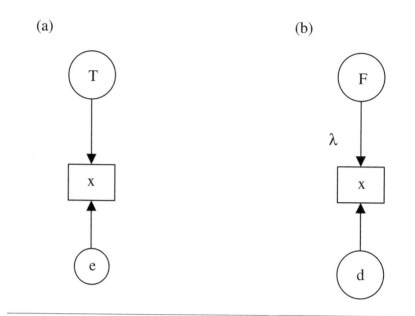

**Figure 3.1**        True-Score and Factor Models

where x is the observed score, T is the true score, and e is random measurement error. When the true score, T, varies, so does the observed score, x,
because the latent construct influences the observed score (i.e., "x" is a reflective indicator). Assuming that the true score and error are uncorrelated (i.e.,
Cov(T,e) = 0), it can be shown that the variance of x is equal to the variance
of the true score plus the variance of the error. That is,

$$Var(x) = Var(T) + Var(e).$$

The reliability of a measurement is defined as the ratio of the variance of the
true score to the variance of the observed score, or in equation form as

$$\text{Reliability} = \rho_{xx} = \frac{Var(T)}{Var(x)} = \frac{\sigma_T^2}{\sigma_x^2} \tag{3.2}$$

where $\rho_{xx}$ is the reliability of x.

**Relationship Between the True-Score**
**Model and the Factor Model**

As shown in Figure 3.1b, in a factor (measurement) model, the relationship between an item and the latent construct is given by

$$x = \lambda F + \delta$$

where x is the observed score, F is the latent factor, $\delta$ is the error, and $\lambda$ (the factor loading) is the extent to which the latent factor F affects the observed score x. Once again, as F varies, so does the observed score; however, the extent to which it varies is determined by the value of $\lambda$. It is clear that the term $\lambda F$ is equivalent to the true score in the true-score model and $\delta$ represents the error.[2] The reliability of the observed measure is given by

$$\text{Reliability} = \frac{\text{Var(T)}}{\text{Var(x)}} = \frac{\lambda^2 \text{Var(F)}}{\text{Var(x)}} = \frac{\lambda^2 \sigma_F^2}{\sigma_x^2}. \tag{3.3}$$

Notice that the numerators in Equations 3.2 and 3.3 are equivalent in the sense that they measure the variance that is due to the effect of the latent construct on the observed score.

## TYPES OF RELIABILITY

Because the true score (i.e., the latent construct) and error are unobservable, reliability has to be inferred from the observed score. Procedures used to assess reliability frequently discussed in the literature can be grouped into three general types: (a) test-retest reliability; (b) alternative-form reliability; and (c) internal consistency reliability. In discussing the three types of reliability, we will use both hypothetical examples and examples with data collected from our own research.

---

[2] In a strict sense, one might argue that conceptually the factor and the true-score models are not equivalent. In the factor model, $\delta$ in addition to measurement error also includes the unique or specific error. Empirically, however, it is impossible to separate the two. Consequently, at an empirical level it is not possible to differentiate between the true-score and the factor model.

**Table 3.1**          Hypothetical Data for Test-Retest Reliability

| Subject | Occasion 1 | Occasion 2 |
|---------|------------|------------|
| 1  | 4 | 5 |
| 2  | 4 | 5 |
| 3  | 6 | 5 |
| 4  | 5 | 3 |
| 5  | 5 | 4 |
| 6  | 3 | 3 |
| 7  | 2 | 3 |
| 8  | 5 | 4 |
| 9  | 3 | 3 |
| 10 | 7 | 7 |

**Test-Retest Reliability**

Suppose one is interested in measuring consumer coupon proneness (CP), and the following item or statement is used to measure it.[3] *Redeeming coupons makes me feel good.* Assume that 10 subjects are asked to indicate their degree of agreement using a 7-point *agree-disagree* Likert-type scale. Now suppose the same 10 subjects are asked to indicate their degree of agreement again after, say, 2 weeks. The resulting hypothetical data are reported in Table 3.1. Assuming that the respondents' coupon proneness does not change during the 2-week period and there is no measurement error, then the correlation between measures taken 2 weeks apart hypothetically should be equal to one. A value of less than one for the correlation coefficient can be attributed to measurement error. The reliability of the measure, then, is given by the correlation of measures taken at occasion 1 and occasion 2, which for the present hypothetical data is equal to 0.74. This measure of reliability is referred to as test-retest reliability.

Note that test-retest reliability is concerned with the stability of item responses over time. A test-retest or "stability" coefficient usually is estimated by the magnitude of the correlation between the same measures (and sample) on different assessment occasions. If the stability coefficient is low in magnitude, with no change in the construct over time, the reliability of the measure

---

[3] See Lichtenstein, Ridgway, and Netemeyer (1993) for further information regarding the CP construct.

is in doubt. If the stability coefficient is high in magnitude, with no change in the construct over time, the reliability of the measure is enhanced. The rationale for test-retest reliability is that if a measure truly reflects its intended construct, it should be able to assess the construct on different occasions. The true score on the latent construct should be reflected by the construct over two occasions in a comparable manner. Thus, test-retest reliability is useful because it offers information on the degree of confidence one has that the measure reflects the construct and is generalizable to other assessment occasions (Haynes et al., 1999). In sum, the test-retest correlation theoretically represents the degree to which the latent construct determines observed scores over time (DeVellis, 1991; Nunnally & Bernstein, 1994).

Some key shortcomings are associated with test-retest reliability that limit its usefulness as a theoretical reliability coefficient. First, how much time should elapse between administrations? There are no clear-cut answers, but for opinion-based (attitudinal) constructs, a period of a minimum of 2 weeks has been advocated (Robinson et al., 1991). Second, and related to the amount of time between administrations, if a low test-retest coefficient is obtained, does this mean that the scale is unreliable, or does it imply that what the scale measures has changed over time? If the latter is the case, then a basic principle of classical test theory has been violated and the test-retest coefficient is not an appropriate measure of reliability (Crocker & Algina, 1986). That is, the nature of the construct and the possibility of it changing over time must be considered. It is possible that a respondent's standing on the construct of interest (his or her true score) has changed over time. On the other hand, if the time interval between administrations is too short, the respondent's score from time 1 to time 2 may just reflect memory or "purposefully" being consistent. Thus, the time period should be long enough to allow the effects of such a memory response bias to fade (a testing effect of purposely being consistent from time 1 to time 2), but not so long as to reflect historical changes in the respondent's true score. (For other shortcomings associated with the test-retest coefficient, the interested reader is urged to consult Kelley and McGrath [1988] and Nunnally and Bernstein [1994]).

## Alternative-Form Reliability

Suppose that the following second statement, preferably developed independently of the first statement, is also available for measuring the

**Table 3.2**       Hypothetical Data for Alternate Form Reliability

| Subject | Occasion 1 (Statement 1) | Occasion 2 (Statement 2) |
|---------|--------------------------|--------------------------|
| 1       | 4                        | 4                        |
| 2       | 4                        | 4                        |
| 3       | 6                        | 5                        |
| 4       | 5                        | 3                        |
| 5       | 5                        | 4                        |
| 6       | 3                        | 5                        |
| 7       | 2                        | 4                        |
| 8       | 5                        | 4                        |
| 9       | 3                        | 5                        |
| 10      | 7                        | 7                        |

coupon proneness (CP) construct: *I enjoy clipping coupons out of the newspaper.* Assume that at occasion 1, the first statement is used, and at occasion 2, the second statement is used. Table 3.2 gives the data for the two *alternate forms* (i.e., statements) for measuring the CP construct. The correlation between the two responses (occasion 1 and occasion 2), which in the present case is equal to 0.41, is referred to as alternative-form reliability.

The similarities and differences between test-retest and alternative-form reliability should be noted. In both cases, reliability is estimated by correlating two sets of responses taken at two occasions. In the test-retest case, the two sets of responses are with respect to the *same* statement or measure. In alternative-form reliability, on the other hand, the two sets of responses are with respect to two different statements developed to measure the construct. The relevant issues for alternative-form reliability are the same as those for test-retest reliability.

## Internal Consistency Methods

It is obvious that because of constraints such as time, cost, and availability of the same subjects at multiple occasions, it is not always possible to

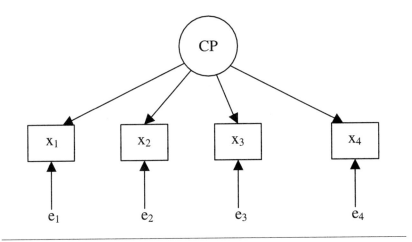

**Figure 3.2**    A One-Factor Model

take repeated measures or use alternate forms. In such cases, the concept of internal consistency can be used to estimate reliability. The internal consistency concept to measure reliability requires only a single administration of the items to respondents; however, it assumes availability of multiple measures or items for measuring a given construct. Before discussing the most widely used measure of internal consistency (coefficient alpha), we first provide a brief discussion of split-half reliability, which is one form of internal consistency reliability.

### Split-Half Reliability

As depicted in Figure 3.2, suppose that the following four items are used to measure the CP construct.

$x_1$—Redeeming coupons makes me feel good.

$x_2$—I enjoy clipping coupons out of the newspaper.

**Table 3.3**          Hypothetical Data for Split-Half Reliability

| Subject | Statements | | | | Total Score | |
| --- | --- | --- | --- | --- | --- | --- |
| | $X_1$ | $X_2$ | $X_3$ | $X_4$ | $X_1-X_2$ | $X_3-X_4$ |
| 1 | 4 | 4 | 5 | 5 | 8 | 10 |
| 2 | 4 | 4 | 5 | 5 | 8 | 10 |
| 3 | 6 | 5 | 6 | 5 | 11 | 11 |
| 4 | 5 | 3 | 5 | 3 | 8 | 8 |
| 5 | 5 | 4 | 3 | 4 | 9 | 7 |
| 6 | 3 | 5 | 5 | 3 | 8 | 8 |
| 7 | 2 | 4 | 5 | 3 | 6 | 8 |
| 8 | 5 | 4 | 3 | 4 | 9 | 7 |
| 9 | 3 | 5 | 5 | 3 | 8 | 8 |
| 10 | 7 | 7 | 7 | 7 | 14 | 14 |

$x_3$—When I use coupons, I feel I am getting a good deal.

$x_4$—I enjoy using coupons, regardless of the amount of money I save by doing so.

Ten subjects are asked to indicate their degree of agreement or disagreement on the above statements using a 7-point Likert-type scale. Table 3.3 gives the data. Now suppose we take the first two statements and compute the total score for each subject, which is given in the second to last column of Table 3.3. Similarly, the last two statements are taken and the total score is computed; these totals are provided in the last column of Table 3.3. The correlation between the two total scores is equal to 0.77 and is referred to as the split-half reliability. It is obvious that numerous split-halves can be formed, and the correlation for each split will be different.[4] Cronbach (1951) has shown that the average correlation of all possible splits is equal to coefficient

---

[4] The number of splits that can be formed is equal to $(2n')!/2(n'!)^2$ where $n' = n/2$ and $n$ is the number of statements.

alpha. Coefficient alpha or Cronbach's alpha ($\alpha$) can be computed using the following formula:

$$\alpha = \frac{k}{k-1}\left(\frac{\sum_{i=1}^{k}\sum_{\substack{j=1\\i\neq j}}^{k} \mathrm{Cov}\,(x_i x_j)}{\sum_{i=1}^{k}\sum_{\substack{j=1\\i\neq j}}^{k} \mathrm{Cov}\,(x_i x_j) + \sum_{i=1}^{k} \mathrm{Var}(x_i)}\right)$$

$$= \frac{k}{k-1}\left(\frac{\sum_{i=1}^{k}\sum_{\substack{j=1\\i\neq j}}^{k} \sigma_{ij}}{\sum_{i=1}^{k}\sum_{\substack{j=1\\i\neq j}}^{k} \sigma_{ij} + \sum_{i=1}^{k} \sigma_i^2}\right). \tag{3.4}$$

where $\alpha$ is the coefficient alpha, $x_i$ is measurement for item $i,$ and $k$ is the number of items. Because $\alpha$ is the most frequently used measure of reliability, in the sections that follow we discuss $\alpha$ and its relationship to reliability, dimensionality, scale length, interitem correlations, and item redundancy.

## COEFFICIENT ALPHA ($\alpha$)

Coefficient alpha is concerned with the degree of interrelatedness among a set of items designed to measure a single construct. It is further concerned with the variance that is *common* among items. For a set of items composing a scale, the variance in that set is composed of "true" variance (the variance across individuals in the construct that the scale measures) and "error" variance (all other variance not accounted for by the true variance, i.e., unshared variance, or *unique* variance). Computing $\alpha$ is a means of partitioning variance of the total score into these true and error components. In very simple terms, 1 – error variance = $\alpha$, and 1 – $\alpha$ = error variance. Therefore, $\alpha$ represents the proportion of a scale's total variance that is attributable to a *common* source— that common source being the true score of the latent construct being measured.

In Figure 3.2, the variance in each item (i.e., $x_i$) that is due to the latent variable CP is considered *common* or shared variance. When CP varies, so do the scores on the individual items, because the latent construct influences the scores on the items. Thus, scores on all items vary jointly with the latent construct CP, theoretically implying that all the items are correlated. The error terms ($e_i$) depicted in Figure 3.2 are considered *unique* to each item. That is, they represent variance that is not attributable to the latent construct CP, and according to classical test theory, the error terms are not correlated. Both the individual item scores and, therefore, the overall scale score vary as functions of two sources: (a) the source of variation *common* to itself (the overall score) and other items and (b) unshared or *unique* variation associated with that particular item. Thus, total scale variance and variance for each item are that which is attributable to *common* and *unique* (error) sources. As discussed below, alpha is conceptually equivalent to the ratio of common source variation to total variation (Cortina, 1993; DeVellis, 1991; Nunnally & Bernstein, 1994).

The covariance matrix of the four-item CP scale is given by

$$\begin{pmatrix} \sigma_1^2 & \sigma_{12} & \sigma_{13} & \sigma_{14} \\ \sigma_{21} & \sigma_2^2 & \sigma_{23} & \sigma_{24} \\ \sigma_{31} & \sigma_{32} & \sigma_3^2 & \sigma_{34} \\ \sigma_{41} & \sigma_{42} & \sigma_{43} & \sigma_4^2 \end{pmatrix}.$$

Suppose we form the total score, TS, as

$$TS = x_1 + x_2 + x_3 + x_4.$$

The variance of TS is equal to

$$\begin{aligned} Var\,(TS) &= s_{TS}^2 \\ &= \sigma_1^2 + \sigma_2^2 + \sigma_3^2 + \sigma_4^2 + \sigma_{12} + \sigma_{13} + \sigma_{14} + \sigma_{21} + \sigma_{23} + \sigma_{24} + \sigma_{31} + \sigma_{32} \\ &\quad + \sigma_{34} + \sigma_{41} + \sigma_{42} + \sigma_{43} \\ &= \sum_{i=1}^{k} \sigma_i^2 + \sum_{i=1}^{k} \sum_{\substack{j=1 \\ i \neq j}}^{k} \sigma_{ij}. \end{aligned}$$

Note that the variance of the summed score, TS, is equal to the sum of all the variances and covariances in the covariance matrix. To partition the total variance into *common* variance (i.e., variance of true score) and *unique* variance (i.e., variance due to measurement error), the following must be considered. The diagonal elements essentially represent the covariance of an item with itself, that is, the variability in the score of an item from a given sample of individuals. As such, the diagonal elements are *unique* sources of variance and not variance that is *common* or shared among items. The off-diagonal elements are covariances that represent the variance that is *common* or shared by any pair of items in the scale. Thus, the entries in the covariance matrix consist of *unique* (error) and *common* (shared/joint) variance. That which is unique is represented along the main diagonal ($\Sigma\sigma_i^2$), that which is common is represented by the off-diagonal elements, and the total variance ($\sigma_{TS}^2$) is equal to the sum of all the entries in the matrix. As such, the ratio of *unique* (non-common) variance to total variance is given by

$$\frac{\sum_{i=1}^k \sigma_i^2}{\sigma_{TS}^2}.$$

It follows from the above expression that the proportion of joint/*common* variation is

$$\text{Reliability} = 1 - \frac{\sum_{i=1}^k \sigma_i^2}{\sigma_{TS}^2}$$

$$= \frac{\sigma_{TS}^2 - \sum_{i=1}^k \sigma_i^2}{\sigma_{TS}^2}$$

$$= \frac{\sum_{i=1}^k \sum_{\substack{j=1 \\ i \neq j}}^k \sigma_{ij}}{\sum_{i=1}^k \sum_{\substack{j=1 \\ i \neq j}}^k \sigma_{ij} + \sum_{i=1}^k \sigma_i^2}. \tag{3.5}$$

Although the above equation captures the concept of common variation inherent in the definition of coefficient alpha, an adjustment for the number of items in a scale must be made. The total number of elements in the covariance matrix is equal to $k^2$, where $k$ is the number of items in a scale. Therefore, the denominator of Equation 3.5 is the sum of $k^2$ items. Similarly, the numerator is based on the sum of $k^2 - k$ items. To adjust the reliability given by Equation 3.5, the numerator is divided by $k^2 - k$ and the denominator by $k^2$. That is,

$$\frac{\sum_{i=1}^{k} \sum_{\substack{j=1 \\ i \neq j}}^{k} \sigma_{ij} / (k^2 - k)}{\left( \sum_{i=1}^{k} \sum_{\substack{j=1 \\ i \neq j}}^{k} \sigma_{ij} + \sum_{i=1}^{k} \sigma_i^2 \right) / k^2}$$

$$= \frac{k}{k-1} \left( \frac{\sum_{i=1}^{k} \sum_{\substack{j=1 \\ i \neq j}}^{k} \sigma_{ij}}{\sum_{i=1}^{k} \sum_{\substack{j=1 \\ i \neq j}}^{k} \sigma_{ij} + \sum_{i=1}^{k} \sigma_i^2} \right) \qquad (3.6)$$

which is the same as coefficient $\alpha$ given by Equation 3.4. Theoretically, $\alpha$ ranges from 0 to 1, and higher values of $\alpha$ are obviously preferable.

There is also a "standardized" item $\alpha$ formula analogous to Equation 3.6 that uses a correlation matrix with "1s" on the main diagonal (i.e., the correlation of an item with itself or standardized variances) and correlations ($r$) among pairs of items as the off-diagonal elements (i.e., standardized covariances). Standardized item $\alpha$ is considered an appropriate assessment of internal consistency if standardized item scores are summed to form a scale. Standardized item $\alpha$ is not considered appropriate, however, when the raw score total of the items are used to sum a scale, because differences in item variances can affect the total score (Cortina, 1993). Standardized item alpha can be computed as follows:

$$\frac{kr}{1 + (k-1)\,r} \qquad (3.7)$$

where $k$ is the number of items in the scale and $r$ is the average correlation among the items in the scale.

Finally, for items that are scored dichotomously, the *Kuder-Richardson 20 (KR-20)* formula is used to compute coefficient alpha. The KR-20 formula is identical to the variance-covariance version of alpha (Equation 3.6) with the exception that $(\Sigma pq)$ replaces $(\Sigma \sigma_i^2)$. The $(\Sigma pq)$ term specifies that the variance of each item is computed, and then these variances are summed for all items, where "$p$" represents each item's mean and "$q$" is ($1$ – item mean). As such, the variance of an item becomes "$pq$." (See Crocker and Algina, 1986, pp. 139-140, for an example of the KR-20 formula.)

$$\alpha = \frac{k}{k-1}\left(1 - \frac{\sum pq}{\sigma_x^2}\right) \qquad (3.8)$$

**Coefficient Alpha Example**

To demonstrate the calculation of coefficient alpha (Equation 3.6) and its standardized item form, we use data for the five-item CP scale of Lichtenstein et al. (1993). The items were measured on 7-point Likert-type scales and are as follow:

CP1: Redeeming coupons makes me feel good.

CP2: I enjoy clipping coupons out of the newspaper.

CP3: When I use coupons, I feel I am getting a good deal.

CP4: I enjoy using coupons, regardless of the amount of money I save by doing so.

CP5: Beyond the money I save, redeeming coupons gives me a sense of joy.

The covariance and correlation matrices for these data are reported in Tables 3.4a and 3.4b.

Using the formula for $\alpha$ given in Equation 3.6,

$$\alpha = \frac{5}{5-1}\left(\frac{42.356}{42.356 + 18.112}\right) = .876$$

where

$k = 5,$

$\sum \sigma_i^2 = 3.6457 + 4.3877 + 2.9864 + 3.7786 + 3.3138 = 18.112,$ and

$\sum_{i=1}^{k}\sum_{\substack{j=1 \\ i \neq j}}^{k} \sigma_{ij} = 2(2.7831 + 2.3934 + 2.2280 + 2.0706 + 2.3973 + 1.9109$
$\qquad + 1.8338 + 2.0782 + 1.6011 + 1.8813) = 42.356.$

**Table 3.4a**       Covariance Matrix for the 5-Item CP Scale

|        | CP1    | CP2    | CP3    | CP4    | CP5    |
|--------|--------|--------|--------|--------|--------|
| CP1    | 3.6457 |        |        |        |        |
| CP2    | 2.7831 | 4.3877 |        |        |        |
| CP3    | 2.3934 | 2.2280 | 2.9864 |        |        |
| CP4    | 2.0706 | 2.3973 | 1.9109 | 3.7786 |        |
| CP5    | 1.8338 | 2.0782 | 1.6011 | 1.8813 | 3.3138 |

**Table 3.4b**       Correlation Matrix for the 5-Item CP Scale

|        | CP1    | CP2    | CP3    | CP4    | CP5    |
|--------|--------|--------|--------|--------|--------|
| CP1    | 1.0000 |        |        |        |        |
| CP2    | .6969  | 1.0000 |        |        |        |
| CP3    | .7254  | .6155  | 1.0000 |        |        |
| CP4    | .5579  | .5888  | .5688  | 1.0000 |        |
| CP5    | .5276  | .5450  | .5089  | .5317  | 1.0000 |

Note that the sum of the off-diagonal elements was multiplied by 2 to reflect the covariances both below and above the diagonal.

Repeating the above procedure for the correlation matrix and using Equation 3.7 gives a value of 0.876 for $\alpha$. Notice that there is no difference between the two values of $\alpha$. This usually will be the case; however, if the variances of the items are very different, then the two values may not be the same. The calculation (with $r = .5865$) is as follows:

$$\frac{kr}{1 + (k - 1)\, r} = \frac{5 \times .5865}{1 + (5 - 1) \times .5865} = .876.$$

## Coefficient Alpha and Dimensionality

Although $\alpha$ is concerned with the degree of interrelatedness among a set of items designed to measure a single construct, there are various other descriptions of coefficient $\alpha$. The most dominant descriptions have been summarized nicely by Cortina (1993): (a) $\alpha$ is the mean of all split-half reliabilities, (b) $\alpha$ is the lower bound reliability of a measure, (c) $\alpha$ is a measure of first-factor saturation, (d) $\alpha$ is equal to reliability under a tau equivalence assumption, and (e) $\alpha$ is a general version of the KR-20 coefficient for dichotomous items. Although these descriptions have been widely used, the validity of some of them rests on certain assumptions (e.g., the use of $\alpha$ in its standardized or unstandardized form as just noted). One conclusion that can be drawn from the various descriptions of $\alpha$ in its relation to dimensionality is as follows (Cortina, 1993):

> It is a function of the extent to which items in a test have high communalities and thus low uniqueness. It is also a function of interrelatedness, although one must remember that this does not imply uni-dimensionality or homogeneity. (p. 100)

Thus, it must be remembered that it is possible for a set of items to be interrelated but not homogeneous. As such, coefficient $\alpha$ is not a measure of unidimensionality and should be used to assess internal consistency *only after* unidimensionality is established (Clark & Watson, 1995; Cortina, 1993; Gerbing & Anderson, 1988; Hattie, 1985; Schmitt, 1996).

As stated in Chapter 2, unidimensionality can be defined as the existence of one latent trait or construct underlying a set of items/measures (Hattie, 1985). Such a set of items has also been termed a "congeneric" measure. The importance of establishing dimensionality prior to establishing other psychometric properties (e.g., internal consistency and nomological validity) should not be understated (Cortina, 1993; Gerbing & Anderson, 1988; Hattie, 1985; Schmitt, 1996). To operationalize latent constructs, researchers often use composite scores, summing or averaging across items designed to measure the construct of interest. The computation and use of such scores are meaningful only if the items have acceptable unidimensionality.

Use of multidimensional scales as if they are unidimensional (i.e., summing or averaging item composites) may result in interpretational ambiguities of the relationships among constructs in a test of theory. That is, if a construct is multidimensional but all item scores are summed/averaged across dimensions into a single composite score and correlated with a criterion variable, such a correlation is ambiguous. Neuberg et al. (1997) offer an eloquent exposition of the cost of treating a multidimensional scale as if it were unidimensional by drawing an analogy with experimental manipulations. A primary goal of experimentation is to create an "un-confounded" manipulation of an independent variable to accurately assess its effect on the dependent variable. If two constructs are actually being manipulated by a single experimental manipulation designed to manipulate one construct, that one construct's effect on the dependent variable cannot be gauged accurately, as disentangling its effect from the unwanted variation of the second construct is problematic.

Similarly, researchers have the goal of developing a scale such that one construct is being assessed. The rationale behind unidimensionality is that the "interpretation of any measure—whether it represents a trait, a mood, an ability, or a need—is clearest if only one dimension underlies the measure" (Neuberg et al., 1997, p. 1022). When only one dimension underlies a measure, that measure's correlation with a criterion is clearer. When more than one dimension exists, possibly suggesting that more than one trait/ individual difference variable is being assessed, a measure's correlation with a criterion may be confounded. In sum, the problem that arises from treating a multidimensional scale as if it were unidimensional (e.g., summing for a total score) is that more than one dimension underlies the total score. This raises the possibilities that any effect on a criterion variable can be attributed to the wrong dimension or that all dimensions are necessary to produce the effect. Given that the goal of much research is to build and test theories, valid construct meaning is required. Unidimensionality therefore is a necessary condition for internal consistency, construct validity, and theory testing.

It should be noted that researchers have offered techniques for combining multiple dimensions of a construct that attempt to "un-confound" the effects of combining the dimensions into a single composite score (Carver, 1989; Hull, Lehn, & Tedlie, 1991). In general, these approaches attempt to estimate the effect of each dimension of a construct on criterion variables via statistical means (e.g., regression and structural equation modeling approaches). It should also be noted that there are special instances for which summing scores across dimensions and forming a composite score may be warranted. For example, if the dimensions do not have differential effects on the criterion variables of interest, then creating an overall composite (summing scores across dimensions) may be warranted (Carver, 1989; Richins & Dawson, 1992).

## Coefficient Alpha, Scale Length,
## Interitem Correlation, and Item Redundancy

It must also be remembered that $\alpha$ is a function of scale length, average interitem correlation (covariance), and item redundancy. First consider scale length. The formulas for $\alpha$ expressed in Equations 3.6 and 3.7 suggest that as the number of items increases, $\alpha$ will tend to increase. Because parsimony is also a concern in measurement, an important question is "What is an appropriate scale length in relation to coefficient $\alpha$?" The answer to this question depends partially on the domain and dimensions of the construct. Naturally, a construct with a wide content domain and multiple dimensions will require more items to adequately tap the domain/dimensions than will a construct with a narrow domain and one dimension. Given that most scales are self-administered and that respondent fatigue and/or noncooperation need to be considered, scale brevity is often a concern (cf. Clark & Watson, 1995; Cortina, 1993; DeVellis, 1991; Nunnally & Bernstein, 1994). To address this concern, various researchers have suggested the use of generalizability theory in designing scales. Generalizability theory and its use in designing scales will be discussed later in the chapter.

Next, consider the effects of item redundancy and average interitem correlation on coefficient $\alpha$. It is widely advocated that item wording be simple and straightforward, that the items tap the content of the construct, and that the respondent derive the researcher's intended meaning of the item. It is also advocated that several items be used to adequately tap the domain of the construct. When the wording of the items is too similar, however, coefficient $\alpha$ (as well as content validity and dimensionality) may be artificially enhanced. Items that are worded too similarly will increase average interitem correlation, which in effect increases coefficient $\alpha$, but without adding substantively to the content validity of the measure (Boyle, 1991; Clark & Watson, 1995). Although some similarity among items of a scale is needed to tap the domain, several items that are just slight wording variations of other items are redundant and contain very little new information about the construct (Clark & Watson, 1995). Redundant items may contribute to the "attenuation paradox" in psychometric theory, whereby increasing coefficient $\alpha$ beyond a certain point does not increase internal consistency (Boyle, 1991; Loevinger, 1957). Given this possibility, researchers must be careful in their interpretation of $\alpha$ by considering its relationship to the number of items in a scale, the level of interitem correlation, item redundancy, and dimensionality.

As further evidence of the interrelatedness of scale length, average level of interitem correlation, and the overredundancy of item wording (and dimensionality), consider the following. A widely advocated level of adequacy for $\alpha$ has been .70, regardless of the issues just discussed. Again, $\alpha$ gives us information about the extent to which each item in a set correlates with other items in that set, and as the number of items and the average interitem correlation increase (*ceteris paribus*), $\alpha$ will increase. Furthermore, the number of items in a scale can have a pronounced effect at lower levels of interitem correlation. For example, in his meta-analysis, Peterson (1994) found that the mean $\alpha$ level for a 3-item scale with an average interitem correlation of .47 was .73. If the .47 level of interitem correlation is applied to a 9-item scale, this 9-item scale would exhibit an $\alpha$ level of .89. For the 9-item scales reviewed, however, Peterson (1994) found an average interitem correlation of .31 and an average $\alpha$ level of .80.

Cortina (1993) further demonstrated the relationships between coefficient $\alpha$, average interitem correlation, scale length, and dimensionality. His findings are based on scales with 1, 2, or 3 dimensions; 6, 12, or 18 items; and average interitem correlations of .30, .50, and .70. Three of his key findings are as follow. First, the number of items heavily affects $\alpha$. If a scale has a large number of items, $\alpha$ can be above .70 even with low interitem correlations. Also, for a unidimensional measure with an average interitem correlation of .50, $\alpha$ will be above .70 regardless of the number of items in the measure. Second, for a scale that has more than 14 items, an $\alpha$ of .70 or higher will result even if two orthogonal (nonrelated) dimensions with an average interitem correlation of .30 are combined. If the two dimensions have average item correlations that are above .70, then $\alpha$ can be greater than .85. Third, given a large number of reasonably correlated items, a scale can have an acceptable $\alpha$ even if it contains three orthogonal dimensions. In sum, $\alpha$ increases as interitem correlation increases, and it decreases as a function of multidimensionality. However, $\alpha$ can still be high in spite of low interitem correlations and the presence of multidimensionality. When interpreting $\alpha$, one must have already established unidimensionality, and then consider the number of items and average interitem correlation.

Still, maximizing alpha is a commendable goal in scale construction—a goal that must be tempered by considering scale length, average interitem correlation, redundancy of item wording, and scale dimensionality/complexity. Although to our knowledge no "hard" statistical criteria exist as to what is the minimum or maximum number of items in a scale, what is a minimum acceptable α, or what is an acceptable level of average interitem correlation, several heuristics exist. For example, Robinson et al. (1991) advocated an α level of .80 or better, and average interitem correlations of .30 or better as exemplary. Clark and Watson (1995) advocated average interitem correlations of .15 to .50 across constructs, and for narrowly defined constructs, they advocated a range of .40 to .50. They also advocated a coefficient α level of at least .80 for a new scale. Once the .80 benchmark is achieved, however, adding items is of little utility to internal consistency and content validity, particularly with a narrowly defined construct. For such constructs, four to seven items could suffice. In our view, these guidelines and heuristics represent solid advice in scale construction.

## GENERALIZABILITY THEORY

In previous sections, we reviewed various procedures for examining scale reliability. Another critical issue facing researchers is that of generalizability. That is, can the scale be generalized to other situation(s) under which it will be used? For example, consider the 17-item consumer ethnocentrism scale (CETSCALE) for measuring consumers' ethnocentric tendencies to purchase imported goods (Shimp & Sharma, 1987). Following are examples of issues that could be raised with respect to this scale. First, the items used in the scale supposedly are taken from a population containing an infinite number of items. Suppose one takes another set of, say, 10 items from the statement population. Will the reliability of the CETSCALE, as measured by the 10 statements, be different or the same? That is, to what extent does selection of statements affect the reliability of the scale? If it does affect reliability, what is the nature of the effect? Second, the CETSCALE was developed in the United States. A valid question is "Does the scale generalize across countries (i.e., cultures)?" Although the scale has been found to be reliable in other cultures (e.g., Netemeyer, Durvasula, & Lichtenstein, 1991; Sharma, Shin, & Shimp, 1995), it is reasonable to ask to what extent culture affects the reliability of the scale. Procedures have been developed, which fall under the general umbrella of "Generalizability Theory," to address the above issues by partitioning the total variance of a scale into different components.[5] The

---

[5] Shavelson and Webb (1991) provide an excellent discussion of Generalizability Theory.

following section discusses these procedures and illustrates how they can be used in scale development.

Suppose an educational toy company has developed a new toy for 3-year-old children. The objective of the toy is to develop social interaction among children. To determine whether the new toy is successful with respect to this objective, the toy company arranges a focus group interview in which ten 3-year-old children are given the toy and the session is videotaped. Three experts in social interaction are asked to view the tape and rate the level of interaction on a 7-point item. The procedure is repeated after 2 weeks; the same children are videotaped, and the same experts are asked to rate the children again. In generalizability terminology, this study is referred to as a *two-facet study*. The two generalization facets are time (i.e., the two time periods during which data are collected) and the raters. These facets or factors are referred to as *generalization factors* because of interest in generalizing the results of the study across these factors. The level of social interaction will vary across children, the object of measurement. Research participants (in this case, children) usually are referred to as the *differentiation* or *universe score* factor, as the children are expected to differ with respect to their level of social interaction.

As depicted in Table 3.5, the total variation in the data can be decomposed into seven sources of variation. The sources of variation and their implications are discussed below.

1. *Variation due to differences in children or subjects (S).* If variation due to this source is high, then there is heterogeneity in children with respect to their social interaction.

2. *Variation due to differences in raters (R).* If this variation is large, then it is assumed that ratings of children differ across raters. That is, inter-rater reliability could be low and, consequently, the rating process used by raters or instructions provided to raters might need further attention. It also is possible that because of the nature of measurement, additional raters are needed. The optimum number of raters can be determined from the results of the study. Procedures for determining optimal levels of a given facet will be discussed in the section presenting an empirical illustration of a generalizability study to identify the optimum number of scale items.

3. *Variation due to the two observation occasions or time (T).* A low variation due to this factor would imply that there is very little variation due to time and test-retest reliability is high. One might conclude from

**Table 3.5** Sources of Variability for a Two-Facet Generalizability Design

| Source of Variation | df | Sum of Squares | Mean Square | Expected Mean Square | Variance Component |
|---|---|---|---|---|---|
| Subjects (S) | $S-1$ | $SS_S$ | $SS_S/df_S$ | $\sigma_\varepsilon^2 + n_T\sigma_{S\times R}^2 + n_R\sigma_{S\times T}^2 + n_R n_T\sigma_S^2$ | $\sigma_S^2$ |
| Raters (R) | $R-1$ | $SS_R$ | $SS_R/df_R$ | $\sigma_\varepsilon^2 + n_S\sigma_{R\times T}^2 + n_T\sigma_{R\times S}^2 + n_S n_T\sigma_R^2$ | $\sigma_R^2$ |
| Time (T) | $T-1$ | $SS_T$ | $SS_T/df_T$ | $\sigma_\varepsilon^2 + n_S\sigma_{R\times T}^2 + n_R\sigma_{S\times T}^2 + n_S n_R\sigma_T^2$ | $\sigma_T^2$ |
| $S\times R$ | $(S-1)(R-1)$ | $SS_{S\times R}$ | $SS_{S\times R}/df_{S\times R}$ | $\sigma_\varepsilon^2 + n_T\sigma_{S\times R}^2$ | $\sigma_{S\times R}^2$ |
| $S\times T$ | $(S-1)(T-1)$ | $SS_{S\times T}$ | $SS_{S\times T}/df_{S\times T}$ | $\sigma_\varepsilon^2 + n_R\sigma_{S\times T}^2$ | $\sigma_{S\times T}^2$ |
| $R\times T$ | $(R-1)(T-1)$ | $SS_{R\times T}$ | $SS_{R\times T}/df_{R\times T}$ | $\sigma_\varepsilon^2 + n_S\sigma_{R\times T}^2$ | $\sigma_{R\times T}^2$ |
| $S\times R\times T$, error[a] | $(R-1)(R-1)(T-1)$ | $SS_{S\times R\times T}$ | $SS_{S\times R\times T}/df_{S\times R\times T}$ | $\sigma_\varepsilon^2$ | $\sigma_{S\times R\times T}^2$ |

a. Because there is only one observation per cell, the three-way interaction is confounded with error.

this that multiple measurement occasions are not needed. On the other hand, large variation due to this source suggests that the measurement occasion does have an effect. It is possible, although highly unlikely, that the children might have changed with respect to their social interaction level. It also is possible that the time of day (i.e., morning, afternoon, evening) might be the reason for variation in children's interaction level, and therefore measurement at each of these times of day is necessary to generalize study findings.

4. *The interaction between subject and raters (S × R).* High variation due to this source suggests inconsistencies of raters in rating subjects, in that the rating of a given subject differs across raters. This usually should not be the case; however, if it is, this might suggest that bias due to the raters and the rating process might need further investigation.

5. *The interaction between subject and time (S × T).* High variation due to this source suggests that a given subject's behavior (i.e., social interaction) changes across the two measurement time periods, suggesting that the time period used could be too long.

6. *The interaction between rating and time (R × T).* Variation in a given rater's evaluation across the two time periods; differences in this interaction among raters suggests that some raters are more consistent than other raters.

7. *The interaction between subject, rating, and time (S × R × T).* The residual variation, which is due to the combination of subjects, rating, and time, and/or effects of factors not taken into consideration and random error.

It should be noted that the first four columns of Table 3.5 are similar to that obtained in regular ANOVA (analysis of variance) results. The fifth column gives the expected mean square, and the last column is the variation due to the respective source. The equations in the fifth column can be solved to obtain an estimate of variation due to the respective sources given in the last column. The following empirical illustration shows how this can be done.

**G-Study Illustration**

Suppose that we are interested in determining the extent to which the generalizability of a scale is affected by the number of statements. As an

**Table 3.6**    ANOVA Results

| Source | df | Sum of Squares | Mean Square | Expected Mean Square | Variance | Percentage |
|--------|-----|--------------|-------------|---------------------|----------|------------|
| Items (I) | 16 | 496.416 | 31.026 | $\sigma^2_{I\times S} + n_s\sigma^2_I$ | 0.422 | 15.8 |
| Subjects (S) | 70 | 1,501.857 | 21.455 | $\sigma^2_{I\times S} + n_I\sigma^2_S$ | 1.200 | 44.9 |
| Error (I × S) | 1,120 | 1,175.466 | 1.050 | $\sigma^2_{I\times S}$ | 1.050 | 39.3 |
| Total | | | | | 2.672 | 100.0 |

example, we return to the aforementioned 17-item CETSCALE, using data collected from 71 subjects (Netemeyer et al., 1991). (Exploratory and confirmatory factor analysis results suggest that the scale is unidimensional and that the scale is highly reliable; coefficient $\alpha = 0.952$.) This is a one-facet study in which the subject is the differentiation factor, as one would expect the subjects to differ with respect to CETSCALE scores.[6] Item is the generalization facet, as one is interested in knowing whether the scale is generalizable with respect to the number of items.

Table 3.6 gives the ANOVA results and the expected mean square. The relationships between variance components and expected mean squares (MS) are given by the following equations:

$$MS_I = \hat{\sigma}^2_{I\times S} + n_S\hat{\sigma}^2_I$$
$$MS_S = \hat{\sigma}^2_{I\times S} + n_S\hat{\sigma}^2_S$$
$$MS_{I\times S} = \hat{\sigma}^2_{I\times S}$$

where $n_S$ is the number of subjects and $n_I$ is the number of items. The solution to the above equations results in the following estimates of the variance components:

$$\hat{\sigma}^2_S = \frac{MS_S - MS_{S\times I}}{n_I} = \frac{21.455 - 1.050}{17} = 1.200$$

$$\hat{\sigma}^2_I = \frac{MS_I - MS_{S\times I}}{n_S} = \frac{31.026 - 1.050}{71} = 0.422$$

$$\hat{\sigma}^2_{S\times I} = MS_{S\times I} = 1.050$$

---

[6] We use the term "subjects" instead of "respondents" to be consistent with its use in the Generalizability Theory literature.

**Table 3.7**      Statements for PROC VARCOMP Procedure in SAS to Compute
                   Variance Components

```
VARIANCE DECOMPOSITION FOR CET STUDY;
DATA TEST;
INPUT SUBJECT ITEM RATING;
CARDS;
insert data here
PROC VARCOMP METHOD=MIVQUE0;
CLASS ITEM PERSON;
MODEL RATING=ITEM|PERSON;
RUN;
```

The above estimates and the percentage of the total variation due to the respective source are also reported in Table 3.6. The results suggest that 44.9% of the total variation is due to differences in CETSCALE scores of subjects, which is to be expected. This essentially means that subjects do differ with respect to their ethnocentric tendencies. The results also suggest that 15.8% of the variation is due to the items. Some variance due to the items is to be expected, as the items tap different aspects of the construct. High variance due to items is not desirable, however, as it suggests that the items may not be internally consistent—that is, that responses to items vary considerably, thereby affecting the generalizability of the scale.

The above procedure of computing the variance components by hand becomes cumbersome for multifacet studies. Procedures in standard statistical packages such as SAS and SPSS are available for computing variance components. Table 3.7 gives the statements for PROC VARCOMP in SAS to compute variance components. The METHOD option specifies the method that should be used in estimating the variance components. The minimum norm quadratic unbiased estimator (MIVQUE0) is the default method and is based on the technique suggested by Hartley, Rao, and LaMotte (1978). Other methods are the maximum likelihood (ML), ANOVA method using type 1 sum of squares (TYPE1), and restricted maximum likelihood method (REML). (See the SAS manual for further details about these methods.) Exhibit 3.1 gives the partial SAS output. As can be seen from the output, the estimates, within rounding error, are the same as those reported in Table 3.6.

In SPSS, the drop-down menu feature can be used to estimate variance components. Exhibit 3.2 gives the dialog boxes resulting from the *Analyze* →

**Exhibit 3.1**     Partial SAS Output

MIVQUE(0) Variance Component
Estimation Procedure

| Variance Component | Estimate RATING |
|---|---|
| Var(ITEM) | 0.42220381 |
| Var(PERSON) | 1.20032844 |
| Var(ITEM*PERSON) | 1.04952361 |
| Var(Error) | 0.00000000 |

*General Linear Model → Variance Components* sequence of commands. Moving the *rating* variable to *Dependent Variable* box and *Items* and *Subjects* to the *Random Factors* box and selecting *Model* gives the next dialog box, in which the ANOVA model is selected. Because only one observation per cell is available, the interaction term is used as the error term. Selecting *Custom* and moving *Subject* and *Item* to the *Model* box specifies the model to be used for estimating variance components. Exhibit 3.2 also gives the resulting output. As can be seen, once again the estimates are the same as those computed by hand and reported by SAS.

*Generalizability Coefficient*

The variance components can be used to compute the generalizability coefficient, which is analogous to the reliability coefficient. In fact, for a single facet design in which the number of items is the differentiation facet, the generalizability coefficient is identical to the reliability coefficient. Generalizability coefficients can be computed for both the relative and absolute error variance components. The relative error component is pertinent when relative decisions are desired. For example, the relative error component is relevant if one is interested in comparing the CETSCALE score of each subject with scores of other subjects. This definition of error assumes that all sources of variation that include subjects are error, which in this case is the interaction between subjects and items. That is,

$$\text{Relative error} = \sigma_{\tilde{a}}^2 = \frac{\sigma_{S \times I}^2}{n_I} \ . \tag{3.9}$$

**Exhibit 3.2**     SPSS Procedure for Estimating Variance Components

---

**Popup screen resulting from** *Analyze* ➔ *General Linear Model* ➔ *Variance Component* **sequence of commands.**

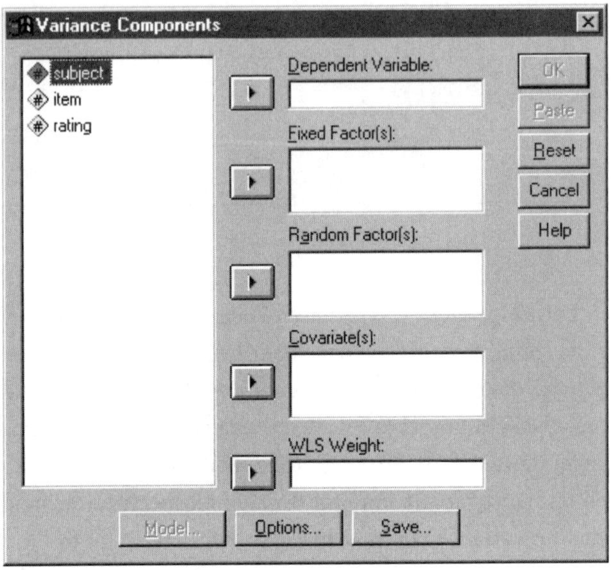

**Popup screen resulting from selecting** *Options*

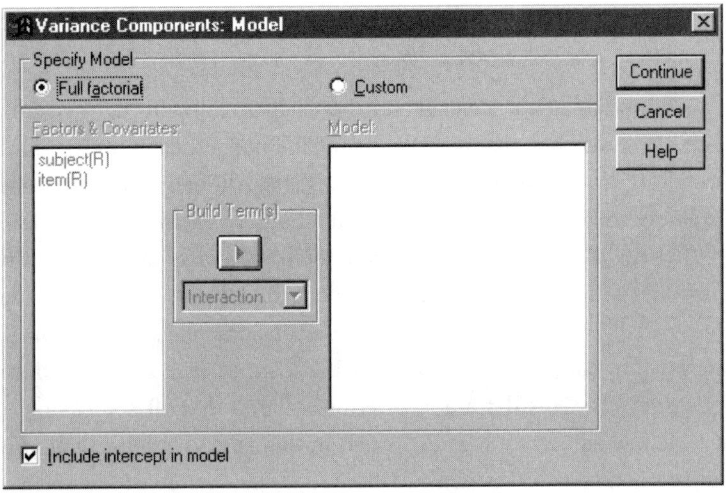

**Variance Estimates**

| Component | Estimate |
|-----------|----------|
| Var (SUBJECT) | 1.200 |
| Var (ITEM) | .422 |
| Var (Error) | 1.050 |

Dependent Variable: RATING
Method: Minimum Norm Quadratic Unbiased estimation
(Weight = 1 for Random Effects and Residual)

The absolute error is used when interest is not in making relative comparisons but in absolute comparisons. For example, situations might arise where one is interested in comparing the CETSCALE score of each subject to a certain value. Absolute error includes all the variances except the variance due to subjects in the design. In the present case it is equal to

$$\text{Absolute error} = \sigma_\Delta^2 = \frac{\sigma_I^2}{n_I} + \frac{\sigma_{S \times I}^2}{n_s} . \tag{3.10}$$

The generalizability coefficient, which would be similar to the reliability coefficient, is based on relative error and is given by

$$G^2 = \frac{\sigma_S^2}{\sigma_S^2 + \sigma_\delta^2} . \tag{3.11}$$

Using the above equation, the generalizability coefficient can be calculated as follows:

$$\sigma_\delta^2 = 1.05/17 = 0.062$$

$$G = \frac{1.20}{1.20 + 0.062} = 0.951$$

which is the same as coefficient $\alpha$ reported earlier.

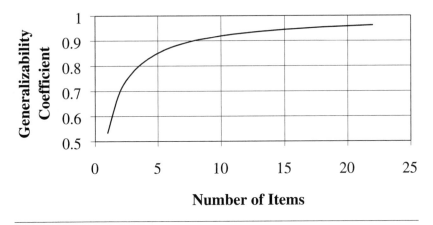

**Figure 3.3**     Relationship Between the Generalizability Coefficient and the
Number of Items

### Decision Studies

Suppose one is interested in using the above results to design a scale with a minimum number of items without sacrificing the generalizability coefficient. Such studies are called decision (D) studies. Equation 3.9 gives the relative error as a function of the number of items, a result that can be used to compute the relative error for a given number of statements and used subsequently in Equation 3.11 to compute the G coefficient. For example, for a scale consisting of two items, the relative error and the G coefficient are equal to

$$\sigma_\delta^2 = 1.05/2 = .53$$

$$G = \frac{1.20}{1.20 + .53} = .694.$$

Table 3.8 gives the relative error and the G coefficient for different numbers of statements, and Figure 3.3 depicts the relationship between the G coefficient and the number of statements. As can be seen from the table and the figure, the increase in the G coefficient becomes negligible after a

**Table 3.8**     Number of Items, Relative Error Variance, and the G Coefficient

| Number of Items | Relative Error Variance | G Coefficient |
| --- | --- | --- |
| 1 | 1.050 | 0.533 |
| 2 | 0.525 | 0.694 |
| 3 | 0.350 | 0.774 |
| 4 | 0.263 | 0.820 |
| 5 | 0.210 | 0.851 |
| 6 | 0.175 | 0.873 |
| 7 | 0.150 | 0.889 |
| 8 | 0.131 | 0.902 |
| 9 | 0.117 | 0.911 |
| 10 | 0.105 | 0.920 |
| 11 | 0.095 | 0.927 |
| 12 | 0.088 | 0.932 |
| 13 | 0.081 | 0.937 |
| 14 | 0.075 | 0.941 |
| 15 | 0.070 | 0.945 |
| 16 | 0.066 | 0.948 |
| 17 | 0.062 | 0.951 |
| 18 | 0.058 | 0.954 |
| 19 | 0.055 | 0.956 |
| 20 | 0.053 | 0.958 |
| 21 | 0.050 | 0.960 |
| 22 | 0.048 | 0.962 |

certain number of statements. In fact, a scale consisting of eight items gives a G coefficient of 0.902. Therefore, one might use a shorter scale consisting of only eight items selected at random rather than 17 items. A shorter scale obviously reduces the size of the questionnaire and the resulting respondent fatigue.

## SUMMARY

This chapter has discussed various forms of reliability, most notably coefficient alpha. It also discussed the relationship between coefficient alpha, unidimensionality, interitem correlation, scale length, and item-wording redundancy. We highlighted the importance of establishing dimensionality prior to assessing internal consistency as well as the effects of interitem correlation and wording redundancy on reliability. We also discussed the concept of generalizability and how it can be used to assess the effects of different variance components on the reliability (and generalizability) of a scale. As we previously acknowledged, dimensionality and reliability are necessary inputs to establishing a scale's validity. The next chapter discusses the various types of validity that come under the term "construct validity" and procedures to establish these types of validity in scale development.

# ⊰ FOUR ⊱

# VALIDITY

---

## OVERVIEW OF CONSTRUCT VALIDITY

This chapter addresses critical issues related to construct validity as applied to measurement development for latent constructs. Construct validity is viewed as the extent to which an operational measure truly reflects the concept being investigated or the extent to which operational variables used to observe covariation in and between constructs can be interpreted in terms of theoretical constructs (Calder, Phillips, & Tybout, 1982). Construct validity can and should be viewed broadly as referring to the degree to which inferences legitimately can be made from measures used in a study to the theoretical constructs on which those operationalizations are based. Similar to the views expressed by Haynes et al. (1999) and Trochim (2002), construct validity represents the overarching quality of a research study or even a program of studies, with other categories or types of validity being subsumed under construct validity. As such, a measure is construct valid (a) to the degree that it assesses the magnitude and direction of a representative sample of the characteristics of the construct and (b) to the degree that the measure is not contaminated with elements from the domain of other constructs or error (Peter, 1981). It is important to note that construct validity for a measure is not assessed directly but is inferred from evidence that the measure's substantive scores perform as expected from theoretically derived tests, as well as from the quality of the procedures that were employed in the development and validation of the measure.

The remainder of the chapter describes the various ways of demonstrating or providing evidence of construct validity. These validity types can be used in measurement development in efforts to generate and develop valid items or indicators of unobservable constructs and in efforts to provide evidence of measure quality. Using classifications similar to those proposed by Haynes et al. (1999) and Trochim (2002), the various types or evidence of validity discussed in the chapter are grouped as follows:

1. Translation validity
   Content validity
   Face validity

2. Criterion-related validity
   Predictive and post-dictive validity
   Concurrent validity
   Convergent validity
   Discriminant validity
   Known-group validity

3. Nomological validity

In addition to these sources of evidence or specific validity types, the chapter concludes with a discussion of the problems associated with socially desirable responding.


## TRANSLATION VALIDITY

Content and face validity reflect the extent to which a construct is *translated* into the operationalization of the construct (Trochim, 2002). The terms are often confused and/or used interchangeably. Although the distinction between face and content validity frequently is unclear, Rossiter (2001) argued that the two validity concepts differ in important ways and should not be confused.


### Face Validity

Evidence of face validity is provided from a post hoc evaluation that the items in a scale adequately measure the construct (cf. Nunnally & Bernstein, 1994; Rossiter, 2001). Face validity can be judged after a measure has been developed, often prior to application in another study, by potential measurement users. An after-the-fact examination of item content for a measure, however, offers only incomplete evidence of validity, because measurement evaluators see only the items that remain and have to infer what may have been omitted and why. Thus, face validity can be considered as one limited aspect of content validity, concerning an inspection of the final product to make sure nothing went wrong in transforming plans into a completed instrument or measure (Nunnally & Bernstein, 1994, p. 110). Furthermore, some argue that face validity is more akin to what a respondent may infer about what an item is intended to measure (Nevo, 1985) and has been referred to as "the mere appearance that a measure has validity" (Kaplan & Saccuzzo, 1997, p. 1320). Thus, high face validity of an instrument enhances its use in practical situations by inducing cooperation among respondents via ease of use, proper reading level, clarity, and appropriate response formats.

### Content Validity

Assurances of content validity are based upon a priori theoretical, item generation, and judging efforts. Specifically, content validity represents the degree to which elements of a measurement instrument are relevant to and representative of the targeted construct for a particular assessment purpose (Haynes et al., 1995, p. 238). Representativeness refers to the degree to which elements are proportional to the facets of the targeted construct and the degree to which the entire domain of the targeted construct has been sampled. That is, the measure should appear consistent with the theoretical domain of the construct in all aspects, including item wording, response formats, and instructions (Haynes et al., 1999; Haynes et al., 1995; Netemeyer, Pullig, & Bearden, 2002; Robinson et al., 1991).

The basic objective, then, is to ensure that the items reflect the content areas encompassed by the target construct. As such, content validity is manifested from procedures at the initial stages of scale development that generate items representative of the domain of the focal construct. Development of a content valid measure is enhanced during the early stages of scale development by effective creation of an "item pool" and the subsequent evaluation of items by lay and/or expert judges.

First, the items in the initial pool should be chosen so as to sample all possible content areas that might be encompassed by the construct according to the complete set of theoretical perspectives underlying the construct

(Clark & Watson, 1995). The initial item pool should be comprehensive in coverage and include a large number of potential items across the a priori theoretical dimensions. The initial item pool undoubtedly will include some items that subsequently will be eliminated in follow-up judging procedures and psychometric analyses. A large number of items for each dimension in the beginning item pool increases the likelihood that all dimensions will be represented adequately. That is, the focus on breadth of the item pool applies to all possible construct areas or dimensions, so that individual areas are not underrepresented in the final scale.

Content validation is particularly important for constructs that are ambiguous or complex. Content validation is enhanced via precise construct definition and conceptualization, including the specification of dimensionality and the individual definitions of the various dimensions that the construct comprises. In addition, content validity is ensured to the extent that lay and expert judges agree that items are reflective of the overall construct and that these judges agree that the items are representative of the domain and facets of the construct.

Items to be included in an item pool may be obtained using any number of sources. The most frequently used sources of items in scale development articles include previously employed statements from prior research involving the construct, open-ended elicitation from samples of representative subjects, and researcher-generated statements based on the researcher's knowledge and understanding of the domain of the construct and its theoretical underpinnings.

As an example, Bearden, Hardesty, and Rose (2001) reported the following efforts in the development of their 31-item, six-dimension measure of consumer self-confidence. Briefly, self-confidence was conceptualized initially as a two-factor higher-order model with seven first-order factors. The a priori higher-order factors (and the hypothesized subdimensions) were as follows:

1. Decision-making self-confidence
   a. Information acquisition
   b. Information processing
   c. Consideration set formation
   d. Personal outcomes
   e. Social outcomes

2. Protection self-confidence
   a. Persuasion knowledge
   b. Marketplace interfaces.

**Table 4.1**     Content Validation Guidelines

1. Carefully define the domain and the dimensions of the construct.

2. Use population and expert sampling for the initial generation of items.

3. Use multiple judges of content validity and quantify judgments using formalized scaling procedures.

4. Examine the proportional representation of items across the various dimensions.

5. Report the results of content validation efforts as indices for researchers to use in evaluating the relevance and representativeness of measurement items.

SOURCE: Adapted from "Content Validity in Psychological Assessment: A Functional Approach to Concepts and Methods," *Psychological Assessment, 7*(3), pp. 244-245, Haynes, Richard, and Kubany, copyright © 1995 by the American Psychological Association.

An initial pool of 145 items was generated from exploratory interviews with adult consumers and a review of items used in earlier studies. In the exploratory interviews, a convenience sample of 43 adult consumers of mixed age and gender were asked to provide descriptive statements of individuals both high and low in the seven a priori dimensions of consumer self-confidence following exposure to the definitions for each dimension. Frequently mentioned statements from the open-ended descriptions were converted to statements and included in the initial item pool. Following development of this initial set of statements, item screening to eliminate redundant, double-barrel, ambiguous, and leading statements reduced the pool of items from 145 to 116 statements.

Fourteen marketing faculty were then used to judge the remaining items. These expert judges were asked to rate how well each of the remaining 116 items reflected the different dimensions of self-confidence using the following scale: 1 = *clearly representative,* 2 = *somewhat representative,* and 3 = *not representative at all.* Each item was evaluated by 7 of the 14 judges, with two sets of judges exposed to the items from either three or four of the hypothesized seven dimensions. Only items evaluated on average as at least somewhat representative were retained. This process reduced the number of items to 97. The number of items remaining per facet ranged from 11 for consideration set formation to 20 for marketplace interfaces. Thus, Bearden et al. (2001) offered a thorough example of item content validity judging. (In Chapter 5, several other marketing and organizational behavior examples are offered.) As a summary, the content validation procedures recommended by Haynes et al. (1995, pp. 244-245) are listed in abbreviated form in Table 4.1 and are expanded upon in Chapter 5.

## CRITERION VALIDITY

Efforts to demonstrate criterion validity involve processes in which measures external to the proposed measurement instrument are employed (Nunnally & Bernstein, 1994). The specific sources of validity that can be used under the larger label of criterion validity include predictive and post-dictive validity, concurrent validity, convergent and discriminant validity, and known-group validity.

### Predictive and Post-dictive Validity

The term *predictive validity* often is used interchangeably with "criterion validity." In traditional applications involving scale development, predictive validity refers to the ability of a measure to effectively predict some subsequent and temporally ordered criterion. Development of a test of consumer persuasion knowledge for use with adolescents (cf. Friestad & Wright, 2001) can be used to illustrate the problem. For example, the validity of such a test could be supported by the size of correlations between a consumer persuasion knowledge test and indices or an observation of effective consumer behaviors occurring after the test has been administered. This is similar to validating pedagogical tests (e.g., a math aptitude test) using follow-up performance or grades in one or more math classes.

Post-dictive criterion validity occurs when the outcome variable is measured before the independent variable. For example, consumer households might be observed for behaviors demonstrating consumers' need for uniqueness (CNFU). Subsequently, a scale designed to measure CNFU is administered to an adult from each household. A significant correlation between an index comprising the observed behaviors and the CNFU scale would offer some evidence of post-dictive validity for the CNFU scale (cf. Tian, Bearden, & Hunter, 2001).

### Concurrent Validity

Evidence of concurrent validity for a measure is provided by sizable correlations between the construct measure under development and a criterion measure collected simultaneously or "concurrently." As an example, Bearden et al. (2001) provided evidence of the concurrent validity of their consumer self-confidence measures using correlations between their self-confidence scales and measures of subjective product knowledge (cf. Park, Mothersbaugh, & Feick, 1994). In addition, these developmental efforts also included demonstration of relative scale validity in that the confidence measures being proposed were more strongly correlated than were competing measures of self-esteem (Rosenberg, 1965) and information processing self-confidence (Wright, 1975). In these later comparisons, evidence of relative concurrent validity was provided from significant differences in tests of dependent correlations, which suggested that the measures being evaluated were more strongly correlated with the concurrent criterion (i.e., subjective knowledge assessments) than were the competing measures.

## Convergent and Discriminant Validity

A measure is said to possess convergent validity if independent measures of the same construct converge, or are highly correlated. Evidence of convergent validity is offered by significant and strong correlations between different measures of the same construct. Discriminant validity requires that a measure does not correlate too highly with measures from which it is supposed to differ (Churchill & Iacobucci, 2002, p. 413). In terms of measure development and validation, evidence of convergent validity typically is provided from correlations between the new measure being developed and existing measures. Obviously, problems in generating evidence of convergent validity often occur in measurement development when alternative measures are not available. These instances are frequently encountered for constructs that have not been studied previously or have been investigated using ad hoc or inadequately developed operationalization methods. When previously validated scales are not available for providing the necessary variety in measurement, measures from other fields, such as psychology, often are employed (Richins, 1983).

Among the most frequently employed methods of investigating convergent validity, as well as discriminant validity, is the multitrait-multimethod matrix (MTMM matrix) proposed by Campbell and Fiske (1959). As Cook and Campbell (1979, p. 61) summarized, at the heart of assessing construct validity are two processes: first, testing for convergence across different measures of the same concept, and second, testing for divergence between measures of related but conceptually distinct concepts.

**Table 4.2**     Multitrait-Multimethod Matrix

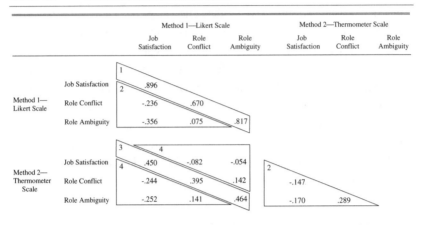

SOURCE: Adapted from "A Paradigm for Developing Better Measures of Marketing Constructs," *Journal of Marketing Research*, *16*(February), p. 17, Churchill, copyright © 1979 by the American Marketing Association.

The typical MTMM matrix displays a series of Pearson correlation coefficients among measures of unobservable constructs. For example, Richins (1983, p. 77) offered a consumer behavior example in which the analysis involved two traits (i.e., consumer assertion and aggression) and two methods (i.e., the Likert-type scales being developed and different scales assessing aggression and assertion borrowed from psychology). Nunnally and Bernstein (1994, p. 93) offered another example, in which the traits are anxiety and depression and the two methods are self-reports of anxiety and depression, and observational scores obtained from external judges. As shown in Table 4.2 and described below, Churchill (1979, pp. 70-71) depicted a sales management example involving three traits (i.e., job satisfaction, role conflict, and role ambiguity) and two methods (i.e., Likert-type and thermometer scales). The pattern of correlations within the matrix (i.e., the relative strength and significance of the correlations included in the matrix) are interpreted for evidence of both convergent and discriminant validity. (Kenny and Kashay [1992] and Widaman [1985] described procedures for using confirmatory factor analysis to analyze multitrait-multimethod data.)

In Table 4.2, the internal consistency reliability estimates are depicted in diagonal 1, in the upper left corner of the table. Evidence of convergent validity is provided by the correlations included in the validity diagonal 3, in the lower left corner. Support for convergent validity is offered in this example by the three correlations in the validity diagonal 3, in that the estimates are significant and large relative to other correlations in the matrix. Evidence of discriminant validity is offered by the correlations in the heteromethod block 4 in the lower left corner (i.e., the correlations among construct measures for which different measurement approaches are employed) and the heterotrait-monomethod triangles 2 in the upper left and lower right corners (i.e., the correlations among the construct measures for which a single measurement approach is employed). Evidence for discriminant validity involves three comparisons (Churchill, 1979, p. 71):

1. The entries in the validity diagonal 3 should be higher than the entries in the heteromethod block 4 that share the same row and column.

2. The correlations in the validity diagonal should be higher than the correlations in the heterotrait-monomethod triangles. This more stringent requirement suggests that the correlations between different measures for a trait should be higher than correlations among traits which have methods in common.

3. The pattern of the correlations should be the same in all the heterotrait triangles (i.e., 2 and 4).

For this example, the first two conditions for discriminant validity are satisfied. An excellent review and series of applications involving lifestyle measures and much different types of methods, including both qualitative and quantitative methods within traits, is provided by Lastovicka, Murry, and Joachimsthaler (1990). As demonstrated effectively by Lastovicka et al. (1990), the use of divergent methods enables more rigorous examination of convergent and discriminant validity.

Other procedures for providing evidence of convergent validity have been employed in the development of measures of unobservable constructs. For example, using procedures similar to those recommended by Bagozzi (1993), Bearden, Hardesty, et al. (2001) provided evidence of convergent validity for their six-dimension measure of consumer self-confidence. They did so via correlations between the multi-item scales being developed and general single-item measures for each dimension based on the conceptual definitions of each dimension. In this study, the multiple-item and the single-item measures enabled correlations among "multiple methods." Bearden et al. (2001) provided additional evidence of convergent validity by correlating spousal scores obtained from surveys of a sample of husband-wife dyads. Husbands provided responses regarding their wives' self-confidence, and wives provided their own responses. The correlation between these spousal ratings (i.e., the different raters' responses) reflected multiple methods.

Evidence of convergent validity is also obtained from factor analyses in which items from a new measure load highly on the same factor as do items from existing measures of the same construct (DeVellis, 1991; Paulhus, 1993). Finally, in validating their measure of consumer frugality, Lastovicka, Bettencourt, Hughner, and Kuntze (1999) employed the direct product model of Browne (1990) in efforts to examine the MTMM requirements for convergent and discriminant validity.

### Known-Group Validity

Known-group validity addresses the extent to which a measure differs as predicted between groups who should score low and high on a trait. Supportive evidence of known-group validity typically is provided by significant differences in mean scores across independent samples. Tian et al. (2001, pp. 56-57) provided several interesting examples in validating their scale to assess "consumers' need for uniqueness" (CNFU). Specifically, the average item score for a large heterogeneous mail survey sample for their 31-item CNFU scale was 2.60 ($n = 621$). Three known-group comparison samples, the type of consumer differentiation that the group represented, and the results for each sample are shown in Table 4.3. The known-group comparison samples were as follows: tattoo artists, reflecting the domain of bodily displays of consumer goods ($M = 3.05$, $n = 39$, $t = 3.22$, $p < .01$); owners of "customized low rider" mini-trucks, reflecting possession of unique objects ($M = 2.99$, $n = 22$, $t = 3.22$, $p < .01$); and members of the Society for Creative Anachronism, representing participation in unique groups that dress differently and enact medieval performances ($M = 2.91$, $n = 21$, $t = 2.49$, $p < .01$). Another interesting example of known-group validity was provided by Saxe and Weitz (1982). In validating their salesperson customer orientation scale (SOCO),

**Table 4.3** Summary of Known-Group Validity Test Results

| Known-Group Validity Test | Sample | Unique Group | | | Comparison Group | | | Value of t | Value of p | Validity Support |
|---|---|---|---|---|---|---|---|---|---|---|
| | | n | Mean | SD | n | Mean | SD | | | |
| Tattoo and body piercing artists | 1 | 39 | 3.05 | .70 | 621 | 2.60 | .56 | 3.22 | <.001 | Supported |
| Owners of customized low rider autos | 2 | 22 | 2.99 | .45 | 621 | 2.60 | .56 | 3.22 | <.001 | Supported |
| Members of medievalist reenactment group | 3 | 21 | 2.91 | .44 | 621 | 2.60 | .56 | 2.49 | <.01 | Supported |
| Student art majors | 4 | 22 | 3.06 | .45 | 273 | 2.71 | .50 | 3.15 | <.01 | Supported |
| Student purchasers of unique poster art | 5 | 78 | 2.83 | .43 | 273 | 2.71 | .50 | 1.89 | <.05 | Supported |

SOURCE: Adapted from "Consumers' Need for Uniqueness: Scale Development and Validation," *Journal of Consumer Research, 28*(June), p. 58, Tian, Bearden, and Hunter, copyright 2001 by the University of Chicago Press.

they found significant differences across samples from sales positions that differed widely in their professional status.

## NOMOLOGICAL VALIDITY

One means of evaluating construct validity for a measure comes from determining the extent to which the measure fits "lawfully" into a network of relationships or a "nomological network" (Cronbach & Meehl, 1955). That is, one aspect of construct validity involves the extent to which a measure operates within a set of theoretical constructs and their respective measures (Nunnally & Bernstein, 1994, p. 91). Nomological (lawlike) validity is based on investigations of constructs and measures in terms of formal hypotheses derived from theory. As such, nomological validation is primarily external and involves investigating both the theoretical relationships between different constructs and the empirical relationships between measures of those constructs. Thus, measures must demonstrate nomological validity to be accepted as construct valid (Peter, 1981, p. 135).

Evidence of nomological validity is provided by a construct's possession of distinct antecedent causes, consequential effects, and/or modifying conditions, as well as quantitative differences in the degree to which a construct is related to antecedents or consequences (Iacobucci, Ostrom, & Grayson, 1995; Tian et al., 2001, p. 59). Certainly, evidence provided from the methods described in preceding sections of this chapter can have implications for nomological validity. For example, differences in scores for a measure of sales force consumer orientation across ineffective and effective groups of salespersons provide some implications for theories of effective selling (i.e., nomological validity), as well as known-group validity.

Structural equation modeling (SEM), regression-based, and/or experimental methods often are used in efforts to provide corroborating evidence of nomological validity (e.g., Bollen, 1989; Hoyle, 1995). As an example, Bearden et al. (2001) employed logistic regression to demonstrate that a subset of their consumer confidence measures moderated (as hypothesized) the relationship between consumer price quality schema and choice of higher- versus lower-priced options in a choice set. Lastovicka et al. (1999) used multiple regression to demonstrate that their measure of frugality explained an index of frugal behaviors beyond alternative explanations for frugal behavior. As another set of examples, Tian (2001) described a large number of tests of differences in relationships involving a series of trait antecedents (e.g., collective individualism), outcomes (e.g., choice of unique versus common exterior designs), and situational moderators (e.g., popularization of unique designs) for their measure of consumers' need for uniqueness.


## SOCIALLY DESIRABLE RESPONSE BIAS

Socially desirable responding (SDR) is a complex issue that has been discussed by psychologists for years. We raise the issue in this chapter to reiterate its importance and to remind readers that SDR warrants consideration in research, particularly when the potential for response bias affects relationships among constructs. Briefly, SDR can be viewed as a response style or bias that reflects tendencies to provide favorable responses with respect to norms and practices (Nederhof, 1985). Mick (1996) defined socially desirable responding as the tendency of individuals to make themselves look good with respect to cultural norms when answering researchers' questions. As discussed below, this aspect of SDR is consistent with Paulhus's (1993) "impression management" concept, which highlights respondents' attempts to shape their answers purposefully to reflect the most positive image.

SDR can affect the measurement of constructs as well as the relationships among constructs (cf. Mick, 1996, pp. 109-110). Briefly, SDR can increase relationships such that correlations between constructs are due to shared variance in SDR. This phenomenon is termed the *spuriousness effect*. In the *suppression effect,* the true correlation between two measures is masked by SDR. A third possible effect of SDR occurs when the form of the relationship between two measured variables is affected. In these latter situations, SDR moderates the relationship between constructs. Procedures for investigating these alternative problems associated with response bias are described by Mick (1996) and Ganster, Hennessey, and Luthans (1983).

The methods for coping with SDR bias were summarized recently by Tian, Bearden, and Manning (2002). The procedures fit into two categories: methods devised to prevent survey participants from responding in a socially desirable manner and methods aimed at detecting and measuring social desirability response bias (Nederhof, 1985; Paulhus, 1991). Techniques employed by researchers to prevent or lessen socially desirable responding in survey research include the use of neutral questions, forced-choice items, the randomized response technique, indirect questioning, and self-administration of the questionnaire. Neutral questions, forced-choice items, and the randomized response technique have not produced convincing evidence of their effectiveness in reducing socially desirable responding in general social science research (Nederhof, 1985). Forced-choice items, for which respondents are made to choose between two items that are approximately equivalent in their social desirability but that are related to different topics, are problematic because some individuals may still perceive a difference in desirability of the items (Nederhof, 1985). Respondents might become antagonized by the use of randomized response techniques, whereby respondents answer one of two randomly selected items, with the researcher not knowing what item was answered. Indirect questioning, a projective technique in which survey respondents are asked to answer structured questions from the perspective of another person or group, has been demonstrated empirically to be an effective technique for reducing social desirability response bias (Fisher, 1993). Self-administration in mail surveys and anonymous mass administrations tend to lessen socially desirable responding in research involving individuals' self-descriptions (Nederhof, 1985; Paulhus, 1984). Self-administration and related techniques that provide anonymity, however, reduce only the socially desirable responding that stems from impression management—they do not reduce self-deceptive bias (Nederhof, 1985).

The second category of methods involves the use of direct measures of socially desirable responding to assess tendencies for individuals to present themselves favorably with respect to norms and standards. Measuring socially desirable responding allows assessment of the extent to which the tendency to overreport desirable behaviors or underreport undesirable behaviors confounds the accurate assessment of content variables and suppresses, inflates, or moderates variable relationships (Ganster et al., 1983; Mick, 1996; Zerbe & Paulhus, 1987). Furthermore, direct measures allow investigation of socially desirable responding as a psychological construct in its own right (see Mick, 1996, and Paulhus, 1991). Although a variety of socially desirable responding measures have been developed, these vary in their ability to independently capture impression management and self-deception dimensions of socially desirable responding and in their applicability to the study of various populations of respondents (Paulhus, 1991).

Paulhus (1984) developed the Balanced Inventory of Desirable Responding (BIDR). In the BIDR, which captured impression management and self-deceptive enhancement, positively and negatively keyed items were balanced across the two dimensions. This model distinguished socially desirable response styles in terms of impression management and self-deception, as two components that are differentially influenced by social pressure and that therefore require different treatment in analyses. Impression management—the tendency to tailor answers to create a positive image as a socially conventional person—varies according to transient motives and situational demands. Thus, impression management should be controlled when it is conceptually independent of the trait or construct being assessed (Paulhus, 1984, 1991). Self-deceptive enhancement—the tendency to provide responses reflecting an honest but inflated positive self-image—does not vary according to the situation. Because self-deceptive enhancement may be linked inextricably to content variance, such as when measuring achievement motivation or perceived control, it should not be controlled in these cases (Paulhus, 1984, 1991). The frequently used Marlowe-Crowne Social Desirability scale (Crowne & Marlowe, 1960) is associated with both factors, with a slightly higher loading emphasis on impression management.

Despite its laudable characteristics, the BIDR scale poses both practical and conceptual problems for researchers investigating many scale-related topics. With respect to practical problems, items on the BIDR scale appear as statements regarding private behaviors and feelings (e.g., "I never read sexy books or magazines," "When I was young I sometimes stole things," "I have sometimes doubted my ability as a lover"). Thus, organizational informants may question the relevance of these items in surveys that emphasize professional judgments. In addition, the length of the BIDR scale, at 40 items, discourages its inclusion in lieu of measured constructs that test theoretical propositions.

## SUMMARY

This chapter discussed issues related to construct validity as applied to measurement development for unobservable concepts. Overall, construct validity represents the extent to which an operational measure truly reflects the concept being investigated or the extent to which operational variables used to observe covariation in and between constructs can be interpreted in terms of theoretical constructs. Construct validity for a measure is not assessed directly but is inferred from evidence that the measure's substantive scores perform as expected, with that evidence coming from theoretically derived tests and from the quality of the procedures that were employed in the development and validation of the measure.

The various types or sources of evidence regarding the validity of measures intended to assess construct validity discussed in the chapter were as follows.

*Content validity*—the degree to which elements of a measurement instrument are relevant to and representative of the targeted construct for a particular assessment purpose. Assurances of content validity are based upon a priori theoretical, item generation, and judging efforts.

*Face validity*—an evaluation that the items in a scale adequately measure the construct. Face validity can be judged after a measure has been developed, often prior to application in another study, by potential measurement users.

*Predictive validity*—the ability of a measure to effectively predict some subsequent and temporally ordered criterion.

*Concurrent validity*—for which evidence is provided by sizable correlations between the construct measure under development and a criterion measure collected simultaneously or "concurrently."

*Convergent validity*—the extent to which independent measures of the same construct converge, or are highly correlated.

*Discriminant validity*—the extent to which measures diverge from other operationalizations from which the construct is conceptually distinct.

*Known-group validity*—the extent to which a measure differs as predicted between groups who should score low and high on a trait.

*Nomological validity*—the extent to which the measure fits "lawfully" into a network of relationships or a "nomological network"; that is, the extent to which a measure operates within a set of theoretical constructs and their respective measures.

In addition to these sources of evidence or specific validity types, the chapter concluded with a discussion of the problems associated with socially desirable responding, as well as a description of methods devised to prevent survey participants from responding in a socially desirable manner and methods aimed at detecting and measuring social desirability response bias (Nederhof, 1985; Paulhus, 1991). In the chapters that follow, these validity types are discussed further within the four recommended steps for scale development.

# FIVE

# STEPS 1 AND 2

## *Construct Definition and Generating and Judging Measurement Items*

———•———

## INTRODUCTION

Chapters 2, 3, and 4 discussed the psychometric principles of dimensionality, reliability, and validity primarily from a conceptual standpoint, as well as offering examples from some more recently developed scales. Chapters 5, 6, and 7 will now offer applications of these principles from an empirical standpoint. These chapters will cover the recommended steps and procedures in scale development and validation from construct definition to generalizability theory. As examples, we will use scales developed and validated within the marketing and organizational behavior literatures. Specifically, we will summarize results from the Consumer Self-Confidence scales (Bearden et al., 2001), the Consumer Frugality Scale (Lastovicka et al., 1999), the Work-Family Conflict (WFC) and Family-Work Conflict (FWC) scales (Netemeyer, Boles, & McMurrian, 1996), the Consumer Price Consciousness scale (Lichtenstein et al., 1993), and the Consumer Ethnocentrism Scale (CETSCALE; Shimp & Sharma, 1987). These scales appear in Appendix 5A of this chapter.

The first part of this chapter discusses the critical step of construct definition and delineation of the construct's content domain. Underscored in this step are the following issues: (a) the role of theory in construct definition and content domain, (b) the importance of a thorough literature review and definition judging by experts and individuals from relevant populations, (c) the focus on effect (reflective) items/indicators, and (d) the importance of an a priori construct dimensionality. The second part of this chapter deals with the second step in scale development: generating and judging an initial pool of items to reflect the construct. With this step, we will briefly cover the theoretical assumptions of domain sampling. We will also discuss issues in the generation of an item pool, question/statement wording options, choice of response formats, and judging the items for content and face validity by both experts and potential respondents from relevant populations. The last part of this chapter uses examples that illustrate and apply many of the procedures recommended for the first two steps in scale development.

## STEP 1: CONSTRUCT DEFINITION
## AND CONTENT DOMAIN

### The Importance of Clear Construct Definition

The importance of a well-defined construct cannot be overstated, as the validity of what is being measured will rest largely on its definition and content domain. Clearly defining the construct—its facets and domains—is an essential first step that many consider the most difficult step in the scaling process (cf. Churchill, 1979; Haynes et al., 1999; Haynes et al., 1995; Nunnally & Bernstein, 1994). In defining constructs, care must be taken as to what is included in the domain of the construct and what is excluded from this domain, as sources of invalidity can have their origins in the construct definition process. A measure may be too narrow and fail to include important facets of the construct. This has been referred to as construct *underrepresentation* (Messick, 1993). If the domain is too broadly defined, extraneous factors or domains of constructs other than the target construct may be included. Although these extraneous domains may be highly correlated with the relevant domains of the construct, they create what has been referred to as *construct-irrelevant variance,* which in turn can create confounds between the target construct and its predictor and criteria variables (Neuberg et al., 1997). The rationale behind a construct's domain is that the interpretation of any measure is clearest when the domain is un-confounded. When extraneous factors are included, possibly suggesting that more than one trait/individual difference variable is being assessed, that construct's correlation with a criterion may be confounded. In sum, when extraneous factors or domains of other constructs are included, more than one construct underlies the total score, and construct validity is threatened. Thus, it is widely believed that the key issue for the content aspect of construct validity is the clear specification of the boundaries of the domain of the construct to be assessed.

### The Importance of Theory, Literature Review, and Judging

In their classic works on measurement and validity, Cronbach and Meehl (1955) and Loevinger (1957) stated the importance of theory in measurement. For measures of latent constructs to have relevance in the social sciences, the constructs should be grounded in a theoretical framework. Even narrowly abstracted constructs based in theory are more useful as antecedents or consequences of other latent constructs or behaviors when embedded in theory. As such, a latent construct's relevance to the social sciences depends in part on the theories in which it is couched: What does the latent construct predict, and what predicts the latent construct? This has been referred to as a latent construct's *nomological net.* Figure 5.1 (Obermiller & Spangenberg, 1998) is a good example of a nomological network. In developing their measure of consumer skepticism toward advertising, Obermiller and Spangenberg posited several personality traits and demographic characteristics as potential antecedents of advertising skepticism. They also posited several information-processing variables, beliefs, attitudes, and behaviors as potential consequences of advertising skepticism. Such a network is instrumental in guiding scale development and assessing validity.

In essence, there can be no construct validity of a measure without a well-specified theory. This well-thought-through theory starts with construct conceptualization/definition based in a thorough review of the literature. Such a literature review ideally serves several important purposes. First, a literature review should alert the researcher to theories in which the construct may prove useful as an independent or dependent variable. A more precise handle on what the construct is—its boundaries, dimensions, and content domain—can be uncovered through a literature review. A literature review may also reveal prior attempts to measure the construct and the strengths and weaknesses of such attempts. Problems with previous attempts to measure the construct can be uncovered and thus avoided in one's own effort.

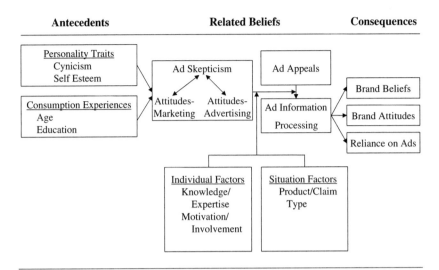

**Figure 5.1**     Nomological Network for Ad Skepticism

SOURCE: From "Development of a Scale to Measure Consumer Skepticism Toward Advertising," *Journal of Consumer Psychology, 7*(2), p. 167, Obermiller and Spangenberg, copyright 1998 by the University of Chicago Press. Reprinted with permission of the University of Chicago Press.

Second, a thorough review can uncover important related constructs to be used in validation. A thorough review can reveal related constructs and measures that can be used to assess discriminant, convergent, and other types of validity.

Finally, given that scale development and validation is a time-consuming and sometimes costly endeavor, a thorough literature review should help answer the following question: Is a scale needed at all? If good measures of a construct already exist, the value of a new measure may be small relative to the costs involved in developing it. A new measure, to be useful, must show some theoretical or empirical advantage over an existing measure of the same construct. For a new scale to have incremental validity over existing measures, it should capture the targeted construct either more accurately or more efficiently (e.g., it is shorter, cheaper, more user friendly, or easier to respond to) than existing measures (Clark & Watson, 1995; Haynes et al., 1999).

Another helpful way to enhance the accuracy and comprehensiveness of construct definition is review by experts and individuals from relevant populations. Although such reviews traditionally have been more associated with item judging, they can help delineate the facets of the construct prior to item generation. For example, in developing a measure of frugality, Lastovicka et al. (1999) conducted six depth interviews with self-professed frugal consumers to derive the definition and dimensionality of their construct. Bearden et al. (2001) conducted exploratory open-ended interviews with 43 adult consumers to help delineate dimensions of consumer self-confidence. (Other qualitative procedures for construct definition and refinement are noted by Crocker and Algina [1986, p. 68]). In sum, both judges with expertise in the subject area and members of relevant populations can be helpful in construct definition and establishing content domain.

### The Focus on Effect Items Versus Formative Indicators

As stated in Chapter 1, this text focuses on measures that are considered to be effect (reflective) indicators of constructs rather than "formative" (causal) indicators. For effect indicators, scores on the items are hypothesized to be driven by the latent construct. That is, individual differences on the construct account for the individual differences in item endorsement. With formative indicators, individual differences on the items account for individual differences on the construct. Two clarifying examples of a formative construct are offered here. First, the construct "life stress in the past year" may be construed as a formative indicator construct, in which indicators are different sources of stress including a job change, death of a loved one, birth of a child, and illness. It is counterintuitive that changes in life stress produce the death of a loved one or birth of a child; the opposite makes sense (Smith & McCarthy, 1995). Likewise, as a second example, socioeconomic status (SES) is best conceptualized as a formative indicator construct. People have high SES because of their wealth or education; they do not become wealthy or educated as a result of high SES (Nunnally & Bernstein, 1994). Thus, the indicators "form" the construct score.

Two other important differences between effect and formative indicators lie in both conceptual and methodological areas. First, for indicators that are conceptualized to form the latent construct, it is believed that the list of indicators must be comprehensive. That is, with formative indicators, a census of indicators—not just a sample—is needed to fully measure the construct. The exclusion of any indicator changes the makeup of the latent construct, and thus, each indicator is important to the validity of the construct (Bollen & Lennox, 1991; MacCallum & Browne, 1993; Neuberg et al., 1997). This is not necessarily the case with effect indicators. With reflective indicators, the items must represent a reasonable sample of items tapping the domain of the construct (Nunnally & Bernstein, 1994).

Second, the fact that the indicators of a formative construct are combined to produce an overall index does not necessarily imply that all individual indicator scores are intercorrelated, and whether they are or are not correlated is irrelevant to the reliability of the measure (Bollen & Lennox, 1991; Smith & McCarthy, 1995). Formative indicators need not be internally consistent, and reliability methods based on internal consistency do not apply. With effect items, the interrelatedness among items, and hence internal consistency, is of concern for the reliability of the measure.

Not only are there conceptual differences between formative and effect indicators, the methods used in developing such measures differ as well. (For an excellent review of these methods, see Diamontopoulus and Winklhofer, 2001.) Here again, the importance of a well-defined and thought-out construct definition is very useful. Theory and a thorough literature review can help determine if the construct is a formative or effect indicator measure.

## The Role of Theory in Specifying Dimensionality

As noted in Chapters 1 and 2, dimensionality is concerned with the homogeneity of items. Unidimensionality can be defined as the existence of one latent trait or construct underlying a set of items/measures (Hattie, 1985). Given that a construct's content domain can be hypothesized as unidimensional or multidimensional, its empirical structure should reflect its hypothesized dimensionality. For a single unidimensional construct, each item/indicator is reflected by its latent construct, or first-order factor. Such a set of items has also been termed a "congeneric" measure, one for which a single dimension underlies the set of items. When a construct is composed of multiple facets that are related, yet distinct, the construct can be classified as multidimensional.

The six-factor Consumer Self-Confidence Scale of Bearden et al. (2001) represents such a multidimensional scale. In contrast, Lastovicka et al.'s (1999) Consumer Frugality Scale is unidimensional. With multidimensional constructs, each dimension is considered a first-order factor represented by a separate latent variable, where each individual item is used to operationalize its respective hypothesized dimension. Within their respective dimensions, the items should show evidence of unidimensionality (i.e., congeneric qualities). To the extent that several first-order factors include common variance, a higher-order factor (also called a second-order factor) could be conceptualized to capture the shared variance across the first-order factors. The first-order factors are considered "reflective" indicators or dimensions of the higher-order construct, and the higher-order construct accounts for the covariance (correlation) among the first-order factors. A higher-order construct suggests that the dimensions (first-order factors) measure the same hierarchical concept, except for random error and measure specificity (Bagozzi & Heatherton, 1994).

The importance of theoretically specifying and empirically testing dimensionality prior to other psychometric properties (e.g., internal consistency and nomological validity) should not be understated (Cortina, 1993; Gerbing & Anderson, 1988; Hattie, 1985). To operationalize latent constructs, researchers often use composite scores, summing or averaging across items designed to measure the construct of interest. The computation and use of such scores are meaningful only if the items have acceptable unidimensionality. As noted in Chapter 3, multidimensional scales, when used as if they are unidimensional (i.e., summed or averaged item composites), may result in interpretational ambiguities of the relationships among constructs in a test of theory. If a construct is multidimensional but all item scores are summed/averaged across dimensions into a single composite score and correlated with a criterion variable, such a correlation is ambiguous (Neuberg et al., 1997). Here again, the role of theory and a thorough literature review should help specify a priori the dimensionality of the construct of interest.

## STEP 2: GENERATING AND JUDGING MEASUREMENT ITEMS

### Domain Sampling

Once the construct has been accurately defined and delineated, the task of generating items to tap the construct's domain begins. A model that is consistent with elements of both classical test theory and generalizability theory for generating items is domain sampling. As a model of measurement error, domain sampling suggests that a measure be composed of a sample of items from a large hypothetical domain of items. There exists a large pool (domain) of items that could tap the domain of the construct, and to arrive at a final scale measure, a sample of items from this domain with desirable psychometric properties must be selected.

As just stated, in theory, this pool is large and the items selected are drawn from what some have termed a "universe" or "population" of items. In practice, items for an initial pool are drawn from extant literature or generated by the scale authors. Expert judges from relevant populations also may contribute items. As long as the initial item pool is sufficiently large relative to the content domain of the construct, the principles of domain sampling still apply (Nunnally & Bernstein, 1994). Content adequacy exists when the content of the measure is a representative random sample of the domain to be measured and when the final items chosen (i.e., sample of items) to represent the construct have the same means and variances as those in the entire population pool of items. As noted in Chapter 4, content validity is relevant to domain sampling because content validity partially represents the degree to which one can generalize from a given set of items to all possible items in the construct's domain. The measurement error considered with domain sampling, then, is the error produced by using a sample of the items rather than the entire domain of items.

## Generating an Item Pool

In generating an item pool, an important goal is to systematically sample all content areas of the construct. Several issues relevant to translation validity must be kept in mind. First, the scale items generated should tap the content domain of the construct and exhibit content validity. As discussed in Chapter 4, the term "content validity" has been defined in many ways, with most definitions stressing that a measure's items are a proper sample of the theoretical domain of the construct (Nunnally & Bernstein, 1994; Peter, 1981). Most definitions are consistent with the following: Content validity reflects "the degree to which elements of an assessment instrument are relevant to and representative of the targeted construct for a particular assessment purpose" (Haynes et al., 1995, p. 238). Elements refer to the content of individual items, response formats, and instructions to respondents. Representativeness refers to the degree to which the elements are proportional to the facets (domains) of the targeted construct and to the degree that the entire domain of the target construct has been sampled. That is, the items should appear consistent with the theoretical domain of the construct in all respects, including response formats and instructions.

Second, in generating items, face validity must also be considered. A highly face valid scale enhances cooperation of respondents because of its ease of use, proper reading level, and clarity, as well as its instructions and response formats. Thus, from a practical perspective, face validity may be more concerned with what respondents from relevant populations infer with respect to what is being measured, and content validity is concerned with face validity as well as what the researcher believes he or she is constructing (Haynes et al., 1995; Nunnally & Bernstein, 1994).

Third, even with the focus on content and face validity, two other issues should be considered in constructing a pool of items. Clark and Watson (1995) advocated that the scale developer go beyond his or her own view of the construct in generating an initial item pool and that the initial pool contain items that ultimately will be only tangentially related to the content domain of the construct. Thus, it is better to be overinclusive of the construct's domain rather than underinclusive in generating an item pool. Care must also be taken to ensure that each content area of the construct has an adequate sampling of items. Although difficult to achieve in practice, broader content areas should be represented by a larger item pool than narrower content areas.

With these issues in mind, item generation can begin with careful thought to (a) what should be the source of the items, (b) item wording issues, and (c) how many items should serve as an initial pool. For these issues, definitive answers do not exist, but some practical guidelines are evident.

### Item Sources

In terms of item sources, it is suggested that scale developers go beyond their view of the target construct and consult several sources. It has been our experience that many existing scales have items with content and face validity that tap the domain of one's construct. Looking at how previous studies have operationalized the construct (or related constructs) can be a valuable source in item generation. For example, to measure work-family conflict (WFC) and family-work conflict (FWC), Netemeyer et al. (1996) culled items from existing WFC measures and measures of work role overload, and Bearden et al. (2001) converted items from various studies of consumer confidence/expertise for their initial pool to assess the dimensions of consumer self-confidence. Another source for item generation is the population of interest (Haynes et al., 1999; Haynes et al., 1995). Those who may be responding to the scale (i.e., members of the population) can offer insights into what the construct might be and how to measure it, thus enhancing face validity. Structured and unstructured interviews with members of the population can provide insights into item wording and response formats. Several scales developed in the marketing literature have used this approach both to help define the construct and to generate items (e.g., Bearden et al., 2001; Lastovicka et al., 1999).

Two more sources of items are experts in the field and the scale developer. Scholars, researchers, and practitioners familiar with the target constructs can be excellent sources for items. Experts in the field can suggest, write, or modify items consistent with the construct's domain. Obviously, the scale developer is also a source of items. This will be particularly true for constructs that are novel or for which very limited extant literature is available. Even with other sources contributing to the initial pool of items, most scale developers will need to write several of their own items to generate an adequate initial pool.

### Item Writing

A second consideration in generating items involves item writing. Several issues must be considered: (a) wording clarity, (b) wording redundancy, (c) positively and negatively worded items, and (d) choice of response formats.

*Wording Clarity.* Item clarity is important. In fact, Nunnally and Bernstein (1994) suggest that the cardinal rule of item writing can be summed up by one word: "clarity." A good item should be unambiguous to the point that its meaning is comprehended by all respondents in the same fashion. Some simple rules of thumb apply. First, use language that is common to the reading level of the target population. Second, keep the item short and simple regardless of the reading level of the population of interest. Although one does not want to sacrifice the meaning of an item for the sake of brevity, length and complexity will tend to diminish item clarity. Third, avoid jargon or trendy slang. The meaning of such language is quickly dated or subject to different interpretation as time passes. Fourth, avoid double-barrel statements that in effect address two issues (or content areas) in one statement. Finally, writing items that everyone will endorse in an extreme manner will be of little use.

Such items produce little item variance and thus little scale variance. As Clark and Watson (1995) noted, items that everyone endorses the same way in a positive manner (e.g., "Sometimes I am happier than other times") or the same way in a negative manner (e.g., "I am always furious") add little to the content validity of a construct.

*Wording Redundancy.* In the item generation phase, some wording redundancy among items is needed. The scale developer must be aware, however, of redundancy that is useless. Creating a new item by changing only a word that is not critical to an item's meaning is not important to the content of the item and therefore reflects useless redundancy. Varying the choice of words and grammatical structure to create new items, such that the content domain of the construct is being tapped differently, reflects useful redundancy. DeVellis (1991, p. 56) offered a good example. In tapping the "degree to which a parent will help his/her child" the items "I will do almost anything to ensure my child's success" and "No sacrifice is too great if it helps my child achieve success" have useful redundancy because both statements express the content of the construct in different ways. In assessing attitude toward pet lovers, however, the statements "In my opinion, pet lovers are kind" and "In my estimation, pet lovers are kind" share common vocabulary and grammar that do not tap the construct in different ways, thus reflecting useless redundancy. Overall, though, in the item-generation phase of scale development, some item redundancy is necessary, but it should not reflect purely trivial wording/grammar differences.

In the final scale, when the wording of the items is too similar and reflects only trivial differences, some psychometric properties actually may be compromised. Items that are worded too similarly will increase average interitem correlation, which in effect increases internal consistency without substantively contributing to the content validity of the measure. As will be discussed in Chapter 7, such items can also contribute to correlated measurement errors in confirmatory factor analyses that, in effect, threaten the dimensionality of a measure (Floyd & Widaman, 1995). Although some similarity among items of a scale is needed to tap the domain, several items that are just slight wording variations of one another yield little more construct-relevant information than any one item individually (Clark & Watson, 1995). Given that, items with useless redundancy may contribute to the "attenuation paradox" in psychometric theory, whereby increasing internal consistency estimates beyond a certain point does not enhance validity.

*Positively and Negatively Worded Items.* The choice of using all positively worded items vs. some positively and some negatively worded items is also of interest. Several scale developers have written items that reflect low levels of, the opposite of, or the absence of the target construct. The primary goal of such a procedure is too "keep the respondent honest" and thus avoid response bias in the form of acquiescence, affirmation, or yea-saying. Cacioppo and Petty's (1982) Need for Cognition scale is an example. They used items that reflect a higher level of the construct, such as " I prefer complex to simple problems," and items that reflect a low level of the construct, such as "I only think as hard as I have to." It has been our experience, however, that negatively worded items either do not exhibit as high a reliability as positively worded items do or can be confusing to respondents. Such items also may contribute to a methods factor in factor analytic models because positively worded items tend to load highly on one factor and negatively worded items tend to load highly on another factor. (See Herche and Engellend [1996] for a discussion and examples.) With that possibility in mind, the researcher must weigh the potential advantages and disadvantages of using negatively worded items in the item pool.

*Choice of Response Format.* Regarding response formats, two basic issues must be considered: (a) dichotomous versus multichotomous scale points and (b) wording of the response scale points. Although there are many types of response formats, including checklists and visual analog, the dominant two forms are dichotomous and multichotomous scale formats. Most dichotomous formats use true-false or yes-no scoring, and most multichotomous use Likert-type or semantic differential (or some variation of) scales with three or more scale points. Given the dominance of their use, our discussion is limited to these two types of scales. (For more information on the use of checklists, forced choice, and visual analog scales, the interested reader is referred to DeVellis [1991]; Green, Goldman, and Salovey [1993]; and Clark and Watson [1995]).

There are disadvantages and advantages to both the dichotomous and multichotomous formats. Dichotomous formats have been criticized for their tendency to have highly unbalanced response distributions, that is, all individuals always answering "true" or all individuals always answering "false" (Comrey, 1988). Careful item judging during the scale development stage can help eliminate such items, and the dichotomous format generally takes less time for a respondent to answer, allowing more items to be responded to in a shorter period of time. Another criticism of dichotomous scales relates to scale variance. A desirable measurement property of a scale is that there is sufficient variance in the overall scale scores for a given sample. Given that any one item for a dichotomous scale produces only limited covariance with another item because of the binary format, overall scale variance will be limited. For a scale composed of dichotomous items, a larger number of items will be needed to produce scale variance similar to that for items using Likert-type and semantic differential scales.

Likert-type scales and semantic differentials may use a number of response options and formats. Likert-type scales generally ask respondents to indicate their level of agreement with a declarative statement (e.g., disagree-agree, or strongly disagree-strongly agree); the degree or extent to which what is expressed in the statement is true of a belief, attitude, or characteristic of the respondent (i.e., not at all-very much, or not true of me-very true of me, or not at all like me-very much like me); or the frequency of a behavior (i.e., never-always). With Likert-type scales, it is also possible to label each scale point as well as scale endpoints. For example, for a 5-point scale, each scale point could be labeled as follows: 1 = *strongly disagree,* 2 = *somewhat disagree,* 3 = *neither agree nor disagree,* 4 = *somewhat agree,* and 5 = *strongly agree.* Such labeling serves to give the respondent a better idea of the endorsement he or she is making. Depending on what is being assessed, the scale points can take on many different wordings. Thus, the researcher must be careful when choosing to label scale points or endpoints (e.g., Clark & Watson, 1995; Comrey, 1988; DeVellis, 1991; Nunnally & Bernstein, 1994). Good Likert-type items should state the opinion, attitude, belief, behavior, or characteristic being assessed in clear terms and use the appropriate wording for scale points. Careful item judging can be very helpful in this regard.

Semantic differential items use adjective-based scale endpoints that are bipolar in nature (e.g., friendly-hostile, good-bad, hot-cold) or unipolar in nature (e.g., friendly-not friendly, good-not good, hot-not hot) (Osgood & Tannenbaum, 1955). Here, the respondent rates the stimulus (e.g., object or person) on a series of semantic differential scales assessing some latent attribute of the stimulus. For both Likert-type and semantic differential items, the scores on the items constituting the scale are summed to form an overall score.

A primary advantage of multichotomous scales is that they create more scale variance relative to a dichotomous scale with a similar number of items. With multichotomous scales, though, one should consider the number of scale points and whether an odd or even number of scale points should be used.

Most multichotomous scales use between 5 and 9 scale points, with some going as low as 3 and as high as 11 scale points. It has been our experience that 5- or 7-point formats suffice, and providing more response alternatives may not enhance scale reliability or validity. If the researcher wants to provide a "label" for each scale, it is easier and probably more meaningful for both scale developer and respondent if 5- or 7-point formats are used. More alternatives may require more effort on the respondent's behalf by forcing him or her to make finer distinctions. This, in turn, can produce random responding and more scale error variance.

Another consideration is using an odd or even number of scale points. With an odd number, the respondent is offered a scale midpoint or "neutral" response. Such a response, in effect, expresses a "no opinion," "not sure," or "neither agree nor disagree" option depending on what is being assessed. The scale developer must be careful in choosing an appropriate wording for such a midpoint if he or she chooses to label each point on the scale. As stated by Clark and Watson (1995, p. 313), a scale midpoint of "cannot say" may actually confound the midpoint of the scale with an uncertainty of what the item means to the respondent. On the other hand, an even number of scale points forces the respondent to have an opinion, or at least make a weak commitment to what is being expressed in an item (i.e., express some level that reflects a preference for endorsing or not endorsing an item), that he or she may not actually have. Although some researchers believe that neither an odd nor an even number of scale points is superior, it would seem that for some items a neutral response is a valid answer, so that an odd number of scale points is appropriate.

Overall, it has been shown that if reliably and validly constructed, dichotomous and multichotomous scales will yield similar results. It is strongly recommended that the format, wording of scale points, and number of scale points be carefully judged by experts and pilot tested prior to other scale construction steps.

### Number of Items in the Initial Pool

As previously stated, it is better to have a pool of items that is overinclusive of the domain of the construct than one that is underinclusive. Consistent with this view, a large pool of items is recommended. Much will depend on the number and complexity of the facets of the construct domain. If the construct is narrowly defined and the resulting scale is to be short (5-10 items), a pool as small as 20-30 items may suffice. In fact, DeVellis (1991) recommends that for narrow constructs, a pool that is twice the size of the final scale will suffice. For broader, multifaceted constructs, many more items will be needed to serve as an initial pool. Some researchers advocate a pool of 250 items as exemplary for item generation for multifaceted constructs (Robinson et al., 1991, pp. 12-13). Still, one must consider other issues, such as item redundancy, a desired level of internal consistency, and respondent cooperation. It is possible for a pool to be so large as to hinder respondent cooperation on a single occasion.

In sum, there are no hard-and-fast rules for the size of an initial item pool. Narrowly defined, single-facet constructs will require fewer items than will complex multifaceted constructs. In general though, a larger number is preferred, as overinclusiveness is more desirable than underinclusiveness.

## Judging Items for Content and Face Validity

Establishing content and face validity varies with how precisely the construct is defined and the degree to which experts agree about the domain and facets of the construct. The wider the discrepancy as to what the construct is, the more difficult the content validation will be. Content validity is threatened if (a) items reflecting any of the domains (facets) were omitted from the measure, (b) items measuring domains (facets) outside the definition of the construct are included in the measure, (c) an aggregate score on the construct disproportionately reflects one domain (facet) over other domains (facets), and (d) the instrument was difficult to administer and respond to for the target populations.

## Guidelines for Content and Face Validation

Several authors offer comprehensive guidelines for judging the content and face validity of the items in an initial pool. The reader is urged to consult these sources (cf. Clark & Watson, 1995; Haynes et al., 1999; Haynes et al., 1995; Nunnally & Bernstein, 1994). In Chapter 4, we touched on these guidelines, and below, we elaborate further.

First, the researcher should have *all* elements of the items judged for face and content validity. The items themselves, the response formats, the number of scale points, and instructions to the respondent all should be judged for representativeness by using multiple expert and population judges via qualitative and quantitative procedures. Some scholars recommend that

3-point categorization ratings be used by at least five expert (for content validity) and five target population (for face validity) judges to assess the degree to which items "represent" the construct's definition and domains (i.e., "not representative," "somewhat representative," "clearly representative"). Some advocate 5- or 7-point evaluation scales that ask five judges or more to rate each item in terms of representativeness (i.e., suitability), specificity, and clarity, and then retain items with high levels of interjudge agreement (Haynes et al., 1995). As a practical rule of thumb, more judges (five or more) are preferred, as the detection of bad or marginal items will be more confident given more raters.

In this regard, both qualitative and quantitative procedures can help identify elements of the items that need to be refined, changed, or deleted. Qualitative procedures include judges writing or verbalizing comments about specific items, as well as focus groups and/or one-on-one interviews with members from relevant populations to assess face validity. Quantitative procedures include categorization statistics assessing the level of agreement among judges (Perreault & Leigh, 1989).

Second, judging results should be reported when new instruments are published. This allows the reader to judge the degree to which the procedures were adequate and make decisions about the appropriateness of the scale for his or her use and/or adjustments needed to the instrument. Finally, some psychometricians advocate that once an item pool has been thoroughly judged, modified, and/or trimmed by expert and population judges, pilot testing the items on a larger sample ($n = 100$-$200$) from a relevant population is in order (Clark & Watson, 1995; Haynes et al., 1999). Here, items can be assessed initially for internal consistency, means, variances, intercorrelations with other items, and factor structure. Items that do not behave empirically as expected then can be adjusted for wording, scale labels, and so on for retention for initial data collection. Some items may require deletion based on these analyses, and if need be, more items can be drafted and judged, such that a sufficient item pool is retained for the scale development studies that follow.

## APPLICATIONS OF STEPS 1 AND 2

The first part of this chapter offered a conceptual review of the first two steps in scale development and validation. The remainder of this chapter will offer examples and an application of these two steps.

Shimp and Sharma's (1987) Consumer Ethnocentrism Scale (CETSCALE) offers an example of construct definition and delineation, as well as item generation and judging. Shimp and Sharma (1987) defined consumer ethnocentrism as "the beliefs held by American consumers about the appropriateness, indeed morality, of purchasing foreign-made products" (p. 208). They further defined the domain of the construct from the view of the consumer (i.e., the relevant population) by surveying 800 consumers and asking them to offer their views on purchasing foreign-made goods. Via content analysis of these responses, Shimp and Sharma delineated their construct by stating that the consumer ethnocentric individuals hold products from other countries in contempt because purchasing foreign-made goods hurts the U.S. economy, causes loss of jobs, and is unpatriotic. Shimp and Sharma also viewed consumer ethnocentrism as a "tendency" rather than as an attitude because "tendency" captures the behavioral element of the construct.

The primary theories that Shimp and Sharma (1987) drew from in defining and delineating the content domain of consumer ethnocentrism are the conceptual frameworks of "ethnocentrism" (Sumner, 1906) and sociocultural "in-groups and out-groups" (Levine & Campbell, 1972). A major premise of these two frameworks is that many individuals view their own in-group (culture and society) as the center of their universe and tend to reject objects and ideas that are dissimilar from those of their in-group while accepting objects that are similar. Using these frameworks as their theoretical base, Shimp and Sharma (1987) defined and delineated their consumer ethnocentrism construct.

Recall that for a construct to be useful in the social sciences, it should be embedded in a nomological net (Cronbach & Meehl, 1955). In their studies, Shimp and Sharma posited that consumer ethnocentrism would be related to patriotism, politico-economic conservatism, and dogmatism (i.e., potential antecedents), as well as to attitudes toward foreign-made products, intention to buy foreign-made products, intention to buy American-made products only, and domestic automobile ownership (i.e., potential consequences). (These relationships were tested in later scale development studies.) In sum, Shimp and Sharma (1987) offered a classic example of construct definition and delineation that is based in theory.

To help generate items, Shimp and Sharma content analyzed the responses (from the 800 consumers) and generated items for a first developmental study. Via this procedure, using their own judgment, and culling items from extant studies that examined American attitudes toward foreign products, they generated a pool of 225 items to tap the domain of consumer ethnocentrism.

Wording of all items used common consumer vernacular, and via the consumer responses and author judgment, 7-point Likert-type *strongly disagree* to *strongly agree* scales were used to evaluate the items. This large item pool was trimmed to a more manageable number for the developmental studies that followed. Statements that were viewed as redundant (i.e., useless redundancy) were trimmed by the authors, resulting in 180 items to be judged by six experts (five holding PhDs and 1 doctoral candidate). Using an a priori decision rule in which at least five of six judges had to agree that an item tapped the construct definition/domains, a total of 117 items were retained for the initial scale developmental study. In sum, Shimp and Sharma aptly followed Steps 1 and 2 in scale development.

Another example of construct definition and item generation and refinement can be found in Lichtenstein et al. (1993). With their construct "price consciousness," a more narrow definition and domain was a major focus to differentiate the construct from other pricing-related concepts. Using theory and extant literature, Lichtenstein et al. (1993) defined price consciousness as the "degree to which the consumer focuses exclusively on paying low prices" (p. 235). A primary theoretical premise was that consumers view the price they pay for a product as having either a negative or positive role, and that each role is represented by a higher-order factor with first-order subcomponents (dimensions). As a first-order factor of the negative role of price, price consciousness is distinct from the positive role of price concepts of price-quality schema (i.e., the higher the price, the higher the quality of the product) and price prestige sensitivity (i.e., the prominence and status that higher prices signal to other people about the purchaser). As such, what was excluded from the domain of price consciousness took on a dominant role in defining the construct and determining its dimensionality within the presence of other constructs. Theoretically then, Lichtenstein et al. (1993) posited price consciousness as a first-order factor of the higher-order factor of "negative role of price."

They further delineated their construct within a nomological network in which other first-order factors of the negative role of price (e.g., coupon proneness and sale proneness) would be highly positively related to price consciousness, and price-quality schema and price prestige sensitivity would be negatively related to price consciousness. Basing their logic in theories of consumer buying and information search/processing, Lichtenstein et al. (1993) further posited consequences of price consciousness including "searching for low prices inside the store" and the "actual quantity" and "dollar amounts" of sale products purchased.

Based on the premise that narrowly defined constructs require fewer items, a small pool of items initially was generated to tap the construct. Lichtenstein et al. (1993) culled or adapted four items from the extant pricing literature and had three expert judges familiar with the pricing literature (two marketing PhDs and one PhD candidate) generate 14 more items based on the theoretical definition of the construct (18 items total). Consistent with recent suggestions in the psychometric literature (Clark & Watson, 1995), a pilot study of 341 consumers with the primary grocery shopping duties for their households was conducted to further refine the pool of items. Via item analyses (inspection of interitem correlations, corrected item-to-total correlations, item means, and variances) and exploratory factor analyses, 13 price consciousness items were retained for the scale development study. (As shown in Appendix 5A, the final form of the price consciousness scale was composed of five items.) Overall, the Lichtenstein et al. (1993) studies offer a reasonable example of construct domain delineation, a priori dimensionality, and item generation and refinement for a narrowly defined construct.

A final example of Steps 1 and 2 in scale development comes from the organizational behavior literature. Netemeyer et al. (1996) developed measures of work-family conflict (WFC) and family-work conflict (FWC). In their studies, it was thought important to differentiate the two constructs, as much of the prior literature had combined WFC and FWC into one overall construct, ignoring the conceptual distinction between the two and their differential relationships with antecedent and consequence variables. Netemeyer et al. (1996) defined WFC as "a form of inter-role conflict in which the general demands of, time devoted to, and strain created by the job interfere with performing family-related responsibilities" (p. 401) and FWC as "a form of inter-role conflict in which the general demands of, time devoted to, and strain created by the family interfere with performing work-related responsibilities" (p. 401). Their literature review also revealed a nomological framework of potential antecedents (e.g., number of children living at home, number of hours worked per week, role conflict, and role ambiguity) and consequences (e.g., organizational commitment, job satisfaction, job burnout, and life satisfaction) of WFC and FWC.

Netemeyer et al. (1996) generated a large pool of items to tap the domains of WFC and FWC. By adapting items from published sources and writing their own items based on recommendations from experts in the field, they generated 18 items to reflect the general demand facet of WFC, 20 for time-based WFC, and 19 for strain-based WFC. For FWC, 18 items were generated to reflect the general demand facet, 19 for time-based, and 16 for strain-based. Over both constructs, 110 items were generated for the initial pool, with about one third of the items being negatively worded. Four expert judges, using both qualitative and quantitative procedures, judged these items for representativeness. The judges were asked to place items in one of three categories based on the construct definition and content domain: (a) very representative of the construct (domain), (b) somewhat representative of the construct (domain), or (c) not representative of the construct (domain). The judges were also asked to change the wording of items so that, when modified, they would be at least somewhat representative of the construct (domain).

Using a variation of Cohen's kappa (Perreault & Leigh, 1989), an interrater reliability coefficient was constructed that ranged from 0 to 1. (Appendix 5B offers the calculations for this interrater reliability index.) For all four judges simultaneously, the value of this coefficient was .51 across items; for two judges at a time, this coefficient ranged from .63 to .79. Based on these results, a decision rule was adopted to retain only those items that all four judges classified as at least "somewhat representative" of the construct (domain). Via further author judging for item redundancy (i.e., useless redundancy), the initial pool for the first developmental study contained 7, 8, and 7 items (22 in total) for the WFC general demand, time-based, and strain-based WFC domain facets, respectively, and 8, 7, and 6 items (21 in total) for the FWC general demand, time-based, and strain-based domain facets. In sum, Netemeyer et al. (1996) used several procedures to generate and judge their item pool. (The final forms of the scales are offered in Appendix 5A.)

## SUMMARY

In this chapter, we have offered several illustrations of the important first two steps in scale development: Step 1 of construct definition and content domain and Step 2 of generating and judging measurement items. We discussed several important issues related to the first step, including the role of theory in construct definition and content domain, the importance of a thorough literature review and definition, and the importance of an a priori construct dimensionality. Issues relevant to the second step also were highlighted, including generating a sufficiently large pool of items to tap the content domain, the various aspects of item writing, and the use of expert and lay judges for judging content and face validity. Chapters 6 and 7 will turn to empirical studies to further develop, refine, and finalize a scale.

# Appendix 5A

---•---

## *Consumer Self-Confidence Scales*

| **INFORMATION ACQUISITION (IA)** | **Factor Loading** |
|---|---|

**INFORMATION ACQUISITION (IA)**          **Factor Loading**

1) I know where to find the information
   I need prior to making a purchase.    .80
2) I know where to look to find the product information I need.    .82
3) I am confident in my ability to research important purchases.    .62
4) I know the right questions to ask when shopping.    .60
5) I have the skills required to obtain needed
   information before making important purchases.    .64

**CONSIDERATION SET FORMATION (CSF)**

1) I am confident in my ability to recognize a
   brand worth considering.    .85
2) I can tell which brands meet my expectations.    .64
3) I trust my own judgment when deciding which
   brands to consider.    .72
4) I know which stores to shop.    .55
5) I can focus easily on a few good brands when making a decision.    .60

**PERSONAL OUTCOMES DECISION MAKING (PO)**

1) I often have doubts about the purchase decisions I make.    .81
2) I frequently agonize over what to buy.    .67
3) I often wonder if I've made the right purchase selection.    .73
4) I never seem to buy the right thing for me.    .50
5) Too often the things I buy are not satisfying.    .65

**SOCIAL OUTCOMES DECISION MAKING (SO)**

1) My friends are impressed with my ability
   to make satisfying purchases.    .89
2) I impress people with the purchases I make.    .89
3) My neighbors admire my decorating ability.    .53
4) I have the ability to give good presents.    .53
5) I get compliments from others on my purchase decisions.    .68

## PERSUASION KNOWLEDGE (PK)

1) I know when an offer is "too good to be true."                              .70
2) I can tell when an offer has strings attached.                              .73
3) I have no trouble understanding the bargaining tactics
   used by salespersons.                                                       .62
4) I know when a marketer is pressuring me to buy.                             .68
5) I can see through sales gimmicks used to get consumers to buy.              .74
6) I can separate fact from fantasy in advertising.                           .61

## MARKETPLACE INTERFACES (MI)

1) I am afraid to "ask to speak to the manager."                              .79
2) I don't like to tell a salesperson something is wrong in the store.        .79
3) I have a hard time saying no to a salesperson.                             .59
4) I am too timid when problems arise while shopping.                         .67
5) I am hesitant to complain when shopping.                                   .77

SOURCE: Reprinted from "Consumer Self-Confidence: Refinements in Conceptualization and Measurement," *Journal of Consumer Research, 28*(June), p. 125 (Table 1), Bearden, Hardesty, and Rose, copyright 2001 by the University of Chicago Press. Reprinted with permission of the University of Chicago Press.
NOTE: The factor loadings based on the six-factor correlated model from the confirmatory factor analysis of the Study Three data are shown in the column to the right.

# Consumer Frugality Scale

## MAXIMUM-LIKELIHOOD ESTIMATES OF A ONE-COMMON-FACTOR MODEL

| | Factor loading estimates: $\lambda_x$ | | |
|---|---|---|---|
| | Study 1: Generation Sample | Study 1: Validation Sample | Study 6: General Population |
| 1. If you take good care of your possessions, you will definitely save money in the long run | .77 | .70 | .69 |
| 2. There are many things that are normally thrown away that are still quite useful | .63 | .66 | .65 |
| 3. Making better use of my resources makes me feel good | .70 | .68 | .68 |
| 4. If you can re-use an item you already have, there's no sense in buying something new | .74 | .66 | .63 |
| 5. I believe in being careful in how I spend my money | .73 | .74 | .73 |
| 6. I discipline myself to get the most from my money | .59 | .53 | .69 |
| 7. I am willing to wait on a purchase I want so that I can save money | .71 | .72 | .72 |
| 8. There are things I resist buying today so I can save for tomorrow | .65 | .74 | .68 |
| | Study 1 (n = 106) | Study 1 (n = 107) | Study 6 (n = 164) |
| Goodness of fit indices: | | | |
| Bentler comparative fit index | .98 | .93 | .96 |
| 90% confidence interval of root mean square error of approximation | .00, .10 | .04, .13 | .00, .09 |
| Tucker-Lewis $\rho$ | .97 | .90 | .94 |
| $\chi^2$, p with $df = 20$ | 25.93, .17 | 31.92, .04 | 30.93, .06 |

SOURCE: Reprinted from "Lifestyle of the Tight and Frugal: Theory and Measurement," *Journal of Consumer Research, 26*(June), p. 89 (Table 2), Lastovicka, Bettencourt, Hughner, and Kuntze, copyright 1999 by the University of Chicago Press. Reprinted with permission of the University of Chicago Press.

# Work-Family Conflict and
# Family-Work Conflict Scales

**WFC:**

**Factor Loading**

1) The demands of my work interfere with
my home and family life.                                                      .83
2) The amount of time my job takes up makes it difficult
to fulfill family responsibilities.                                          .79
3) Things I want to do at home do not get done because of
the demands my job puts on me.                                               .81
4) My job produces strain that makes it difficult
to fulfill family duties.                                                    .66
5) Due to work-related duties, I have to make changes to
my plans for family activities.                                             .75

**FWC:**

1) The demands of my family or spouse/partner
interfere with work-related activities.                                      .73
2) I have to put off doing things at work because of demands
on my time at home.                                                          .89
3) Things I want to do at work don't get done because of
the demands of my family or spouse/partner.                                 .83
4) My home life interferes with my responsibilities at
work such as getting to work on time, accomplishing
daily tasks, and working overtime.                                           .83
5) Family-related strain interferes with my ability
to perform job-related duties.                                              .75

SOURCE: Reprinted from "Development and Validation of Work-Family Conflict and Family-Work Conflict Scales," *Journal of Applied Psychology, 81*(4), p. 410, Netemeyer, Boles, and McMurrian, copyright 1996 by the American Psychological Association. Reprinted with permission from the American Psychological Association.

NOTE: The factor loadings are based on the two-factor correlated model from the confirmatory factor analysis of the Study Three (real-estate sample).

# Consumer Price Consciousness

|  |  | Factor Loading |
|---|---|---|
| 1) | I am not willing to go to extra effort to find lower prices. | .65 |
| 2) | I will grocery shop at more than one store to take advantage of low prices. | .62 |
| 3) | The money saved by finding low prices is usually not worth the time or effort. | .71 |
| 4) | I would never shop at more than one store to find low prices. | .68 |
| 5) | The time it takes to find low prices is usually not worth the effort. | .76 |

SOURCE: Reprinted from "Price Perceptions and Consumer Shopping Behavior: A Field Study," *Journal of Marketing Research, 30*(May), pp. 233-234, Lichtenstein, Ridgway, and Netemeyer, copyright 1993 by the American Marketing Association. Reprinted with permission of the American Marketing Association.

# CETSCALE Items

**Factor Loading**

1) American people should always buy American-made products instead of imports. .81
2) Only those products that are unavailable in the U.S. should be imported. .79
3) Buy American-made products. Keep America working. .71
4) American products, first, last, and foremost. .81
5) Purchasing foreign-made products is un-American. .80
6) It is not right to purchase foreign products because it puts Americans out of jobs. .85
7) A real American should always buy American-made products. .84
8) We should purchase products manufactured in America instead of letting other countries get rich off us. .82
9) It is always best to purchase American products. .77
10) There should be very little trading or purchasing of goods from other countries unless out of necessity. .73
11) Americans should not buy foreign products, because this hurts American business and causes unemployment. .82
12) Curbs should be put on all imports. .72
13) It may cost me in the long-run but I prefer to support American products. .74
14) Foreigners should not be allowed to put their products on our markets. .72
15) Foreign products should be taxed heavily to reduce this entry into the U.S. .76
16) We should buy from foreign countries only those products that we cannot obtain within our own country. .77
17) American consumers who purchase products made in other countries are responsible for putting their fellow Americans out of work. .81

SOURCE: Reprinted from "Consumer Ethnocentrism: Construction and Validation of the CETSCALE," *Journal of Marketing Research, 24*(August), p. 282 (Table 1), Shimp and Sharma, copyright 1987 by the American Marketing Association. Reprinted with permission from the American Marketing Association.
NOTE: The factor loadings are based on the four-area study from the source cited above.

# Appendix 5B

After compiling the results across all items, Netemeyer et al. (1996) constructed their interrater reliability index based on Perreault and Leigh's (1989, p. 141) variation of Cohen's kappa. The equation is as follows:

$$IR = \{[(F/N) - (1/k)] \; [k/(k-1)]\}^{.5}$$

where IR is the interrater reliability coefficient,

F is the absolute level of observed agreement among all judges for each item placed in the same category,

$N$ is the total number of items judged, and

$k$ is the number of coding categories.

All four judges placed 56 of the 110 items (for both WFC and FWC) into the same category. Thus, the equation is solved as follows:

$$
\begin{aligned}
IR \; &= \{[(F/N) - (1/k)] \; [k/(k-1)]\}^{.5} \\
&= \{[(56/110) - (1/3)] \; [3/(3-1)]\}^{.5} \\
&= .51
\end{aligned}
$$

For two judges, where they placed 82 of the 110 items into the same category, the equation is solved as follows:

$$
\begin{aligned}
IR \; &= \{[(F/N) - (1/k)] \; [k/(k-1)]\}^{.5} \\
&= \{[(82/110) - (1/3)] \; [3/(3-1)]\}^{.5} \\
&= .79
\end{aligned}
$$

# SIX

# STEP 3

## *Designing and Conducting Studies to Develop a Scale*

―――・・―――

### INTRODUCTION

Chapter 5 focused on construct definition and generating, judging, and refining an initial item pool—that is, Steps 1 and 2 in scale development. This chapter focuses on designing and conducting initial studies to develop the scale and further trim the item pool—that is, Step 3 in scale development. Specifically, we address the following objectives: pilot testing a pool of items as an item trimming and initial validity testing procedure, and conducting multiple studies for scale development. Within this second objective we highlight (a) the importance of including constructs for assessing the various types of validity, (b) exploratory factor analyses (EFA) over multiple data sets to refine the scale and examine a theoretical a priori initial factor structure, and (c) item and reliability analyses. Finally, we offer examples from recently developed scales to illustrate how EFA and item and reliability analyses can be used in scale development.

### PILOT TESTING

As stated in Chapter 5, a pool of items should be generated and judged for content and face validity prior to being administered to samples from relevant populations. As also stated in Chapter 5, the initial item pool should be sufficiently large, with the appropriate size varying depending on the dimensionality and the complexity of the construct definition. With a large pool of items, it will be useful to trim the pool for the developmental studies that follow and to obtain some initial estimates of reliability and validity. In this regard, pilot testing can be helpful. Given that the scale will be administered to further samples for refinement, a pilot study can reduce the number of items in an initial pool to a more manageable number by deleting items that do not meet certain psychometric criteria. Pilot testing also can serve the purpose of initially testing for validity. Subsequently, a nomological net can be partially assessed by including measures/scales of relevant constructs with a pilot sample.

Four issues to consider in pilot testing include (a) the size of the sample, (b) sample composition, (c) initial item reliability estimates, and (d) the number and type of validity-related scales to include. First, consider the size of the sample of respondents in the pilot test. Some suggest that pilot samples should be in the $n = 300$ range (DeVellis, 1991), whereas others suggest that $n = 100$ to 200 will suffice (Clark & Watson, 1995). An issue to consider with sample size is how many items are in the initial pool. For pools with small numbers of items (e.g., 20 items or less) associated with narrowly defined constructs, the $n = 100$ to 200 range seems reasonable, as initial item and factor analyses can be performed with such sample sizes. For larger pools, however (and for complex and/or multidimensional constructs), larger sample sizes in the 300 range are preferred.

A second consideration is sample composition. For pilot testing, convenience samples (e.g., college students) may suffice, but it is preferable to use a sample from a relevant population of interest. Given that a goal of pilot testing is to reduce the number of items to a more manageable number for the larger development studies, sample representativeness is a plus. An item that performs well (poorly) with a sample from a relevant population will be more confidently assessed as a candidate for inclusion (deletion) for developmental samples that follow. Thus, samples from relevant populations are preferred.

Third, items can be assessed initially for internal consistency, means, variances, average interitem correlation, and factor structure. Items that do not behave empirically as was expected can then be adjusted for wording, scale labels, and otherwise for retention in developmental data collection efforts. Some items may require deletion based on these analyses, and if need be, more items can be drafted and judged, such that a sufficient item pool is retained for the scale development studies that follow.

Fourth, an initial assessment of some aspects of validity can be made via a pilot sample. Here, a few key construct measures can be very useful for obtaining initial estimates of validity (i.e., part of the construct's nomological net). As previously stated, a thorough literature review should alert the scale developer to those constructs and accompanying measures that the focal construct should be related to (and differentiated from). Thus, three or four key construct measures should be included for examining initial estimates of validity. At this stage, an initial estimate of social desirability bias may also be considered if the focal construct has the potential for such bias. As noted in Chapter 4, Paulhus (1993) and Mick (1996) offered some useful techniques and ideas for assessing social desirability bias.

As a final note on pilot testing, it is better to have a pool of items that is overinclusive of the domain of the construct than one that is underinclusive. Given that a goal of pilot testing is to trim items, an important question is "How many items should be retained from the pilot test?" We believe it is best to "err on the high side." That is, it is best to have a larger rather than a smaller pool to be carried over for the developmental samples. Thus, if an item performs marginally in item and factor analyses in a pilot test but is judged as having content and face validity, it is best to retain that item for further samples. This will be particularly the case if the pilot sample was one of convenience and not necessarily entirely representative of the population of interest.

### Example of a Pilot Test

Lichtenstein et al. (1993) offered a useful example of pilot testing with their price-consciousness construct and measure. These authors used a pilot sample of 341 consumers with primary grocery shopping duties for their households to further refine their initial pool of 18 items. Via item analyses (e.g., inspection of interitem correlations, corrected item-to-total correlations, item means and variances) and exploratory factor analyses, 13 items were retained for their primary scale development study. (The final form of the price-consciousness scale was composed of 5 items.) Lichtenstein et al. (1993) also included several validity-related measures (e.g., sale proneness, value consciousness, coupon proneness) that were conceptualized as theoretical antecedents or outcomes of their price-consciousness measure. Overall, the Lichtenstein et al. (1993) studies offer a reasonable example of pilot testing for a narrowly defined construct.

# CONDUCTING MULTIPLE STUDIES
# FOR INITIAL DEVELOPMENT AND VALIDATION

## Including Constructs for Assessing Validity

Including constructs for validation purposes is a highly recommended procedure even with the first developmental studies. Recall from the previous chapters that for a construct to be useful, a theoretical framework (nomological net) should be considered. Furthermore, several studies are needed to more confidently infer a construct's validity. A single study, even if it assesses multiple aspects of validity, will not be enough to infer construct validity. Multiple applications over time are needed. Given this, it is not uncommon for numerous studies to be conducted to initially derive and examine a measure in a scale development paper. For example, Lastovicka et al. (1999) used six studies to develop and validate their measure of consumer "frugality." Shimp and Sharma (1987) and Bearden et al. (2001) both used six samples to develop and validate their measures of "consumer ethnocentrism" and "consumer self-confidence," respectively. It is important, as can be seen from the studies above, that theory guides the choice of related constructs for validity testing and that multiple studies be conducted to test for the hypothesized relations of these constructs with the focal construct (Clark & Watson, 1995; Smith & McCarthy, 1995).

As stated in previous chapters, specifying related constructs should be given thought at both the initial and later stages of scale development. Given that multiple studies are needed to infer validity, two questions come to mind in choosing validity-related constructs for Step 3: what types of validity to test for? and how many validity constructs to include? The simple answers to these questions would be to test for all types of validity and include all validity constructs that may be theoretical antecedents or consequences of the focal construct. In practice, though, survey length considerations must be taken into account and, therefore, "judgment calls" on the part of the scale developer must be made. A strategy that seems practical is to test the various types of validity in different studies, such that those types most relevant to the scale have been assessed multiple times. The following two examples illustrate such a strategy.

In deriving their measure of consumer ethnocentrism, Shimp and Sharma (1987) tested for *convergent validity* of their 17-item CETSCALE by correlating it with another "maximally dissimilar" measure of consumer ethnocentrism. Two years prior to conducting one of their validation studies, Shimp and

Sharma collected data from a portion of that study's sample with the following open-ended question: "Please describe your views of whether it is right and appropriate to purchase products that are manufactured in foreign countries." Responses were coded by two independent judges as "ethnocentric" or "non-ethnocentric" with a 93% agreement rate. Then, the correlation between this dichotomously scored variable and the CETSCALE was calculated ($r = .54$, $n = 388$). Although this result may be considered modest in terms of convergent validity, the measures on which it was based were separated by a 2-year time difference, and the correlation was between a continuous and a dichotomous measure.

Shimp and Sharma also tested for *discriminant validity*. They correlated the CETSCALE with measures of patriotism, politico-economic conservatism, and dogmatism (i.e., potential antecedents that should be distinct from consumer ethnocentrism). Correlations ranged from .39 to .66, providing evidence of discriminant validity. *Nomological validity* and elements of *predictive validity* were also tested in all six studies, using attitudes toward foreign-made products, intention to buy foreign-made products, intention to buy American-made products only, and domestic automobile ownership (i.e., potential consequences) as correlates. Of the 28 relationships hypothesized, 26 were significant in the predicted direction, demonstrating evidence of the nomological and predictive validity of the CETSCALE. Finally, in one of their studies, Shimp and Sharma (1987) showed that the CETSCALE demonstrated aspects of *known-group validity*. Theory strongly suggested that those whose economic livelihood (i.e., job) is most threatened by foreign products would show higher mean-level scores on the CETSCALE than those whose economic livelihood is less threatened. This hypothesis was supported, as a sample from Detroit (home of the U.S. auto industry) showed significantly higher mean scores on the CETSCALE than those from three other areas of the country. Known-group validity thus was supported.

A second example of a validation strategy comes from the consumer self-confidence scales developed Bearden et al. (2001). They assessed aspects of convergent, discriminant, nomological, predictive, and known-group validity. They also examined an often-overlooked aspect of validity testing—contamination from social desirability bias (Mick, 1996). In terms of *convergent validity*, in one of their samples, Bearden et al. (2001) presented respondents with definitions of the facets and then asked them to rate the degree to which their behaviors were characteristic of each definition on 7-point scales. Two weeks later, the same sample responded to all facets of the consumer self-confidence scales. The summed scores of these ratings (for each facet) were correlated with the respective definition-based rating of consumer self-confidence scale. The correlations, ranging from .39 to .63, showed evidence of convergence.

Bearden et al. (2001) examined the *discriminant validity* among the six facets via confirmatory factor analysis (CFA) in two of their studies. For each possible pair of facets, two discriminant validity tests were performed. In the first test, if the average variance extracted (AVE) by each facet's measure was greater than the shared variance between the facets (i.e., the square of the correlation between the facets as separate factors), evidence of discriminant validity was deemed to exist. In the second test, if a two- factor model (where the items of the two facets are treated as distinct yet correlated constructs) fit significantly better than a one-factor model (where the items of two facets are combined into one factor), evidence of discriminant validity was deemed to exist (Anderson & Gerbing, 1988). Both tests supported the discriminant validity among the facets of consumer self-confidence. (Chapter 7 expands on the use of CFA for testing discriminant validity.)

In three of their studies, Bearden et al. (2001) included measures to test aspects of *nomological* and *predictive validity*. In two of the studies, they correlated the facets of consumer self-confidence with susceptibility to normative influence, subjective product knowledge, price-quality schema, and trait self-esteem. The pattern of correlations supported the nomological validity of the consumer self-confidence scales. In another study, Bearden et al. (2001) assessed the relations between the facets of consumer self-confidence and state self-esteem, information processing confidence, and product-specific self-confidence for five product categories via multiple regression analyses. The pattern of results for these equations supported the predictive validity of the consumer self-confidence measures. *Known-group validity* was tested by comparing the mean scores between the respondents of two of the samples (i.e., the general population) with a sample of professionals with an average of 23.4 years of experience in sales and marketing ($n = 44$). For two facets of consumer self-confidence (persuasion knowledge and protection), the mean score differences between these two groups were significant in the predicted direction ($t$ values ranged from 3.52 to 7.16).

Given that individuals tend to overestimate their desirable characteristics and underestimate their undesirable characteristics, Bearden et al. (2001) tested for *social desirability bias* in one of their studies. Paulhus's (1993) impression management scale was correlated with the facets of consumer self-confidence. Only two of the six facets were significantly (but lowly) correlated with impression management ($r = .18$ and $r = .21$), suggesting that the scales are mostly free of social desirability bias. In sum, the Shimp and Sharma (1987) and Bearden et al. (2001) examples demonstrate strategies for designing multiple studies for validity assessment.

### Initial Item Analyses: Exploratory Factor Analysis (EFA)

Exploratory factor analyses (EFA) can be used for two primary purposes in scale development: (a) to reduce the number of items in a scale so that the remaining items maximize the explained variance in the scale and maximize the scale's reliability and (b) to identify potential underlying dimensions in a scale. These two uses are related, and in the case of scale development, they can be used in a complementary fashion. The following sections will discuss the use of EFA, focusing on how it can be used to evaluate a potential a priori theoretical factor of measures and as a tool to reduce the number of items. We then apply common factor analysis to the data collected by Netemeyer et al. (1996) from their work-family conflict (WFC) and family-work conflict (FWC) scales to demonstrate the use of common factor analysis in scale development.

### EFA Options

The goal of data reduction is a primary use of EFA. Typically, principal components factor analysis (PCA) is used for such a purpose in place of common factor analysis (Floyd & Widaman, 1995; Hair, Anderson, Tatham, & Black, 1998). With PCA, the components (or factors) are estimated in such a manner as to represent the variances among the items in the scale as economically as possible, with the fewest number of meaningful components (dimensions) as possible. PCA analyzes the correlation matrix among the observed variables (items) with ones on the main diagonal. By doing so, PCA maximizes *all* the variance in the items, regardless of whether it is common to a factor (component) or unique to an item. Those items for which little variance is explained are considered as candidates for deletion (i.e., to reduce the number of items in the scale).

In contrast, common factor analysis (in scale development) is more often associated with finding underlying dimensions for a set of items. Common factor analysis also uses a matrix of correlations (or covariances) among the observed scores on the items to identify a set of latent variables (factors) that explain the correlations among the items. Common factor analysis, however, uses the communality estimates of the items on the main diagonal. Furthermore, the variance in a given item is partitioned into that which is common to a factor or latent variable (based on the shared variance with other items in the analysis) and variance that is unique to a given item—a combination of specific variance and random error variance. Common factor analysis can be used to identify the theoretical construct(s) whose effects are reflected by responses to items in a scale. Common factor analysis also can offer information as to what items to delete or retain, similar to that of PCA.

Many authors report that the solutions derived from PCA and common factor analyses tend to be quite similar. This is particularly the case when the number of items exceeds 30 or commonalities exceed .60 for most items (e.g., Hair et al., 1998). Others have questioned the finding that PCA and common factor analyses yield similar results. Differences may be most pronounced with a small number of items and low commonalities. In fact, in such a case, PCA and common factor analyses can offer divergent results (Floyd & Widaman, 1995). Some authors therefore suggest that common factor analyses are preferred over PCA, as most scale development applications look to understand a construct in terms of the number of latent factors that underlie it, as well as to reduce the number of items in a scale. Furthermore, given that confirmatory factor analysis (CFA) is a widely used tool in scale finalization, EFA-based common factor analyses may generalize better to CFA than does PCA (Floyd & Widaman, 1995).

*Number of Factors to Extract*

There are various criteria for extracting factors. Hair et al. (1998), Floyd and Widaman (1995), and Sharma (1996) offer eloquent expositions of these criteria. We will only briefly review them here. Although some statistical tests are available for factor extraction, they generally are restricted to estimation techniques more closely aligned with CFA (e.g., maximum likelihood estimation). (This issue will be discussed in Chapter 7.)

For EFA, psychometric criteria and "rules of thumb" are most often applied. As noted in Chapter 2, the "eigenvalue-greater-than-1" rule (Kaiser-Guttman criterion or Latent Root criterion) is often used as a psychometric criterion. Each component (factor) has an eigenvalue that represents the amount of variance accounted for by the component, where the sum of all eigenvalues is equal to the number of items analyzed. An eigenvalue less than 1 indicates that that component accounts for less variance than any single item. Thus, with data reduction as a goal, a component with an eigenvalue less than 1 is not considered meaningful. It should be noted that the Kaiser-Guttman criterion can underestimate the number of components in some circumstances and may not be reliable. Cliff (1988) showed that the eigenvalue-greater-than-one rule is flawed, and it is probably best used as a guide rather than as an absolute criterion to extract factors.

Other rules of thumb are often advocated for factor extraction. The first of these involves the scree test. The scree test plots the eigenvalues and shows the slope of a line connecting the eigenvalues. Factors are retained where the slope of this line approaches zero, and at which point a sharp "elbow" occurs. Deleting a factor well below this elbow will show little loss of explained variance. Such a procedure may be particularly the case with PCA, but with common factor analyses, eigenvalues less than 1 may be worth examining because the judgment of the elbow is subjective. In fact, Floyd and Widaman (1995) suggested that for common factor analysis, when two or more factors are near the elbow cutoff, alternative factor solutions with differing numbers of factors should be examined in efforts to avoid a useful factor. Because determining the elbow is very subjective, Horn (1965) proposed the use of parallel analysis to identify the elbow. (See Chapter 2 for more details.) The parallel analysis computes the eigenvalues of variables for a given sample size assuming that the correlations among the variables are the result solely of sampling error. That is, this analysis provides an estimate of the eigenvalues for items that have no common factors. (Equation 2.3 of Chapter 2 can be used to determine these eigenvalues.)

A second rule of thumb for retaining factors pertains to the number of items that substantially load on a factor. What is considered substantial is somewhat open for debate, but loadings in the .40 range and above have been classified as substantial (Floyd & Widaman, 1995), and loadings above .50 have been considered as "very significant" (Hair et al., 1998). Factors with only a single substantial loading will be of little consequence because only the specific factor variance associated with that item is being accounted for, and it has been suggested that at least three items that load highly are needed to identify a factor (Comrey, 1988). Still, many authors suggest that sample size must be considered in judging not only the size of the factor loading but also its stability. Rules of thumb for EFA techniques range from a minimum sample size of 100 to a size of 200 to 300; another recommendation is a sample size of 5 to 10 respondents per item (Clark & Watson, 1995; Comrey, 1988; Floyd & Widaman, 1995; Hair et al., 1998).

A third rule of thumb involves the amount of variance being explained by an extracted factor in relation to the total variance explained by the entire factor solution. Some advocate that the number of factors extracted should account for 50% to 60% of the variance in the items and that for any one factor to be meaningful, at least 5% of the total variance explained should be attributable to that factor (Hair et al., 1998). A fourth rule of thumb that seems appropriate for scale development involves a priori criteria. Most scale developers will have some idea as to the number of factors (dimensions) that underlie a set of items. Thus, restricting the factor solution to a prespecified number of factors (consistent with theory) can offer valuable information regarding how much variance the factors account for and the strength of the loadings of items on respective factors (Floyd & Widaman, 1995; Hair et al., 1998). This approach also can give information as to the level of cross-loading of an item to a factor that it should not load on (theoretically), and thus reveal an item that may be a candidate for deletion.

In practice, no single rule of thumb or psychometric criterion should be relied upon in deciding the number of factors to extract. Most EFA extraction criteria should be used in conjunction with other criteria, and the scale developer should use a priori theory and common sense as guides in deciding the number of factors to extract. We do recommend that factor analyses that restrict a solution to an a priori theoretically derived number of factors be conducted, with those results compared with solutions not restricted to an a priori number. Again, scale developers should have some idea as to the number of factors that underlie a set of items. Restricting the solution to that number can offer valuable diagnostic information.

## *Rotational Methods*

To make factors more interpretable (and item retention and deletion more meaningful), factors are "rotated" after extraction. A basic goal for scale developers is to look for simple structure after rotation. Simple structure occurs when each item loads highly on as few factors as possible, or, more preferably, has a substantial loading on only one factor. Rotation can be specified either as orthogonal or as oblique, where orthogonal rotation keeps factors uncorrelated and oblique rotation allows factors to correlate. VARIMAX is the most common form of orthogonal rotation for EFA and will show simple structure in most cases. Given, however, that a goal of EFA for scale development is to look for the degree to which multiple scales/dimensions correlate, oblique rotation methods (such as PROMAX) are advised. Oblique rotation will reveal (in most cases) the more meaningful theoretical factors. Both methods can help reveal what items to retain and delete for future studies, which brings us to our next issue in the application of EFA as a scale development tool.

### Item Retention via EFA

Given that EFA can be used as a method to reduce the number of items in a scale, questions arise regarding how many items should be deleted and what criteria to use in deleting items. As stated above, obtaining simple structure is a goal of EFA achieved by looking for loadings that are substantial (.40 and above). This goal should be used with EFA across *multiple* data sets (i.e., at least two). Furthermore, scale developers must also look for extremely high loadings, as items with such loadings may be indicative of wording redundancy that does not add substantively to a scale's internal consistency or validity. Thus, in general, we advocate retaining items via multiple EFAs with loadings no less than .40 but no greater than .90. At this stage, however, we caution against deleting items that may not meet this criterion but still are judged to have face and/or content validity. Furthermore, item deletion and retention in the early studies of scale development should simultaneously consider reliability and item-based statistics such as corrected item-to-total correlations, average interitem correlations, and item variances.

## Initial Item and Reliability Analyses

At the earlier stages of scale development, it is wise to examine a number of internal consistency– and item-based statistics in conjunction with EFA to use in decisions to retain and delete items. These internal consistency estimates include coefficient alpha average interitem correlations, corrected item-to-total correlations, item variances, and item-wording redundancy. Several heuristics or rules of thumb have been advocated for items as candidates for retention/deletion. Robinson et al. (1991) advocated an average interitem correlation of .30 or better as exemplary. Clark and Watson (1995) advocated average interitem correlations of .15 to .50 across constructs; for narrowly defined constructs, they advocated a range of .40 to .50. They also advocated a coefficient alpha level of at least .80 for a new scale and suggested that retaining items with greater variances relative to other items will help to increase overall scale variance. Bearden and Netemeyer (1998) advocated corrected item-to-total correlations of .50 and above and alpha levels of .80 or above (subject to scale length considerations).

These heuristics make sense, but it must also be remembered that coefficient alpha is related to scale length, average interitem correlation (covariance), item redundancy, and dimensionality. First, consider scale length. It was noted in Chapter 3 that as the number of items increases, alpha will tend to increase. Because parsimony is also a concern in measurement and most scales are self-administered, scale brevity is often a concern.

Item redundancy and average interitem correlation also affect coefficient alpha. Although it is advocated that several items are needed to adequately tap the domain of the construct, when the wording of the items is too similar, coefficient alpha (as well as content validity and dimensionality) may not be enhanced. Items that are worded too similarly will increase average interitem correlation and coefficient alpha; however, such items may just contribute to the "attenuation paradox" in psychometric theory, whereby increasing coefficient alpha beyond a certain point does not increase internal consistency (see Chapter 3). With these considerations in mind, researchers must be careful in their interpretation of alpha and consider its relationship to the number of items in a scale, the level of interitem correlation, and item redundancy. Last, and as discussed in Chapters 2 and 3, it must also be remembered that it is possible for a set of items to be interrelated but not unidimensional. Coefficient alpha is not a measure of unidimensionality and should be used to assess internal consistency *only after* unidimensionality is established (Clark & Watson, 1995; Cortina, 1993).

## A Final Caveat

Although EFA and internal consistency– and item-based statistics can be used in the early studies of scale development as means to decide which items to retain and delete, it is *always* better to retain many items at this stage for further studies. That is, *items that do not meet certain statistical criteria or rules of thumb but have face and/or content validity should be retained for the next "round" of studies.* If they continue to perform poorly, they can always be deleted when deriving the final form of the scale.


## EFA AND ITEM AND
## RELIABILITY ANALYSES
## EXAMPLES FROM THE LITERATURE

Numerous marketing and organizational behavior–based scale development articles illustrate the use of EFA and item and reliability analyses for trimming and retaining items. For example, in developing their CETSCALE, Shimp and Sharma (1987) used common factor analysis and item-based statistics over five large samples to trim an initial pool of CETSCALE items from 100 to 25. With the first sample, they used a "decision rule" of a loading less than .50 to delete items, and in the remaining studies, they used a decision rule of loadings greater than .70 to retain items. They further finalized their scale to 17 items via CFA pooled over their last four samples.

Bearden et al. (2001) took 97 items initially judged for content and face validity and used two samples (*n* = 221 and *n* = 204) to reduce this pool of items in deriving their consumer self-confidence scales. Using EFA and item- and reliability-based statistics, they trimmed this pool to 39 items for other developmental studies that followed. They employed the following decision rules for retaining items: (a) an average corrected item-to-total correlation greater than or equal to .35, (b) an average interitem correlation greater than .20, and (c) average factor loadings greater than .50. Items with a judged degree of high face validity were retained if they did not meet criteria a, b, and c. Bearden et al. (2001) also used CFA to trim eight more items from their measures in finalizing the consumer self-confidence scales and testing the scale's dimensionality. Below, we offer a more detailed empirical example of using EFA and item analyses in scale development.


### An Empirical Example of EFA

In scale development, the consistency of results from study to study is an important indicator of how well the scale may perform across samples from relevant populations. Given this, examining the stability of factor structure from sample to sample is recommended. To demonstrate such a procedure, we again use data from Netemeyer et al. (1996). In developing their WFC and FWC scales, they used EFA in the form of common factor analyses to determine if a two-factor structure of WFC and FWC as separate factors was tenable. The 22 WFC and 21 FWC items retained from the item judging procedure (see Chapter 5) were used for these analyses. (The following EFA analyses were not reported by Netemeyer et al. [1996] because of considerations of article length.)

First, Netemeyer and colleagues (1996) used common factor analysis with an oblique rotation method (PROMAX) where no restrictions were placed on the number of factors extracted across two samples (i.e., small business owners and real estate salespeople). SPSS was used to analyze the data. In Tables 6.1 through 6.4, WFC1 to WFC7 represent the "general" content items of work-family conflict; WFCT1 to WFCT8 represent the "time-based" content items of work-family conflict; and WFCS1 to WFCS7 represent the "strain-based" content items of work-family conflict. Likewise, FWC1 to FWC8 represent the "general" content items of family-work conflict; FWCT1 to FWCT7 represent the "time-based" content items of family-work conflict; and FWCS1 to FWCS6 represent the "strain-based" content items of family-work conflict. (Recall from Chapter 5 that the content domain of the constructs was felt to encompass a general-, time-, and strained-based conflict of work interfering with family and family interfering with work.)

Although for each sample, seven and six eigenvalues (latent roots) with values greater than 1 were extracted, the first two were the largest, accounting for the majority of the variance in the data across the samples (50% and 54%, respectively). The scree plots show a noticeable break (e.g., elbow) after the second factor, but the scree plot, along with parallel analysis, suggested a three-factor solution. However, the rotated factor matrix for these seven and six eigenvalue structures showed that only two factors were interpretable (not shown here in Tables 6.1 and 6.2). Given that theory suggested a priori that WFC and FWC were conceptually distinct yet correlated constructs, common factor analysis with an oblique rotation method (PROMAX) restricting the solution to two factors was then performed across the samples. Tables 6.1b and 6.2b show these rotated solutions (i.e., the pattern matrix). For interpretation purposes, only loadings greater than .40 in

**Table 6.1a**     Sample of Small Business Owners: Total Variance Explained

| Factor | Initial Eigenvalues | | | Extraction Sums of Squared Loadings | | | Rotation Sums of Squared Loadings | | |
|---|---|---|---|---|---|---|---|---|---|
| | Total | % of Variance | Cumulative % | Total | % of Variance | Cumulative % | Total | % of Variance | Cumulative % |
| 1 | 15.648 | 36.390 | 36.390 | 15.201 | 35.352 | 35.352 | 11.887 | 27.643 | 27.643 |
| 2 | 6.854 | 15.938 | 52.329 | 6.396 | 14.873 | 50.226 | 9.710 | 22.582 | 50.226 |
| 3 | 2.644 | 6.149 | 58.477 | | | | | | |
| 4 | 1.660 | 3.860 | 62.337 | | | | | | |
| 5 | 1.628 | 3.787 | 66.124 | | | | | | |
| 6 | 1.326 | 3.083 | 69.207 | | | | | | |
| 7 | 1.204 | 2.800 | 72.006 | | | | | | |

SCREE PLOT

EIGENVALUE

FACTOR NUMBER

**Table 6.1b**    Sample of Small Business Owners: Pattern
Matrix for Two-Factor Solution

| Factor | 1 | 2 |
|--------|------|------|
| WFC1 | .811 | |
| WFC2 | .735 | |
| WFC3 | .834 | |
| WFC4 | .871 | |
| WFC5 | .694 | |
| WFC6 | .647 | |
| WFC7 | .808 | |
| WFCT1 | .662 | |
| WFCT2 | .545 | |
| WFCT3 | .675 | |
| WFCT4 | .794 | |
| WFCT5 | .692 | |
| WFCT6 | .753 | |
| WFCT7 | .828 | |
| WFCT8 | .866 | |
| WFCS1 | .481 | |
| WFCS2 | | |
| WFCS3 | .755 | |
| WFCS4 | .828 | |
| WFCS5 | .698 | |
| WFCS6 | .593 | |
| WFCS7 | .706 | |
| FWC1 | | .584 |
| FWC2 | | .755 |
| FWC3 | | .550 |
| FWC4 | | .465 |
| FWC5 | | .775 |
| FWC6 | | .823 |
| FWC7 | | .750 |
| FWC8 | | .752 |
| FWCT1 | .518 | |
| FWCT2 | | .526 |
| FWCT3 | | .658 |
| FWCT4 | | .779 |
| FWCT5 | | .886 |
| FWCT6 | | .750 |
| FWCT7 | | .767 |
| FWCS1 | | .692 |
| FWCS2 | | .804 |
| FWCS3 | | |
| FWCS4 | | .549 |
| FWCS5 | | .588 |
| FWCS6 | | .628 |

**Table 6.1c**       Sample of Small Business Owners: Factor
                    Correlation Matrix

| Factor | 1 | 2 |
|---|---|---|
| 1 | 1.000 | .403 |
| 2 | .403 | 1.000 |

magnitude are printed. (Because the sample sizes were within the 150 to 200 range, loadings of .40 to .45 are statistically significant; Hair et al. [1998, pp. 111-112]).

It is clear from these tables that most items loaded highly on their intended factor, and this pattern was consistent across the samples. Inconsistencies for the samples were noted for the following items. For the small business owner sample, WFCS2 did not load above .40 on the WFC factor, FWCT1 loaded higher on the WFC factor than on the FWC factor, and FWCS3 did not load above .40 on the FWC factor. For the real estate salespeople sample, WFCT2 and WFCS2 did not load above .40 on the WFC factor, and FWCS3 did not load above .40 on the FWC factor. These items were considered as candidates for deletion in later item analyses. Furthermore, across the two samples, three high loadings were found: FWCT5 (.89 and .94) and, to a lesser extent, FWCT6 (.75 and .93) and FWC7 (.75 and .93). These items were also examined as candidates for deletion in later item analyses. Still, the primary purpose here was to determine if a two-factor solution was tenable, and common factor analysis revealed a consistent pattern of results across the samples for the hypothesized two-factor WFC-FWC structure underlying the data.

## Reliability and Item-Based Statistics

As previously stated, reliability and item-based statistics should also be used in conjunction with EFA during developmental studies. Tables 6.3a-d and 6.4a-d show the results of initial reliability and item analyses for the afore-mentioned small business owner and real estate salespeople examples. The

*(Text continued on page 137)*

**Table 6.2a**   Sample of Real Estate Salespeople: Total Variance Explained

| Factor | Initial Eigenvalues | | | Extraction Sums of Squared Loadings | | | Rotation Sums of Squared Loadings | | |
|---|---|---|---|---|---|---|---|---|---|
| | Total | % of Variance | Cumulative % | Total | % of Variance | Cumulative % | Total | % of Variance | Cumulative % |
| 1 | 17.741 | 41.259 | 41.259 | 17.337 | 40.320 | 40.320 | 12.761 | 29.676 | 29.676 |
| 2 | 6.117 | 14.225 | 55.484 | 5.702 | 13.260 | 53.580 | 10.278 | 23.903 | 53.580 |
| 3 | 2.371 | 5.514 | 60.998 | | | | | | |
| 4 | 1.766 | 4.107 | 65.105 | | | | | | |
| 5 | 1.311 | 3.048 | 68.153 | | | | | | |
| 6 | 1.169 | 2.718 | 70.871 | | | | | | |

Scree Plot

Factor Number

**Table 6.2b**      Sample of Real Estate Salespeople: Pattern
Matrix for Two-Factor Solution

| Factor | 1 | 2 |
|---|---|---|
| WFC1 | | .754 |
| WFC2 | | .749 |
| WFC3 | | .788 |
| WFC4 | | .874 |
| WFC5 | | .766 |
| WFC6 | | .774 |
| WFC7 | | .774 |
| WFCT1 | | .772 |
| WFCT2 | | |
| WFCT3 | | .474 |
| WFCT4 | | .607 |
| WFCT5 | | .478 |
| WFCT6 | | .614 |
| WFCT7 | | .673 |
| WFCT8 | | .650 |
| WFCS1 | | .628 |
| WFCS2 | | |
| WFCS3 | | .776 |
| WFCS4 | | .792 |
| WFCS5 | | .667 |
| WFCS6 | | .495 |
| WFCS7 | | .618 |
| FWC1 | .750 | |
| FWC2 | .768 | |
| FWC3 | .747 | |
| FWC4 | .651 | |
| FWC5 | .896 | |
| FWC6 | .889 | |
| FWC7 | .932 | |
| FWC8 | .824 | |
| FWCT1 | .709 | |
| FWCT2 | .755 | |
| FWCT3 | .813 | |
| FWCT4 | .891 | |
| FWCT5 | .939 | |
| FWCT6 | .929 | |
| FWCT7 | .777 | |
| FWCS1 | .816 | |
| FWCS2 | .670 | |
| FWCS3 | | |
| FWCS4 | .603 | |
| FWCS5 | .518 | |
| FWCS6 | .698 | |

**Table 6.2c**    Sample of Real Estate Salespeople: Factor
                  Correlation Matrix

| Factor | 1 | 2 |
|--------|-------|-------|
| 1 | 1.000 | .482 |
| 2 | .482 | 1.000 |

**Table 6.3a**    Sample of Small Business Owners: WFC Scale, Reliability Analysis
                  Scale (Alpha)

|  |  | Mean | Std. Dev. | Cases |
|------|------|------|-----------|-------|
| 1. | WFC1 | 4.1154 | 2.0319 | 156.0 |
| 2. | WFC2 | 3.3462 | 2.0966 | 156.0 |
| 3. | WFC3 | 3.1410 | 1.9426 | 156.0 |
| 4. | WFC4 | 3.4038 | 1.9798 | 156.0 |
| 5. | WFC5 | 4.1923 | 1.9939 | 156.0 |
| 6. | WFC6 | 3.6282 | 1.9780 | 156.0 |
| 7. | WFC7 | 3.2179 | 1.9684 | 156.0 |
| 8. | WFCT1 | 3.8910 | 2.1630 | 156.0 |
| 9. | WFCT2 | 3.6026 | 1.9599 | 156.0 |
| 10. | WFCT3 | 3.6218 | 1.9587 | 156.0 |
| 11. | WFCT4 | 3.0641 | 1.8723 | 156.0 |
| 12. | WFCT5 | 3.8590 | 2.0711 | 156.0 |
| 13. | WFCT6 | 2.6218 | 1.7973 | 156.0 |
| 14. | WFCT7 | 2.5833 | 1.7523 | 156.0 |
| 15. | WFCT8 | 2.5769 | 1.6964 | 156.0 |
| 16. | WFCS1 | 3.6987 | 1.9157 | 156.0 |
| 17. | WFCS2 | 3.8590 | 1.9689 | 156.0 |
| 18. | WFCS3 | 3.3397 | 1.8991 | 156.0 |
| 19. | WFCS4 | 2.8654 | 1.8000 | 156.0 |
| 20. | WFCS5 | 2.5192 | 1.6322 | 156.0 |
| 21. | WFCS6 | 3.0769 | 1.8051 | 156.0 |
| 22. | WFCS7 | 2.7885 | 1.8352 | 156.0 |

Statistics for Scale

| Mean | Variance | Std Dev | Variables |
|------|----------|---------|-----------|
| 73.0128 | 948.3869 | 30.7959 | 22 |

Item Means

| Mean | Minimum | Maximum | Range | Max/Min | Variance |
|------|---------|---------|-------|---------|----------|
| 3.3188 | 2.5192 | 4.1923 | 1.6731 | 1.6641 | .2666 |

**Table 6.3a**     (Continued)

Item Variances

| Mean | Minimum | Maximum | Range | Max/Min | Variance |
|------|---------|---------|-------|---------|----------|
| 3.6815 | 2.6641 | 4.6784 | 2.0142 | 1.7561 | .2462 |

Interitem Correlations

| Mean | Minimum | Maximum | Range | Max/Min | Variance |
|------|---------|---------|-------|---------|----------|
| .5157 | .1363 | .8562 | .7199 | 6.2817 | .0201 |

**Table 6.3b**     Sample of Small Business Owners: WFC Scale, Item-Total Statistics

| | *Scale Mean if Item Deleted* | *Scale Variance if Item Deleted* | *Corrected Item-Total Correlations* | *Squared Multiple Correlation* | *Alpha if Item Deleted* |
|------|------|------|------|------|------|
| WFC1 | 68.8974 | 858.2217 | .7227 | .6644 | .9560 |
| WFC2 | 69.6667 | 855.9656 | .7175 | .6898 | .9560 |
| WFC3 | 69.8718 | 860.3706 | .7392 | .6489 | .9558 |
| WFC4 | 69.6090 | 849.2719 | .8250 | .7756 | .9547 |
| WFC5 | 68.8205 | 863.5418 | .6901 | .6530 | .9564 |
| WFC6 | 69.3846 | 864.9737 | .6833 | .7024 | .9564 |
| WFC7 | 69.7949 | 851.0544 | .8137 | .8205 | .9549 |
| WFCT1 | 69.1218 | 860.2883 | .6575 | .5969 | .9569 |
| WFCT2 | 69.4103 | 885.1596 | .5092 | .4977 | .9585 |
| WFCT3 | 69.3910 | 867.6977 | .6660 | .7411 | .9566 |
| WFCT4 | 69.9487 | 857.7522 | .7945 | .6868 | .9551 |
| WFCT5 | 69.1538 | 863.8342 | .6593 | .6788 | .9568 |
| WFCT6 | 70.3910 | 869.8010 | .7108 | .6998 | .9561 |
| WFCT7 | 70.4295 | 863.0853 | .7987 | .8224 | .9552 |
| WFCT8 | 70.4359 | 861.7830 | .8406 | .8705 | .9548 |
| WFCS1 | 69.3141 | 881.9459 | .5517 | .6725 | .9579 |
| WFCS2 | 69.1538 | 899.7955 | .3785 | .2764 | .9600 |
| WFCS3 | 69.6731 | 859.9505 | .7616 | .8075 | .9555 |
| WFCS4 | 70.1474 | 858.4362 | .8221 | .8412 | .9549 |
| WFCS5 | 70.4936 | 876.5483 | .7157 | .8162 | .9562 |
| WFCS6 | 69.9359 | 872.3572 | .6824 | .7190 | .9564 |
| WFCS7 | 70.2244 | 866.8977 | .7229 | .7896 | .9560 |

Reliability Coefficients: 22 items
Alpha = .9582        Standardized item alpha = .9591

**Table 6.3c**     Sample of Small Business Owners: WFC Scale, Reliability Analysis
Scale (Alpha)

|     |       | *Mean* | *Std. Dev.* | *Cases* |
|-----|-------|--------|-------------|---------|
| 1.  | FWC1  | 2.1316 | 1.4679      | 152.0   |
| 2.  | FWC2  | 1.8355 | 1.0945      | 152.0   |
| 3.  | FWC3  | 2.5724 | 1.8109      | 152.0   |
| 4.  | FWC4  | 1.6711 | 1.2490      | 152.0   |
| 5.  | FWC5  | 1.8289 | 1.2856      | 152.0   |
| 6.  | FWC6  | 1.8947 | 1.2563      | 152.0   |
| 7.  | FWC7  | 1.8816 | 1.3319      | 152.0   |
| 8.  | FWC8  | 2.1776 | 1.4877      | 152.0   |
| 9.  | FWCT1 | 2.1184 | 1.4139      | 152.0   |
| 10. | FWCT2 | 1.9539 | 1.2987      | 152.0   |
| 11. | FWCT3 | 1.7566 | 1.0918      | 152.0   |
| 12. | FWCT4 | 1.9868 | 1.2969      | 152.0   |
| 13. | FWCT5 | 1.7763 | 1.1229      | 152.0   |
| 14. | FWCT6 | 1.9408 | 1.2672      | 152.0   |
| 15. | FWCT7 | 1.8618 | 1.2398      | 152.0   |
| 16. | FWCS1 | 2.0724 | 1.3911      | 152.0   |
| 17. | FWCS2 | 2.1382 | 1.4468      | 152.0   |
| 18. | FWCS3 | 3.5921 | 2.1664      | 152.0   |
| 19. | FWCS4 | 2.0526 | 1.3800      | 152.0   |
| 20. | FWCS5 | 2.3750 | 1.5260      | 152.0   |
| 21. | FWCS6 | 2.0000 | 1.2867      | 152.0   |

Statistics for Scale

| Mean    | Variance | Std Dev | Variables |
|---------|----------|---------|-----------|
| 43.6184 | 354.5422 | 18.8293 | 21        |

Item Means

| Mean   | Minimum | Maximum | Range  | Max/Min | Variance |
|--------|---------|---------|--------|---------|----------|
| 2.0771 | 1.6711  | 3.5921  | 1.9211 | 2.1496  | .1466    |

Item Variances

| Mean   | Minimum | Maximum | Range  | Max/Min | Variance |
|--------|---------|---------|--------|---------|----------|
| 1.9516 | 1.1920  | 4.6934  | 3.5014 | 3.9375  | .6058    |

Interitem Correlations

| Mean  | Minimum | Maximum | Range | Max/Min  | Variance |
|-------|---------|---------|-------|----------|----------|
| .4232 | −.1055  | .8505   | .9560 | −8.0599  | .0391    |

**Table 6.3d**     Sample of Small Business Owners: WFC Scale, Item-Total Statistics

| | Scale Mean if Item Deleted | Scale Variance if Item Deleted | Corrected Item-Total Correlations | Squared Multiple Correlation | Alpha if Item Deleted |
|---|---|---|---|---|---|
| FWC1 | 41.4868 | 322.9932 | .5571 | .4850 | .9261 |
| FWC2 | 41.7829 | 325.0982 | .7157 | .7194 | .9238 |
| FWC3 | 41.0461 | 320.0972 | .4809 | .5361 | .9286 |
| FWC4 | 41.9474 | 335.2687 | .3873 | .4322 | .9289 |
| FWC5 | 41.7895 | 323.0415 | .6459 | .7354 | .9245 |
| FWC6 | 41.7237 | 319.5125 | .7448 | .7838 | .9228 |
| FWC7 | 41.7368 | 321.4800 | .6551 | .7032 | .9242 |
| FWC8 | 41.4408 | 317.3210 | .6605 | .6767 | .9240 |
| FWCT1 | 41.5000 | 325.2980 | .5342 | .5755 | .9265 |
| FWCT2 | 41.6645 | 324.4363 | .6074 | .7119 | .9251 |
| FWCT3 | 41.8618 | 325.6960 | .7018 | .8159 | .9240 |
| FWCT4 | 41.6316 | 319.5985 | .7173 | .7114 | .9232 |
| FWCT5 | 41.8421 | 321.1272 | .7990 | .8402 | .9224 |
| FWCT6 | 41.6776 | 319.3325 | .7420 | .7203 | .9228 |
| FWCT7 | 41.7566 | 319.9205 | .7460 | .7679 | .9228 |
| FWCS1 | 41.5461 | 317.4416 | .7094 | .8399 | .9231 |
| FWCS2 | 41.4803 | 312.3705 | .7836 | .8376 | .9216 |
| FWCS3 | 40.0263 | 346.4231 | .0425 | .1162 | .9424 |
| FWCS4 | 41.5658 | 321.6513 | .6260 | .7862 | .9247 |
| FWCS5 | 41.2434 | 318.6357 | .6163 | .8380 | .9249 |
| FWCS6 | 41.6184 | 320.5422 | .7020 | .8222 | .9235 |

Reliability Coefficients: 22 items
Alpha = .9286     Standardized item alpha = .9390

same items used for the preceding EFA analyses were used here. These tables show recommended levels of average interitem correlations for both the WFC and FWC items (.42-.58 across samples), as well as initial corrected item-to-total correlations mostly in the .50 to .80 range. (Coefficient alpha estimates were all above .90.) These two tables also show results consistent with those from the restricted two-factor EFA; that is, those items that did not load highly on their intended EFA factors also showed low corrected item-to-total correlations. For the small business owner sample, WFCS2 and FWCS3 had low

**Table 6.4a**     Samples of Real Estate Salespeople: FWC Scale, Reliability
                   Analysis Scale (Alpha)

|      |         | Mean    | Std. Dev. | Cases   |
|------|---------|---------|-----------|---------|
| 1.   | WFC1    | 3.9836  | 1.7556    | 183.0   |
| 2.   | WFC2    | 3.0984  | 1.7607    | 183.0   |
| 3.   | WFC3    | 3.1366  | 1.6368    | 183.0   |
| 4.   | WFC4    | 3.4590  | 1.6829    | 183.0   |
| 5.   | WFC5    | 4.0929  | 1.8118    | 183.0   |
| 6.   | WFC6    | 3.9016  | 1.7229    | 183.0   |
| 7.   | WFC7    | 3.3607  | 1.7068    | 183.0   |
| 8.   | WFCT1   | 3.7213  | 1.7491    | 183.0   |
| 9.   | WFCT2   | 3.8251  | 1.8042    | 183.0   |
| 10.  | WFCT3   | 4.3333  | 1.8645    | 183.0   |
| 11.  | WFCT4   | 3.0328  | 1.5756    | 183.0   |
| 12.  | WFCT5   | 4.2951  | 1.9188    | 183.0   |
| 13.  | WFCT6   | 2.6612  | 1.6391    | 183.0   |
| 14.  | WFCT7   | 2.7814  | 1.6261    | 183.0   |
| 15.  | WFCT8   | 2.6667  | 1.5418    | 183.0   |
| 16.  | WFCS1   | 3.7814  | 1.8653    | 183.0   |
| 17.  | WFCS2   | 4.1694  | 1.7693    | 183.0   |
| 18.  | WFCS3   | 3.3388  | 1.7525    | 183.0   |
| 19.  | WFCS4   | 3.0000  | 1.6575    | 183.0   |
| 20.  | WFCS5   | 2.5027  | 1.5187    | 183.0   |
| 21.  | WFCS6   | 2.8525  | 1.7557    | 183.0   |
| 22.  | WFCS7   | 2.5628  | 1.5496    | 183.0   |

Statistics for Scale

| Mean     | Variance   | Std Dev   | Variables |
|----------|------------|-----------|-----------|
| 74.5574  | 643.4239   | 25.3658   | 22        |

Item Means

| Mean    | Minimum  | Maximum  | Range   | Max/Min  | Variance  |
|---------|----------|----------|---------|----------|-----------|
| 3.3890  | 2.5027   | 4.3333   | 1.8306  | 1.3571   | .3571     |

Item Variances

| Mean    | Minimum  | Maximum  | Range   | Max/Min  | Variance  |
|---------|----------|----------|---------|----------|-----------|
| 2.9427  | 2.3063   | 3.6817   | 1.3754  | 1.5963   | .1413     |

Interitem Correlations

| Mean    | Minimum  | Maximum  | Range   | Max/Min   | Variance  |
|---------|----------|----------|---------|-----------|-----------|
| .4335   | .0552    | .8758    | .8206   | 15.8783   | .0298     |

**Table 6.4b**      Sample of Real Estate Salespeople: FWC Scale, Item-Total Statistics

| | Scale Mean if Item Deleted | Scale Variance if Item Deleted | Corrected Item-Total Correlations | Squared Multiple Correlation | Alpha if Item Deleted |
|---|---|---|---|---|---|
| WFC1 | 70.5738 | 586.7294 | .6304 | .6412 | .9397 |
| WFC2 | 71.4590 | 585.7222 | .6407 | .6149 | .9395 |
| WFC3 | 71.4208 | 585.3989 | .6988 | .6750 | .9387 |
| WFC4 | 71.0984 | 576.8254 | .7888 | .7623 | .9373 |
| WFC5 | 70.4645 | 580.3160 | .6854 | .6269 | .9388 |
| WFC6 | 70.6557 | 579.3149 | .7372 | .7204 | .9380 |
| WFC7 | 71.1967 | 575.9941 | .7875 | .7290 | .9373 |
| WFCT1 | 70.8361 | 581.6983 | .6953 | .5770 | .9387 |
| WFCT2 | 70.7322 | 609.5378 | .3438 | .3538 | .9441 |
| WFCT3 | 70.2240 | 595.4825 | .4887 | .5946 | .9420 |
| WFCT4 | 71.5246 | 590.4156 | .6599 | .5651 | .9393 |
| WFCT5 | 70.2623 | 597.3374 | .4521 | .5034 | .9427 |
| WFCT6 | 71.8962 | 590.1925 | .6346 | .5880 | .9396 |
| WFCT7 | 71.7760 | 585.2517 | .7058 | .7220 | .9386 |
| WFCT8 | 71.8907 | 586.2297 | .7342 | .7146 | .9383 |
| WFCS1 | 70.7760 | 583.5814 | .6254 | .5453 | .9398 |
| WFCS2 | 70.3880 | 622.4805 | .2018 | .1542 | .9461 |
| WFCS3 | 71.2186 | 576.4575 | .7593 | .8071 | .9377 |
| WFCS4 | 71.5574 | 577.2591 | .7962 | .8381 | .9372 |
| WFCS5 | 72.0546 | 588.8871 | .7086 | .7376 | .9387 |
| WFCS6 | 71.7049 | 590.1872 | .5879 | .6421 | .9403 |
| WFCS7 | 71.9945 | 587.9176 | .7067 | .7384 | .9387 |

Reliability Coefficients: 22 items
Alpha = .9422      Standardized item alpha = .9439

corrected item-to-total correlations, and for the real estate salespeople sample, WFCT2 and FWCS3 had low item-to-total correlations. Furthermore, those items from the EFA that had consistently high loadings were also found to have corrected item-to-total correlations consistently above .80. A close inspection of these items revealed that they had wording that was redundant with other items and that they had extremely high correlations with the items of similar wording (.85-.90). Thus, based on the EFA and reliability and item-based statistics of two development studies, items WFCT2, WFCS2, FWCT1,

**Table 6.4c**    Sample of Real Estate Salespeople: FWC Scale, Reliability Analysis
Scale (Alpha)

|     |       | Mean | Std. Dev. | Cases |
|-----|-------|------|-----------|-------|
| 1.  | FWC1  | 2.3425 | 1.6172 | 181.0 |
| 2.  | FWC2  | 2.5801 | 1.6399 | 181.0 |
| 3.  | FWC3  | 2.7348 | 1.8216 | 181.0 |
| 4.  | FWC4  | 1.5414 | 1.1029 | 181.0 |
| 5.  | FWC5  | 2.1547 | 1.5629 | 181.0 |
| 6.  | FWC6  | 2.2044 | 1.5696 | 181.0 |
| 7.  | FWC7  | 2.1160 | 1.5502 | 181.0 |
| 8.  | FWC8  | 2.6685 | 1.8229 | 181.0 |
| 9.  | FWCT1 | 2.6685 | 1.6966 | 181.0 |
| 10. | FWCT2 | 2.7127 | 1.6143 | 181.0 |
| 11. | FWCT3 | 2.3094 | 1.4350 | 181.0 |
| 12. | FWCT4 | 2.3757 | 1.6029 | 181.0 |
| 13. | FWCT5 | 2.0884 | 1.4503 | 181.0 |
| 14. | FWCT6 | 2.4088 | 1.6360 | 181.0 |
| 15. | FWCT7 | 2.2486 | 1.5417 | 181.0 |
| 16. | FWCS1 | 2.2044 | 1.5229 | 181.0 |
| 17. | FWCS2 | 2.2762 | 1.5638 | 181.0 |
| 18. | FWCS3 | 2.9448 | 1.7503 | 181.0 |
| 19. | FWCS4 | 1.9945 | 1.4083 | 181.0 |
| 20. | FWCS5 | 2.3315 | 1.6057 | 181.0 |
| 21. | FWCS6 | 2.0497 | 1.4192 | 181.0 |

Statistics for Scale

| Mean | Variance | Std Dev | Variables |
|------|----------|---------|-----------|
| 48.9558 | 651.8869 | 25.5321 | 21 |

Item Means

| Mean | Minimum | Maximum | Range | Max/Min | Variance |
|------|---------|---------|-------|---------|----------|
| 2.3312 | 1.5414 | 2.9448 | 1.4033 | 1.9104 | .0989 |

Item Variances

| Mean | Minimum | Maximum | Range | Max/Min | Variance |
|------|---------|---------|-------|---------|----------|
| 2.4831 | 1.2163 | 3.3228 | 2.1065 | 2.7319 | .2236 |

Interitem Correlations

| Mean | Minimum | Maximum | Range | Max/Min | Variance |
|------|---------|---------|-------|---------|----------|
| .5824 | .1835 | .9020 | .7185 | 4.9159 | .0221 |

**Table 6.4d**     Sample of Real Estate Salespeople: FWC Scale, Item-Total Statistics

|  | Scale Mean if Item Deleted | Scale Variance if Item Deleted | Corrected Item-Total Correlations | Squared Multiple Correlation | Alpha if Item Deleted |
|---|---|---|---|---|---|
| FWC1 | 46.6133 | 590.9607 | .7416 | .7528 | .9644 |
| FWC2 | 46.3757 | 592.2581 | .7133 | .7858 | .9647 |
| FWC3 | 46.2210 | 587.1287 | .6960 | .7319 | .9651 |
| FWC4 | 47.4144 | 616.1107 | .6312 | .5768 | .9656 |
| FWC5 | 46.8011 | 586.0936 | .8372 | .8565 | .9634 |
| FWC6 | 46.7514 | 584.7878 | .8515 | .8912 | .9632 |
| FWC7 | 46.8398 | 585.5797 | .8518 | .8832 | .9632 |
| FWC8 | 46.2873 | 580.9392 | .7696 | .7682 | .9642 |
| FWCT1 | 46.2873 | 584.8170 | .7823 | .7964 | .9640 |
| FWCT2 | 46.2431 | 587.1961 | .7936 | .7962 | .9638 |
| FWCT3 | 46.6464 | 591.7521 | .8318 | .8204 | .9635 |
| FWCT4 | 46.5801 | 585.5783 | .8217 | .7867 | .9635 |
| FWCT5 | 46.8674 | 590.0268 | .8482 | .8439 | .9634 |
| FWCT6 | 46.5470 | 580.9381 | .8657 | .8480 | .9630 |
| FWCT7 | 46.7072 | 589.8971 | .7960 | .7797 | .9638 |
| FWCS1 | 46.7514 | 589.7212 | .8091 | .8157 | .9637 |
| FWCS2 | 46.6796 | 594.4856 | .7207 | .6845 | .9646 |
| FWCS3 | 46.0110 | 616.4554 | .3724 | .3367 | .9688 |
| FWCS4 | 46.9613 | 603.3929 | .6722 | .6868 | .9651 |
| FWCS5 | 46.6243 | 602.5914 | .5926 | .7036 | .9660 |
| FWCS6 | 46.9061 | 597.2856 | .7581 | .8003 | .9643 |

Reliability Coefficients: 21 items
Alpha = .9660     Standardized item alpha = .9670

FWCS3, FWCT5, FWCT6, and FWC7 were primary candidates for deletion for the next set of studies to finalize the scale.

## SUMMARY

This chapter addressed the following issues in Step 3 of the scale development process: pilot testing a pool of items as an item trimming and initial validity testing procedure, and conducting multiple studies for scale development. Within the second issue, we highlighted (a) the importance of including constructs for assessing the various types of validity, (b) EFAs over multiple data sets to refine the scale and examine a theoretical a priori initial factor structure, and (c) item and reliability analyses. Finally, we offered an example from a recently developed scale as to how EFA and item and reliability analyses can be used in scale development. Chapter 7 focuses on procedures in scale finalization.

# SEVEN

# STEP 4

## *Finalizing a Scale*

―――――•◦•―――――

## INTRODUCTION

This chapter focuses on procedures to finalize the scale and further establish its psychometric properties—our recommended fourth step in scale development. We will specifically address the following: (a) exploratory factor analysis (EFA) and additional item analyses as precursors to confirmatory factor analysis (CFA), (b) CFA to help finalize and confirm a theoretical factor structure and test for the invariance of the factor structure over multiple data sets, (c) additional validity testing, (d) establishing norms, and (e) applying generalizability theory. As part of the chapter, we again offer examples from recent published scale development articles in the marketing and organizational behavior literatures. The material in the chapter thus provides additional elaboration for many of the issues discussed in our previous chapters.

## EFA AND ADDITIONAL ITEM ANALYSES

As part of the process of selecting items to include in scales being developed, researchers often are faced with decisions regarding EFA results, corrected item-to-total correlations, interitem correlations, and scale length. Again, these issues are often considered across the first series of studies in a scale development effort and prior to the collection of subsequent data for use in CFA.

## EFA

As stated (and illustrated) in Chapter 6, EFA can be used to trim the number of items in scale development prior to using CFA to confirm a scale's hypothesized structure. Numerous marketing and organizational behavior–based scale development articles illustrate the use of EFA for trimming items and retaining items for the final form of a scale. For example, in measuring consumer frugality, Lastovicka et al. (1999) first used EFA with a decision rule of retaining items with loadings greater than .50 to reduce a 60-item pool to 25 items. (They later used CFA to further reduce their scale to 8 items.) As shown in Chapter 6, Netemeyer et al. (1996) used common factor analysis to examine the initial structure of 22 work-family conflict (WFC) and 21 family-work conflict (FWC) items. Via several criteria advocated in the psychometric literature (e.g., retaining items with factor loadings greater than .50, deleting items with factor loadings greater than .90, and deleting items with high cross-loadings on a factor (e.g., FWC) other than the intended factor (e.g., WFC), 7 WFC and 8 FWC items were considered as candidates for deletion in the CFA analyses that followed.

### Additional Item Analyses

#### *Item-to-Total Correlations*

Corrected item-to-total correlations are routinely provided from scale reliability procedures. These correlations reflect the extent to which any one item is correlated with the remaining items in a set of items under consideration. These analyses typically are done within each dimension for multidimensional scales. As previously stated, items with low corrected item-to-total correlations are candidates for deletion. For multidimensional scales, items that do not have higher correlations with the dimension to which they are hypothesized to belong than they do with the remaining dimensions are also candidates for deletion (Ruekert & Churchill, 1984). A review of recent marketing and organizational behavior scales provides several examples and decision rules for item-to-total correlations. For example, Tian et al. (2001), in the item refinement stages of their development of the three-factor Consumer Need for Uniqueness scale (CNFU), deleted items that did not have corrected item-to-total correlations above .50 for each item's appropriate dimension. Obermiller and

Spangenberg (1998) deleted items with corrected item-to-total correlations below .50 in the development of their scale to measure consumer skepticism toward advertising. Bearden et al. (2001) used a decision rule of item-to-total correlations greater than .35 to retain items in their first two developmental studies. Finally, Netemeyer et al. (1996) considered items for retention that showed initial item-to-total correlations in the .50 to .80 range. In general, all these applications used corrected item-to-total correlations as a means of deleting/retaining items prior to CFA to confirm a scale's structure.

*Interitem Correlations*

Another important early consideration in scale development (e.g., often before final CFA) is consideration of interitem correlations. In fact, Clark and Watson (1995, p. 316) argued that average interitem correlation is a more useful index of internal consistency reliability than is coefficient alpha. They also suggested that the range of interitem correlations should depend upon the specificity of the construct being measured. That is, if the researcher is measuring a broad, higher-order construct, these authors suggest that a mean interitem correlation as low as .15 to .25 might be desirable. In contrast, a valid measure of a construct with a much more narrow focus might require a higher intercorrelation range of perhaps .40 to .50 (Clark & Watson, 1995, p. 316). In their criteria for evaluating attitude scales, Robinson et al. (1991, p. 13) suggested ".30 and better" and ".20 to .29" as providing exemplary evidence or extensive evidence, respectively. Importantly, the arguments of these authors further point out that, to ensure dimensionality, interitem correlations should be moderate in magnitude and cluster around the mean. A cursory review (cf. Bearden & Netemeyer, 1998) of marketing and consumer behavior articles reveals that researchers in these areas infrequently provide evidence regarding averages and the range of interitem correlations.

*Scale Length Considerations*

As we have noted, the reliability of a measure is a function of both the average interitem correlation and the number of items in a scale. Given that, researchers faced with the task of developing valid measures are confronted with decisions regarding scale length. A construct that has a broad content domain and multiple dimensions will require more items to adequately tap the domain/dimensions of the construct (e.g., the 31-item three-dimension Consumer Need for Uniqueness scale, CNFU; Tian et al., 2001), as opposed to a construct with a narrow domain and a single dimension (e.g., the eight-item, single-dimension measure of consumer frugality Lastovicka et al., 1999). Given that most scale uses involve respondent self-administration, scale brevity is often a concern. Part of the researcher's efforts are directed both to encouraging respondent cooperation and to limiting respondent fatigue. Obviously, maximizing reliability by adding items makes the burden on the respondent greater, and the developer needs to give some thought to the trade-off between brevity and reliability.

Decisions regarding the number of items to include in a scale often are subjective. On the low end, each factor or dimension should include four or more items, so that one-factor CFA models are overidentified. With only three items, CFA one-factor models will be perfectly identified, and little insight is provided for measurement fit. Clark and Watson (1995, p. 317) suggested that, once a benchmark of .80 reliability has been reached with an appropriate number of items as low as four or five items for very narrow constructs and up to 35 items for broad concepts, there is little need to strive for higher reliability. Again, shorter scales are preferred as long as the domain of the construct has been adequately covered or tapped. Issues related to content validity and item redundancy affect scale length considerations as well. That is, the content quality of items is more important than the quantity or number of items. Including items worded too similarly will increase average interitem correlation and coefficient alpha but will not enhance the content validity of the measure. Researchers must be careful in their interpretation of coefficient alpha by considering its relationship to the number of items in a scale, the level of interitem correlation, item redundancy, and dimensionality (Netemeyer et al., 2002).

The meta-analysis of Peterson (1994) describes a large distribution of measures taken from marketing and psychology journals in terms of scale length and the values of coefficient alpha at various levels of scale length. The results of this meta-analysis revealed only a weak relationship between scale length and estimates of coefficient alpha ($R^2 = .10$). The major difference in mean alpha coefficients was between scales with two or three items (alpha = .73) and those with more than three items (alpha = .78). Scales with 11 or more items exhibited the largest average coefficient (alpha = .81) (Peterson, 1994, p. 386). It should be noted that these results are based on a wide range of multi-item scales and include many more measures than those developed employing the rigorous scale development procedures described in this volume.

Bagozzi (personal correspondence, February 1, 2002) suggested that, for scales measuring personality traits or similar constructs, 8 to 10 items per construct, or per dimension for multifactor constructs, might represent an ideal. A related issue involves decisions regarding the number of indicators to use per factor in CFA or structural equation modeling (SEM) with structural paths. Again, some researchers argue for a minimum of four indicators, and others for a minimum of three. The problem becomes even more troublesome when sample size is small relative to the number of parameters to be estimated. In these cases, researchers have on occasion combined indicators. At least two options are tenable. First, a composite index or a single construct indicator can be formed by averaging all the indicators or items in a scale and then setting construct error terms based on the reliability of the construct (i.e., set error at 1 minus the square root of alpha). A second approach involves combining subsets of indicators into "parcels" (cf. Bagozzi & Edwards, 1998; Kishton & Widaman, 1994). In these instances, a smaller number of indicators per dimension is employed in SEM analyses, where each parceled indicator is actually a composite of multiple indicators as well. Finally, scale length considerations were also addressed earlier, at the end of Chapter 3, in our discussion of the generalizability coefficient and how a scale can be developed with a minimum number of items without sacrificing the generalizability coefficient.

## CONFIRMATORY FACTOR ANALYSIS (CFA)

### Overview

Our discussion of confirmatory factor analysis is limited to its use as a scale development tool, and we have borrowed heavily from three sources. The interested reader is urged to consult these three sources for more detail (Comrey, 1988; Floyd & Widaman, 1995; Hair et al., 1998). For a more thorough discussion of CFA and SEM practices, the reader is urged to consult some of the numerous books and book chapters on the subject (e.g., Bollen, 1989; Byrne, 2001; Hair et al., 1998; Hoyle, 1995; Schumacker & Lomax, 1996; Sharma, 1996).

At its essence, CFA for scale development is used to confirm an a priori hypothesis about the relationship of a set of measurement items to their respective factors (sometimes referred to as a *measurement model*). CFA differs from EFA primarily in that a confirmatory structure is specified prior to using the technique, and a primary form of estimation with CFA is maximum likelihood estimation (MLE). CFA has become a useful technique for the later stages in scale development to test the internal consistency and validity of a measure. CFA also can be used to detect individual items that may threaten the dimensionality of the scale; these items may be trimmed (Floyd & Widaman, 1995; Hair et al., 1998). Many times, the scale items selected and the corresponding number of factors specified will be the result of extensive EFA and item analyses that have led the scale developer to a set of items (and/or factors) that can be confirmed successfully (i.e., Step 3 of the scale development process). That is, EFA should be used prior to CFA, as EFA can reveal items that load poorly in terms of magnitude on an intended factor or load highly on more than one factor. Although CFA also can be used to examine competing factor structures, we will focus on three key issues for CFA in scale development. We will also focus on criteria for evaluating CFA and offer an example of evaluation and CFA measurement invariance across samples.

### Three Key Issues to Consider

With CFA, a theoretical factor structure is specified and tested for its degree of correspondence (or "fit") with the observed covariances among the items in the factor(s). Confirming a factor structure depends on many issues. Three of these issues are addressed here. First, the level of interitem correlation and the number of items come into play. (We speak of correlations here, but it is important to note that covariances among items should be used as input to the CFA, particularly in tests of measurement invariance over multiple samples.) Pairs of items that are highly correlated and that share variance beyond that variance that is accounted for by their factor(s) can result in correlated measurement errors in CFA. These instances violate a basic tenet of classical test theory (true-score model) that error terms among items are uncorrelated. When a substantial number of error terms are highly correlated, scale dimensionality is threatened. Threats to dimensionality often reveal themselves in a number of CFA diagnostics, including fit indices, standardized residuals, and modification indices. A high level of correlation among items can result from item wording redundancy. That is, some of the correlation (covariation) between the items may be due to a "common methods" (common wording) factor. Although the high level of intercorrelation results in a high level of internal consistency, highly disproportionate correlations among some items relative to others also can result in correlated measurement errors. Thus, although item intercorrelation is desirable and multiple items that tap the domain of the constructs are needed, adequately "fitting" such items to a CFA structure can be problematic (Floyd & Widaman, 1995). As we have stated consistently, the scale developer must balance the issues of interitem correlation and scale length in scale construction. (For an interesting discussion of, and potential solution to, the issues discussed above, the interested reader is referred to the "parceling" strategies of Bagozzi [1993] and Kishton and Widaman [1994]).

A second issue of interest is sample size, given that some evaluative criteria for CFA are more affected by sample size than others (Bearden et al., 1982; Fan, Thompson, & Wang, 1999). As with EFA, sample size recommendations or "rules of thumb" vary. In general, CFA sample sizes should be large. A minimal CFA requirement is that sample size must be at least greater than the number of covariances (or correlations) in the data matrix. Some researchers suggest a minimum of 10 observations per parameter estimated (Jöreskog & Sörbom, 1989), although guidelines as low as 5 to 10 observations per parameter estimated also have been suggested (Floyd & Widaman, 1995). Still others suggest that MLE-based estimation of CFA should be at a sample size of 200 or more (Hair et al., 1998). (For a more detailed discussion of the factors that should be considered in determining an appropriate sample size for a CFA, see Raykov and Widaman [1995]). It should also be noted that some suggest that a "more is better" strategy may not always be appropriate because very large samples may show trivial differences between the observed and implied covariance matrices (or parameter estimates) to be significant.

The third issue is related to the first two and involves CFA not only as a tool to confirm a structure but also as a tool to further trim items from a scale. Although we strongly advocate the use of EFA and item analyses to trim/retain items for the final form of a scale, these techniques will tell us little about one potential threat to dimensionality, namely, the presence of correlated measurement errors among items. That is, EFA and item-based statistics can inform the scale developer as to the magnitude of an item loading, as well as the potential cross-loading of an item to another factor (i.e., the item loads highly on a factor other than its intended factor). EFA and item statistics, however, do not always reveal potential correlated errors among items. Given that correlated errors are a violation of the true-score model, they may threaten the dimensionality of a scale. CFA can be very useful in detecting correlated measurement error. Thus, CFA can be used as a means of scale reduction to finalize a scale and then confirm the scale's final form (Floyd & Widaman, 1995). Later in this chapter, we offer examples of articles that used CFA not only to confirm a scale structure but also to trim items from the scale.

### Evaluating CFA Models

Several criteria can be used to evaluate CFA models. We focus on five:

1. model convergence and an "acceptable range" of parameter estimates,

2. fit indices,

3. significance of parameter estimates and related diagnostics,

4. standardized residuals and modification indices, and

5. measurement invariance across multiple samples.

*Model Convergence and an*
*"Acceptable Range" of Parameter Estimates*

CFA is most often conducted with structural equation modeling (SEM) packages that use maximum likelihood estimation (MLE). MLE involves an iterative process in which the observed covariance matrix (among the items) is compared with an implied or theoretical matrix to minimize the differences (or residuals) between the observed and implied matrices. The SEM package iterates until these differences are minimized. When the differences can no longer be reduced further, convergence occurs. Thus, an initial step in model evaluation is to determine if the CFA solution converges. SEM packages generally issue a warning if the solution has not converged. Still, a converged solution may contain out-of-range parameter estimates ("offending estimates"). Offending estimates typically are negative error variances of items (called Heywood cases) and/or completely standardized parameter estimates (item loadings, correlations among factors) greater than 1. Nonconvergence and out-of-range estimates may result from a common problem (e.g., ill-conditioned data, a strong linear combination among items, model size/complexity). When nonconvergence and/or out-of-range estimates occur, some respecification of the model is likely needed (cf. Anderson & Gerbing, 1988; Hair et al., 1998). In our view, EFA and item analyses prior to CFA to determine which items are candidates for deletion are called for to avoid nonconvergence and/or out-of-range estimate problems.

*Fit Indices*

If the solution converges without any offending estimates, model fit is assessed. Numerous indices assess the "goodness of fit" of the CFA to the data. Most of these indices assess the degree to which the observed covariances in the data equate to the covariances implied by the data. The most common fit index is the "chi-square" ($\chi^2$) index. Because some studies have showed that $\chi^2$ is susceptible to numerous sampling fluctuations (including sample size), a number of other indices have been advanced to assess model fit (cf. Hair et al., 1998; Hoyle, 1995). These have been classified as *stand-alone or absolute, comparative or incremental,* and *parsimony-based* fit indices.

Stand-alone or absolute indices assess overall model fit without any adjustment for overfitting. These include (but are not limited to) the goodness-of-fit (GFI) and adjusted goodness-of-fit (AGFI) indices (Jöreskog & Sörbom, 1989) that theoretically range from 0 to 1, where values closer to 1 are indicative of better fit. A number of simulation studies have examined the properties of fit indices and their sensitivity to sample size, number of indicators in the model (e.g., model complexity), size of factor loadings, and model misspecification. The results suggest that GFI and AGFI may not be the most optimal measures of fit and therefore should not be solely relied upon when assessing fit. (See Hoyle [1995] for several chapters that discuss this issue.) In fact, Hu and Bentler (1999) have advocated against the use of GFI and AGFI in evaluating model fit. A stand-alone or absolute measure of fit that has received a wider level of acceptance in recent years is the root-mean-square-error-of-approximation (RMSEA). (Although RMSEA does include an adjustment for parsimony, it is still commonly classified as a stand-alone index.) Originally formulated by Steiger and Lind (1980),

RMSEA attempts to correct for the tendency of the chi-square statistic to reject (as unacceptable) a model estimated with a sufficiently large sample size. RMSEA values of .08 and less have been advocated as indicative of acceptable fit, and values over .10 have been viewed as unacceptable (Browne & Cudeck, 1993). More recently, a value of .06 or less has been proposed as desirable (Hu & Bentler, 1999).

Incremental (or comparative) measures of fit compare the proposed model (CFA structure) to another model specified by the researcher, typically referred to as the baseline model. Most often, this other model represents a "null" model of no relationships whatsoever in the data—the covariances among the items are assumed to be zero. Often-used incremental indices of fit based on the null model are the comparative fit index (CFI; Bentler, 1990) and the non-normed fit index (NNFI). Although the NNFI can exceed a value of 1, acceptable levels of fit for CFI and NNFI are values close to 1, notably .90 and above. More recently, a value of .95 or greater has been proposed for these indices (Hu & Bentler, 1999).

Parsimony-based indices adjust fit to compare models with differing numbers of estimated parameters, to determine the improvement in fit of one model over another (i.e., fit per coefficient). As such, these indices are particularly useful for comparing models. Although not often used in assessing confirmatory factor models (i.e., measurement models), parsimony indices of interest include (but are not limited to) the Akaike information criteria (AIC) and the parsimonious fit index (PFI). Although definitive rules of thumb are rarely offered for AIC and PFI, values close to 0 are preferred for AIC, and given that PFI can range from 0 to 1, higher values are preferred for PFI (Schumacker & Lomax, 1996).

### *Significance of Parameter Estimates and Related Diagnostics*

If the CFA model fits well, the parameter estimates are used to further evaluate the model. In scale development, individual item loadings should be assessed for both statistical significance and magnitude. Clearly, items that do not load significantly on their intended factors should be deleted. The statistical significance of an item's loading and its magnitude have been referred to as the *convergent validity* of the item to the construct (Anderson & Gerbing, 1988; Fornell & Larcker, 1981). In CFA, a statistically significant loading at the .01 level will have a $t/z$ value greater than 2.57. A rather rigorous rule of thumb for completely standardized item-to-factor loading magnitude is an average of .70 (Hair et al., 1998). It also should be noted that it may not be desirable to have several loadings at very high levels. As previously noted, such loadings may be indicative of item wording redundancy and/or result in correlated measurement error that lower fit values, lead to high modification indices/standardized residuals, and threaten dimensionality. Thus, a range of loadings between .60 and .90 seems reasonable (Bagozzi & Yi, 1988).

Several related diagnostics can be used in model evaluation. The first is composite (or construct) reliability. Analogous to coefficient alpha, composite reliability is a measure of the internal consistency of items in a scale. Although thresholds for a composite reliability have been advocated (e.g., .70 by Hair et al [1998] and .60 by Bagozzi and Yi [1988]), the number of items in the scale must be considered. Again, longer scales, *ceteris paribus,* generally will result in higher internal consistency estimates than shorter scales. Consistent with more recent writings (Clark & Watson, 1995; Netemeyer et al., 2002), even with narrowly defined constructs with five to eight items, a composite reliability level of .80 does not seem unreasonable. The composite reliability of a construct is calculated as follows (Fornell & Larcker, 1981; Hair et al., 1998):

where $\lambda_i$ = the completely standardized loading for the $i$th indicator,

$V(\delta_i)$ = variance of the error term for the $i$th indicator, and

$p$ = the number of indicators.

$$\frac{\left(\sum_{i=1}^{p} \lambda_i\right)^2}{\left(\sum_{i=1}^{p} \lambda_i\right)^2 + \sum_{i}^{p} V(\delta)}$$

Another internal consistency–based diagnostic is the average variance extracted estimate (AVE). It assesses the amount of variance captured by a set of items in a scale relative to measurement error. A rigorous level of .50 or above has been advocated for AVE (Fornell & Larcker, 1981). Given the calculation of AVE below, this corresponds to an average completely standardized item loading of about .70. For newly developed scales, values near the .50 threshold (> .45) seem reasonable. A short-form calculation (i.e., the average squared loading) of the AVE of a construct's measure can be performed as follows:

$$\frac{\sum_{i=1}^{p} \lambda_i^2}{p}$$

A third diagnostic involves the disattenuated (corrected for measurement error) correlations among constructs (factors) to assess discriminant validity among scales (measures). As stated previously, some scales may be multidimensional, and the scale developer may want to demonstrate discriminant validity among the dimensions. The scale developer also may want to provide evidence that a new scale for a construct is distinct from a different, yet related, construct's measure. Rules of thumb for assessing discriminant validity are as follow:

1. If the confidence interval (+ 2 standard errors) around the disattenuated correlation does not contain a value of 1, evidence of discriminant validity exists (Anderson & Gerbing, 1988).

2. If the parameter estimate (disattenuated correlation) for two factors (measurement scales) is constrained to 1 (constrained model) and compared with a factor model where this parameter is freely estimated (unconstrained model), evidence of discriminant validity exists if the chi-square value of the unconstrained model is significantly lower than the chi-square value of the constrained model (Anderson & Gerbing, 1988).

3. Discriminant validity for two factors (measurement scales) is established if the average variance extracted for the two factors is greater than the square of the correlation between the two factors (Fornell & Larcker, 1981).

### Standardized Residuals and Modification Indices

Other evaluative criteria include standardized residuals (SRs) and modification indices (MIs). Simply stated, SRs represent differences between the implied (theoretical) covariance matrix and the observed covariance matrix that are statistically significant and reflect a potential source of "misfit." SRs greater than + 2.57 generally are considered statistically significant (Hair et al., 1998). Modification indices assess the statistical significance of an unspecified model relationship and represent the approximate reduction in $\chi^2$ that would be obtained by estimating the unspecified parameter of interest. MIs greater than 3.84 are considered statistically significant ($p < .05$), and thus freeing a parameter with an MI of 3.84 or greater would significantly improve model fit.

Both SRs and MIs can be useful for assessing items that have correlated measurement errors or load strongly on a factor other than their intended factor. As such, SRs and MIs can be useful to assess threats to unidimensionality. Although we are aware of no definitive guideline as to what constitutes a high MI for a correlated measurement error, it seems reasonable to suggest that the correlated error term in question be significant and high across multiple samples to consider it as a threat to unidimensionality. We are also unaware of definitive guidelines regarding what constitutes a high loading on a construct other than the intended construct (i.e., a "cross-loading"). In our view, two recommendations seem reasonable: (a) to threaten dimensionality, the potential cross-loading of interest should be apparent across multiple samples; and (b) the cross-loading should be as strong (or stronger) as the loading of the item to its intended construct. Thus, if across several data sets some items show high SR and high MI values that consistently indicate threats to dimensionality, such items may be considered candidates for deletion. It should be noted that there are caveats associated with "freeing" parameters associated with significant MIs with regard to correlated measurement errors. For a more full discussion of correlated measurement errors, the problems they cause, and potential solutions, see Gerbing and Anderson (1984, 1988) and MacCallum, Roznowski, and Necowitz (1992).

### Measurement Invariance Across Samples

A fifth criterion for evaluating scales via CFA involves measurement invariance testing. Increasingly, scale developers are using CFA to test the invariance of their measures across samples. When parallel data exist across samples, multigroup CFA offers a powerful test of the invariance of factor loadings, factor variances and covariances (correlations), and error terms for individual scale items. If evidence for invariance exists, the generalizability of the scale is enhanced (Bollen, 1989; Marsh, 1995; Steenkamp & Baumgartner, 1998).

In general, models of measurement invariance are tested hierarchically, where the hierarchy begins with the least restrictive model—the same pattern of fixed and nonfixed parameters across groups. If this model shows reasonable fit, shows that all loadings to their respective factors are significant, and shows evidence of discriminant validity among the factors, this model is then used as a "baseline" for comparison with subsequent models in the hierarchy. The second model tested in the hierarchy is a model specifying invariant factor loadings across samples. If this second model does not differ statistically from the baseline model, the factor loadings are invariant across samples. The third model in the hierarchy specifies that the factor loadings and the factor covariances are invariant across samples. If the fit of this third model does not differ from that of the baseline model, then the factor loadings and factor covariances are considered equal. Establishing invariance for the second and third models is generally considered the most important criterion in measurement invariance testing across samples (Bollen, 1989). The fourth model in the hierarchy specifies that the factor loadings, the covariances among factors, and factor variances are invariant across samples. If the fit of this fourth model does not differ from that of the baseline model, then factor loadings, factor variances, and covariances are considered equal. The last model in the hierarchy specifies that the factor loadings, the covariances among factors, factor variances, and error terms for individual item loadings are invariant across samples (i.e., a full measurement invariance model). If the fit of this last model does not differ from that of the baseline model, then all measurement parameters are statistically invariant across samples.

Before presenting an application of the above hierarchy, the following should be noted. First, though desirable, the statistical significance invariance of factor loadings across multiple samples is rare in practical applications (Marsh, 1995; Steenkamp & Baumgartner, 1998). Such a finding is more likely as the number of samples and the number of items in the scale(s) becomes larger. As such, "partial measurement invariance" has been advocated as acceptable for measurement invariance models (Byrne, Shavelson, & Muthen, 1989; Steenkamp & Baumgartner, 1998). Partial measurement invariance requires that some of, but not all, the factor loadings be invariant before examining the relationships among constructs in a nomological model (i.e., validity). Thus, partial invariance models represent another class of models in the invariance hierarchy. Second, and as previously noted, the issue of sample size must be considered. It is important to note that statistical tests of invariance have the same limitations as statistical tests for other confirmatory models. That is, "invariance constraints are *a priori* false when applied to real data with a sufficiently large sample size" (Marsh, 1995, p. 12). Given this, fit indices also should be used to judge the invariance of parameter estimates across samples. If the fit indices are adequate and do not change appreciably from one model to the next in the hierarchy, reasonable evidence of parameter equivalence exists.

## CFA Examples From the Literature

Several examples from the literature highlight the use of CFA for deleting potentially problematic items and confirming a scale's structure. As previously noted, Shimp and Sharma (1987) used EFA to trim the number of CETSCALE items from 100 to 25. Based on several of the criteria noted above (CFA loadings greater than .70 and problematic correlated measurement errors), they further finalized their scale to 17 items via CFA. After trimming their pool of items from 97 to 39 via EFA (and item-based statistics), Bearden et al. (2001) trimmed another eight items via CFA. Using MIs that indicated high cross-loadings and/or correlated measurement errors, 31 items were retained to represent the 6-factor scale. Then, CFA was again used to further confirm their 31-item, 6-factor measure of consumer self-confidence. Their confirmed structure showed reasonable fit for the CFI (.90) and NNFI (.89). Lastovicka et al. (1999) first used EFA to trim their consumer frugality scale (from 60 to 25 items), then used CFA to further refine the scale down to an 8-item, 1-factor measure. They also used MIs to delete items that threatened dimensionality. Their final scale showed fit indices in the very high range (CFI = .98, NNFI = .97, and RMSEA < .08).

Netemeyer et al. (1996) used CFA to trim and then confirm their measures of WFC and FWC. They reported an iterative CFA procedure to retain 5 WFC items (from a pool of 22) and 5 FWC items (from a pool of 21) via several CFA criteria involving MIs over three samples. Specifically, in the first iteration, items were deleted that (a) showed consistent high cross-loadings on an unintended factor (e.g., a WFC item loading highly on the FWC factor), (b) showed consistent correlated measurement errors or a large number of standardized residuals greater than 2.57 in absolute value, (c) consistently showed completely standardized loadings less than .50, (d) were redundant in terms of wording with other items, or (e) consistently showed extremely high factor loadings (greater than .90). In subsequent iterations, more rigorous criteria for item retention were employed, until the 5-item WFC and FWC scales were derived. They then confirmed the 2-factor WFC-FWC structure with fit indices above .90 for NNFI and CFI.

### An Empirical Example of Evaluating a CFA Model

To demonstrate the use of the above evaluative criteria, we use data from the small business owners and real estate salespeople samples of Netemeyer et al. (1996). As stated above, the final versions of their WFC and FWC scales represented two distinct 5-item factors. Thus, over both samples, the hypothesized 2-factor WFC-FWC structure was estimated separately via LISREL8. Appendix 7A shows the LISREL input file and portions of the output file printouts for these models.

As per the first criterion (model convergence and "acceptable range" of parameter estimates), no convergence warnings were noted. Furthermore, and as shown on the printouts under **COMPLETELY STANDARDIZED SOLUTION LAMBDA-X,** all estimates were in acceptable ranges across the two samples (i.e., no negative error variances or loadings/correlations among factors greater than 1). As per the second criterion (i.e., fit indices), these two samples showed good fit, as RMSEA was $\leq .10$ and CFI and NNFI were $\geq .90$ for both samples, as indicated in the **GOODNESS OF FIT STATISTICS** section of the printouts. As per the third criterion (i.e., significance of parameter estimates and related diagnostics), acceptable levels were found. First, and as shown in the **LISREL ESTIMATES (MAXIMUM LIKELIHOOD)** section of the printouts, the $t$ values across measurement items ranged from 7.19 to 14 .96 ($p < .01$). As shown in the **COMPLETELY STANDARDIZED SOLUTION LAMBDA-X** section of the printouts, the magnitude of loadings ranged from .58 to .89 across samples. Second, composite reliability for the WFC and FWC scales ranged from .83 to .89, and the AVE estimates ranged from .48 to .64. The estimates needed to calculate composite reliability and AVE are found in the **COMPLETELY STANDARDIZED SOLUTION LAMBDA-X** and the **COMPLETELY STANDARDIZED SOLUTION**

**THETA-DELTA** sections of the printouts. For WFC, from the small business owners sample, composite reliability and AVE are as follows:

$$\text{Composite Reliability} = \frac{\left(\sum_{i=1}^{p} \lambda_i\right)^2}{\left(\sum_{i=1}^{p} \lambda_i\right)^2 + \sum_{i}^{p} V(\delta)}$$

$$= \frac{(.87 + .77 + .70 + .79 + .80+)^2}{(.87 + .77 + .70 + .79 + .80+)^2 + (.24 + .40 + .51 + .37 + .36)} = .89.$$

$$\text{AVE} = \frac{\sum_{i=1}^{p} \lambda_i^2}{p}$$

$$= \frac{.87^2 + .77^2 + .70^2 + .79^2 + .80^2}{5} = .62.$$

Next, the WFC and FWC scales showed evidence of discriminant validity for the three recommended rules of thumb. First, he disattenuated correlations ("phi") between the two scales were .33 and .42 in the small business owners and real estate salespeople samples, respectively. These phi estimates can be found in the **LISREL ESTIMATES (MAXIMUM LIKELIHOOD)** section of the printouts. The confidence interval around phi (±2 standard errors) did not contain a value of 1. Second, when phi for the two factors was constrained to 1 (constrained model) and compared with the hypothesized model where phi was freely estimated (unconstrained model), the unconstrained model showed a significantly lower $\chi^2$ than the constrained model. Third, the AVE for WFC (.60 and .59 in the small business owners and real estate salespeople samples) was greater than the square of the WFC-FWC parameter estimate (phi = .33, phi$^2$ = .10 in the small business owners sample; phi = .42, phi$^2$ = .17 in the real estate salespeople sample), and the AVE for FWC (.48 and .64 in the small business owners and real estate salespeople samples) was greater than the square of the WFC-FWC parameter estimate (phi = .33, phi$^2$ = .10 in the small business owners sample; phi = .42, phi$^2$ = .17 in the real estate salespeople sample).

Estimates relevant to the fourth criterion pertain to SRs and MIs. The SR estimates can be found in the **LARGEST NEGATIVE STANDARDIZED RESIDUALS** and **LARGEST POSITIVE STANDARDIZED RESIDU-ALS** sections of the printouts. The MI estimates associated with correlated measurement error can be found in the **MODIFICATION INDICES FOR THETA-DELTA** section of the printouts. Although several SRs were significant (greater than 2.57 in absolute value) and several MIs for correlated measurement errors were greater than 3.84, none was considered to be a consistent substantial threat to unidimensionality. As for MIs for loading highly on a factor other than the intended factor—the **MODIFCATION INDICES FOR LAMBDA-X** section of the printouts—none was significant for the small business owners sample (greater than 3.84) and two were significant for the real estate salespeople sample: WFC5 and WFCT4 loaded on the FWC factor. Still, the completely standardized loadings for these items to their intended factors were .79 (WFC5) and .66 (WFCT4), whereas their expected loadings on the FWC factor were only −.12 (WFC5) and .19 (WFCT4). (See the **COMPLETELY STANDARDIZED EXPECTED CHANGE FOR LAMBDA-X** section of the printouts.)

Overall, then, the finalized WFC and FWC scales met the first four evaluative criteria for CFA in scale development. Given this evidence, the measurement invariance hierarchy can be tested: the fifth evaluative criterion. Appendix 7B shows the LISREL8 input for an invariance hierarchy. (Note that the model specified toward the bottom of the second sample in Appendix 7B represents a full measurement invariance model.) To specify each model in the hierarchy, the procedure is as follows. First, the baseline mode is specified by placing LX=PS on the MO line of the second sample. Second, the factor loadings invariant model is specified by placing LX=IN on the MO line of the second sample. Third, the factor loadings and factor covariances invariant model is specified by placing LX=IN on the MO line of the second sample plus a separate line stating EQ PH (1,2,1) PH (2,1) in the second sample. Fourth, the factor loadings, factor covariances, and factor variances invariant model is specified by LX=IN PH=IN on the MO line of the second sample. Finally, the factor loadings, factor covariances and variances, and individual item error terms invariant model is specified by LX=IN PH=IN TD=IN on the MO line of the second sample (i.e., the full measurement invariance model as shown in Appendix 7B).

Table 7.1 presents the estimates for the models in the invariance hierarchy. The baseline model was supported, as adequate levels of fit for the CFI, NNFI, and RMSEA were found; all loadings of items to their respective factors were significant across cultures ($p < .01$); and discriminant validity between the two factors was supported. (Note that the $\chi^2$ and degrees of freedom ($df$) for the baseline model are the sum of the two chi-square and $df$ values from samples one and two separately.) Next, the model constraining the factor loadings to be invariant across groups was estimated. The difference between this model and the baseline model was not significant ($\chi^2_{\text{diff}} = 7.68$, $df_{\text{diff}} = 8$, $p > .05$), and the fit indices (RMSEA, CFI, and NNFI) were at adequate levels. The model constraining the factor loadings and factor covariances to be invariant across groups was estimated next. The difference between this model and the baseline model was not significant ($\chi^2_{\text{diff}} = 9.08$, $df_{\text{diff}} = 9$, $p > .05$), and the fit indices were adequate. Next, the model constraining the factor loadings, factor covariances, and variances to be invariant across groups was estimated. The difference between this model and the baseline model was significant ($\chi^2_{\text{diff}} = 26.34$, $df_{\text{diff}} = 11$, $p < .05$), but the fit indices were still at adequate levels. Last, the model constraining the factor loadings, factor covariances, factor variances, and item loading error terms to be invariant across groups was estimated. The difference between this model and the baseline model was significant ($\chi^2_{\text{diff}} = 40.72$, $df_{\text{diff}} = 21$, $p < .05$), but the fit was adequate. In sum, evidence for the statistical invariance of factor loadings and factor covariances was found, and the other two models showed reasonable levels of fit across the RMSEA, CFI, and NNFI, suggesting a "practical" level of invariance of factor variances and item error term loadings.

## ADDITIONAL EVALUATIONS OF VALIDITY

Researchers often provide corroborating evidence of validity from measures assessed in new and/or additional studies or from the inclusion of "other" measures included as part of studies used in the developmental aspects of scale development. As an example regarding the latter, Bearden et al. (2001) included a major section of their results description in their article describing the development of measures for assessing the various dimensions of consumer self-confidence entitled "Additional Evidence From Studies 1 and 2." That is, Studies 1 and 2 were conducted primarily as part of the scale development process (e.g., item validation, CFA); however, a number of measures of other

**Table 7.1**     Multiple Group Invariance Models

| Model | $\chi^2$ | df | $\chi^2_{diff}$ | RMSEA | CFI | IFI | NNFI |
|-------|----------|-----|-----------------|-------|-----|-----|------|
| Baseline | 154.94 | 68 | — | .06 | .95 | .95 | .93 |
| Factor loadings invariant | 162.58 | 76 | 7.68 | .06 | .95 | .95 | .94 |
| Factor loadings and factor covariances invariant | 163.98 | 77 | 9.08 | .06 | .95 | .95 | .94 |
| Factor loadings, factor covariances, and factor variances invariant | 181.24 | 79 | 26.34 | .06 | .95 | .94 | .93 |
| Factor loadings, factor variances, and variance of error terms invariant | 195.62 | 89 | 40.72 | .06 | .94 | .93 | .92 |

validating constructs (e.g., Rosenberg's [1965] 10-item self-esteem scale, subjective product knowledge) were also included in the surveys used in the two studies for subsequent use in demonstrating the relative predictive validity, as well as discriminant validity, of the self-confidence measures being developed.

In a similar vein, a number of example procedures and suggestions beyond those included in Chapter 4 for providing additional evidence of convergent, discriminant, predictive, and concurrent validity are described in the following two sections of this chapter. That is, we now present a series of examples described by our marketing and consumer research colleagues. These examples were selected to be representative of the many approaches available from the articles that we have used as the basis for this text.

## Convergent and Discriminant Validity

Earlier, methods described in Chapters 4 and 6 for demonstrating convergent validity included the MTMM approach of Campbell and Fiske (1959), the overall definitional procedure of Bagozzi (1993), the use of spousal dyad data (e.g., Bearden et al., 2001), and the open-ended question approach of Shimp and Sharma (1987). Other interesting and insightful examples taken from the extant scale development literature include the following. First, Richins (1983) used assertiveness and aggressiveness scales borrowed from psychology as measures for assessing convergent validity of her own consumer interaction style variables. Bearden, Netemeyer, and Teel (1989) used student judges to evaluate close friends in terms of their susceptibility to interpersonal influences. Correlations between the friends' responses with those of the judges' evaluations of their friends were offered as evidence of convergent validity.

As evidence of discriminant validity, Lastovicka et al. (1999) demonstrated that their measure of frugality was not redundant with a simple non-materialistic tendency using the Richins and Dawson (1992) scale. Tian et al. (2001, p. 58) provided evidence of the discriminant validity of their measure of consumers' need for uniqueness via a moderate correlation between the CNFU scale and a measure of optimum stimulation level (Steenkamp & Baumgartner, 1992).

## Predictive and Concurrent Validity

From Chapter 4, tests of predictive validity imply some external criterion separated in time and context from the antecedent measure being developed. Richins (1983, pp. 78-79) described a novel application study that provides evidence of predictive validity. In efforts to validate her measures of consumer assertiveness and aggressiveness, respondents to an earlier survey were called under the guise of a telephone solicitation attempt. As predicted, subjects scoring above the median on both aggression and assertion took the shortest time to "get off the phone" (i.e., an indicator of resisting compliance). The reverse pattern held for those scoring low in the two focal constructs.

Bearden and Rose (1990, pp. 467-478) also demonstrated a unique approach in their validation of the Attention-to-Social-Comparison scale (ATSCI) of Lennox and Wolfe (1984) as a measure of consumer sensitivity to interpersonal information. The ATSCI measure was collected at time period 1 using different researchers and a research guise. During a second phase, student subjects were exposed to a situation that heightened perceptions of normative pressure. As predicted, subjects scoring high in ATSCI were more likely to provide conforming choices to an evaluation task that required public display of their choices. In another example, Obermiller and Spangenberg (1998) reported negative correlations between their advertising skepticism measures and three variables reflecting responses to advertising. In this case, the ad response variables were collected 4 weeks after the initial administration of the ad skepticism measure.

Evidence of concurrent validity typically is offered by correlations between the focal construct measures being developed and other measures collected during a single administration. Again, scale developers often anticipate these tests and collect responses to "additional measures" to be used later as data are collected for initial scale development, including item analyses and CFA. Zaichkowsky (1985, pp. 346-347) demonstrated the validity of her involvement measure by demonstrating that subject responses to a series of items differed as expected across low- and high-involvement subgroups. In this study, her 20-item measure was collected simultaneously with items predicted to vary with involvement differences. Bearden et al. (2001) reported negative correlations between their consumer self-confidence measures and susceptibility to interpersonal influence. These findings were consistent with the prediction that individuals high in consumer self-confidence should be less affected by persuasion from others. Lastovicka et al. (1999, p. 92) offered evidence of the concurrent validity of their frugality measure through correlations of their 8-item scale and a series of usage measures (e.g., reusing foil, eating leftovers) combined into a single behavioral index. Finally, Richins and Dawson (1992) tested a series of four propositions concerning materialism based on data from multiple consumer surveys. Like many concurrent validity tests, these results also offered strong support for nomological validity.

## ESTABLISHING NORMS

### Means and Standard Deviations

The interval nature of most marketing and organizational behavior measures makes the evaluation of mean scores problematic, particularly for new measures. As such, it is important that absolute scale values be interpreted cautiously and that means and standard deviations across studies and samples be recorded in efforts to assist in interpreting subsequent results from scale applications over time and by new researchers. In addition, researchers on occasion describe estimates of scale skewness and kurtosis. Churchill (1979, p. 72) appropriately reminded researchers that norm quality is a function of both the number of cases on which the norms are based and the representativeness of the samples for which means and standard deviations are noted. Relatedly, and as explained in the next section, known-group comparisons also provide useful norm information for evaluating scale results and enhance subsequent comparisons between samples.

Researchers vary in the extent to which they present scale means as a summed score for all items in a scale or as the average of the items composing the scale. McDonald (1999) recommended reporting average item scores. Although these differences will affect the absolute range of scores, as well as the absolute values for means and standard deviations, correlations with other constructs will not be affected. Moreover, and in either case, the items are equally weighted. In the selection of items to retain in the development of the "need to evaluate" scale, Jarvis and Petty (1996) deleted items in their developmental efforts that had mean scores below 2.0 and above 4.0 on their 5-point response format scales. Although not strictly final scale norms, these procedures ensure that items vary across respondents and lead to mid-range final scale norms. In instances where item and scale scores are expected to elicit extreme values (e.g., many customer satisfaction assessments), mean values closer to scale endpoints might be the norm.

The provision of meaningful scale norms is based on the researcher's ability to administer the scales being developed to representative groups. A review of the extant scale development literature in marketing offers a number of examples. Three scale norm descriptions from this literature are as follows. In the development of their measure of consumer skepticism toward advertising, Obermiller and Spangenberg (1998) reported an average score across five diverse samples of 28.8 for their 9-item scale, operationalized using a 5-point *disagree-agree* response format (i.e., a potential range of 9 to 45). Lastovicka et al. (1999) reported a mean score of 40.43 for their general population sample and 8-item measure of frugality, with each item assessed using 6-point Likert-type agreement response scales. Tian et al. (2001) reported an average item score of 2.60 (range of 1.06 to 4.55) across their 31 5-point statements designed to assess consumers' need for uniqueness based on the responses from their consumer mail survey.

**Known-Group Differences**

As explained in Chapter 4, in efforts to demonstrate the validity of their measures, researchers often report differences in scale mean scores across groups for which the measure being developed and/or validated is expected to differ in a predicted direction. (Again, efforts to demonstrate known-group validity also provide additional evidence regarding scale norms to the extent that summary scale statistics are reported and particularly when unique groups are compared with representative samples.) Earlier, in Chapter 4, known-group differences reported by Tian et al. (2001) for the Consumers' Need for Uniqueness scale and by Saxe and Weitz (1982) for the salesforce consumer orientation scale were offered as example mean comparisons involving known-group differences. Two other examples from the published scale development literature demonstrate further the usefulness of conducting additional studies in demonstrations of known group validity. First, Bearden et al. (2001) described significant differences in terms of consumer self-confidence between samples of the general population and members of the American Council on Consumer Interests (ACCI), a professional organization that focuses on the well-being of consumers. As predicted, the mean scores in consumer self-confidence were significantly higher for the ACCI member sample than for the general population sample. Zaichkowsky (1985) reported significantly higher means across two groups in terms of purchase involvement (i.e., her Personal Involvement Inventory) involving the selection of wine for everyday consumption (mean = 78 for the predicted low group) versus the selection of wine for a special dinner party (mean = 106 for the predicted high group).

## APPLYING GENERALIZABILITY THEORY

As discussed in Chapter 3, generalizability theory (G-Theory) can be used to determine the extent to which the scale, and therefore scale items, can be generalized across various factors. In the following section, we illustrate the use of G-Theory to assess the generalizability of the WFC and FWC scales across multiple groups using two data sets of Netemeyer et al. (1996).

Earlier in the chapter, it was demonstrated that the WFC and FWC scales had measurement equivalency across groups; that is, the loadings, error

**Table 7.2**    Estimates of Variance Components

| | WFC Scale | | FWC Scale | |
|---|---|---|---|---|
| Source | Variance Estimate | Percentage | Variance Estimate | Percentage |
| Items | 0.231 | 6.62 | 0.016 | 0.69 |
| Group | 0.000[a] | 0.00 | 0.026 | 1.13 |
| Subjects:Group | 2.000 | 57.27 | 1.281 | 55.45 |
| Group × Items | 0.002 | 0.06 | 0.002 | 0.09 |
| Subjects:Group × Items | 1.259 | 36.05 | 0.985 | 42.64 |
| Total | 3.492 | | 2.310 | |

SOURCE: These results are from data in Netemeyer et al. (1996).
a. Negative estimates are assumed to be equal to zero.

variances, factor variances, and factor covariances were equal across the two groups. We now illustrate that similar conclusions can be reached using generalizability theory. In addition, use of generalizability theory gives an estimate of the degree to which scale items differ across groups. For the Netemeyer et al. (1996) data, *group* is the differentiation factor, and *scale items* and *subjects* are the generalization factors. Group is chosen as the differentiation factor because we would like to determine the extent to which the groups are different with respect to WFC and FWC. *Scale items* and *subjects* are generalization factors because one would like to generalize the findings across *scale items* and *subjects*. That is, we are interested in determining the extent to which the subjects and/or the scale items are different across the groups. In estimating variance that is due to the different sources, it is desirable to have a balanced design—that is, equal cell sizes. An unbalanced design (i.e., unequal cell sizes) complicates the estimation of variance. In cases in which the cell sizes are not equal, Finn and Kayande (1997) suggested randomly dropping subjects in the cells. The following procedure was used to obtain equal cell sizes: (a) values for missing data were replaced by mean values, and (b) observations from the larger group were randomly chosen to be equal to the number of observations in the smaller group. Table 7.2 gives the variance estimates obtained using the PROC VARCOMP procedure in SAS.

From the table, it can be seen that for the WFC scale, almost 57% of the variance is due to variation in subjects' response across groups. This is to be expected, as one would expect subjects to differ in their responses across groups. The variance estimate of interest, however, is due to the Group × Items interaction, which is only 0.06%. High variance due to this effect would suggest that the pattern of responses to items differs across groups, and low variance would suggest similarity of the pattern of responses across groups, which is the desired outcome. That is, the scale items can be generalized across groups. Similar conclusions can be reached for the FWC scale. The variance decomposition analysis leads us to conclude that the WFC and FWC scales can be generalized across groups, reinforcing the conclusion reached earlier using multigroup analysis. But what if multigroup analysis suggests only partial or no equivalency? In such cases, generalizability analysis provides further insights into the degree to which the scale cannot be generalized across groups. The following section presents the results of the CETSCALE administered in multiple countries. (For a detailed discussion, see Sharma and Weathers [2002].)

The data for this empirical illustration are taken from Netemeyer et al. (1991). The 17-item CETSCALE was administered to samples of 71 subjects in the United States, 70 subjects in France, 76 subjects in Japan, and 73 subjects in Germany. In the present case, because 70 was the minimum number of subjects from any given country (France), 70 subjects were randomly selected from the United States, Japan, and Germany. Tables 7.3a and 7.3b summarize the confirmatory factor analysis results. As can be seen from the $\chi^2$ difference tests in the tables, only partial equivalence is achieved.

To assess the degree to which the scale items vary across countries, generalizability theory was employed to estimate the variance component analysis using the PROC VARCOMP procedure in SAS. Table 7.4 summarizes these results. As can be seen from the table, the Country factor accounts for only 7% of the total variation. Of greater interest is the Items × Countries interaction. For the data analyzed, the variance due to the Items × Countries interaction accounts for the lowest percentage of total variation (5.51%), suggesting that there is consistency in response patterns to items across countries. That is, the items measuring the construct do *not* appear to be country-specific, suggesting that violation of complete equivalency is not severe and that the scale can be generalized across countries.

**Table 7.3a** Results of Measurement Equivalency Using Confirmatory Factor Analysis: Unconstrained and Constrained Models

| Model | Chi-Square | df |
|---|---|---|
| 1. Unconstrained | 1089.42 | 476 |
| 2. Equal loadings ($\Lambda^1 = \Lambda^2 = \cdots = \Lambda^j$) | 1152.82 | 524 |
| 3. Equal construct variances ($\phi^1 = \phi^2 = \cdots = \phi^j$) | 1091.75 | 479 |
| 4. Equal error variances ($\Theta_\delta^1 = \Theta_\delta^2 = \ldots \Theta_\delta^j$) | 1326.08 | 527 |
| 5. Equal loadings, equal construct variances ($\Lambda^1 = \Lambda^2 = \cdots = \Lambda^j$ and $\phi^1 = \phi^2 = \cdots = \phi^j$) | 1159.62 | 527 |
| 6. Equal loadings, equal error variances ($\Lambda^1 = \Lambda^2 = \cdots = \Lambda^j$ and $\Theta_\delta^1 = \Theta_\delta^2 = \ldots \Theta_\delta^j$) | 1393.90 | 575 |
| 7. Equal loadings, equal construct variances, equal error variances ($\Lambda^1 = \Lambda^2 = \cdots = \Lambda^j$ and $\phi^1 = \phi^2 = \cdots = \phi^j$) and $\Theta_\delta^1 = \Theta_\delta^1 = \cdots = \Theta_\delta^1$) | 1400.35 | 578 |

SOURCE: These results are from data in Netemeyer et al. (1991).

**Table 7.3b** Results of Measurement Equivalency Using Confirmatory Factor Analysis: Chi-Square Difference Tests

| Equivalency Tests | Model Comparison | Difference in $\chi^2$ | Difference in df | p value | Conclusion |
|---|---|---|---|---|---|
| Metric equivalency | (2) − (1) | 63.40 | 48 | .07 | Yes |
| Factor variance equivalency | (3) − (1) | 2.33 | 3 | .51 | Yes |
| Error variance equivalency | (4) − (1) | 236.66 | 51 | .00 | No |
| Metric and factor variance equivalency | (5) − (1) | 70.20 | 51 | .04 | No |
| Metric and error equivalency | (6) − (1) | 304.48 | 99 | .00 | No |
| Metric, factor variance, and error variance equivalency | (7) − (1) | 310.93 | 102 | .00 | No |

SOURCE: These results are from data in Netemeyer et al. (1991).

## SUMMARY

This chapter focused on procedures to finalize the scale and further establish its psychometric properties. We highlighted the following: (a) the role of

**Table 7.4**        Estimates of Variance Components

| Source | Variance | Percentage |
| --- | --- | --- |
| Country | 0.1727 | 7.01 |
| Subjects within country | 0.8608 | 34.92 |
| Items | 0.2286 | 9.27 |
| Items × Country | 0.1357 | 5.51 |
| Subjects within countries × Items, error | 1.0670 | 43.29 |
| Total | 2.4648 | |

SOURCE: These results are from data in Netemeyer et al. (1991).

exploratory factor analysis (EFA) and other additional item analyses as precursors to confirmatory factor analysis (CFA), (b) the use of CFA to help finalize and confirm a theoretical factor structure and test for the invariance of the factor structure over multiple data sets, (c) the need for additional validity testing, (d) the importance of establishing norms, and (e) applying generalizability theory. We view each of these issues as important in scale finalization. Chapter 8 will offer some concluding remarks about this text and scale development in general.

# Appendix 7A

---

## *LISREL Input for Small Business Owners Sample*

```
la
  wfc4 wfc5 wfc6 wfct4 wfcs4
  fwc1 fwc6 fwc8 fwct4 fwcs1   /
  mo nx=10 nk=2 ph=st
  fr lx(1,1) lx(2,1) lx(3,1) lx(4,1) lx(5,1) lx(6,2)
    lx(7,2) lx(8,2) lx(9,2) lx(10,2)
  st .5 all
  path diagram
  OU sc rs mi ss tv it=800 tm=1000
```

---

```
NOTE: The following input (MO) could have also been used:
mo nx=10 nk=2

fr lx(2,1) lx(3,1) lx(4,1) lx(5,1) lx(7,2) lx(8,2)
    lx(9,2) lx(10,2)
va 1.00 lx(1,1) lx(6,2)
```

The above input gives a statistical significance estimate for the factor (scale) variances, but not for the first item in each scale.

## *LISREL Output for Small Business Owners Sample*

**LISREL ESTIMATES (MAXIMUM LIKELIHOOD)**

|        | KSI 1   | KSI 2   |
| ------ | ------- | ------- |
| wfc4   | 1.72    | - -     |
|        | (0.13)  |         |
|        | 13.04   |         |
| wfc5   | 1.55    | - -     |
|        | (0.14)  |         |
|        | 10.87   |         |
| wfc6   | 1.38    | - -     |
|        | (0.15)  |         |
|        | 9.43    |         |
| wfct4  | 1.49    | - -     |
|        | (0.13)  |         |
|        | 11.22   |         |
| wfcs4  | 1.44    | - -     |
|        | (0.13)  |         |
|        | 11.41   |         |
| fwc1   | - -     | 0.96    |
|        |         | (0.12)  |
|        |         | 8.29    |
| fwc6   | - -     | 0.97    |
|        |         | (0.09)  |
|        |         | 10.25   |
| fwc8   | - -     | 1.05    |
|        |         | (0.12)  |
|        |         | 9.10    |
| fwct4  | - -     | 0.98    |
|        |         | (0.10)  |
|        |         | 9.97    |
| fwcs1  | - -     | 0.81    |
|        |         | (0.11)  |
|        |         | 7.19    |

**PHI**

|        | KSI 1   | KSI 2   |
| ------ | ------- | ------- |
| KSI 1  | 1.00    |         |
| KSI 2  | 0.33    | 1.00    |
|        | (0.09)  |         |
|        | 3.91    |         |

**THETA-DELTA**

| wfc4   | wfc5   | wfc6   | wfct4  | wfcs4  | fwc1   |
| ------ | ------ | ------ | ------ | ------ | ------ |
| 0.92   | 1.60   | 2.01   | 1.32   | 1.17   | 1.24   |

|        |        |        |        |        |        |
|--------|--------|--------|--------|--------|--------|
| (0.17) | (0.22) | (0.26) | (0.19) | (0.17) | (0.17) |
| 5.53   | 7.21   | 7.75   | 7.03   | 6.92   | 7.37   |

**THETA-DELTA**

| fwc6   | fwc8   | fwct4  | fwcs1  |
|--------|--------|--------|--------|
| 0.65   | 1.12   | 0.73   | 1.28   |
| (0.11) | (0.16) | (0.11) | (0.16) |
| 6.11   | 6.95   | 6.35   | 7.78   |

NOTE: For each parameter estimate, three numbers are given: (a) the unstandardized parameter estimate, (b) a standard error estimate (in parentheses), and (c) a z/t-value.

**GOODNESS OF FIT STATISTICS**
CHI-SQUARE WITH 34 DEGREES OF
FREEDOM = 85.58 (P = 0.0000025)
ESTIMATED NON-CENTRALITY PARAMETER (NCP) = 51.58
MINIMUM FIT FUNCTION VALUE = 0.57
POPULATION DISCREPANCY FUNCTION VALUE (F0) = 0.34
**ROOT MEAN SQUARE ERROR OF APPROXIMATION (RMSEA) = 0.10**
P-VALUE FOR TEST OF CLOSE FIT (RMSEA < 0.05) = 0.0015
EXPECTED CROSS-VALIDATION INDEX (ECVI) = 0.85
ECVI FOR SATURATED MODEL = 0.73
ECVI FOR INDEPENDENCE MODEL = 5.10
CHI-SQUARE FOR INDEPENDENCE MODEL WITH 45
DEGREES OF FREEDOM = 744.93
INDEPENDENCE AIC = 764.93
MODEL AIC = 127.58
SATURATED AIC = 110.00
INDEPENDENCE CAIC = 805.10
MODEL CAIC = 211.94
SATURATED CAIC = 330.95
ROOT MEAN SQUARE RESIDUAL (RMR) = 0.16
STANDARDIZED RMR = 0.060
GOODNESS OF FIT INDEX (GFI) = 0.90
ADJUSTED GOODNESS OF FIT INDEX (AGFI) = 0.83
PARSIMONY GOODNESS OF FIT INDEX (PGFI) = 0.55
NORMED FIT INDEX (NFI) = 0.89
**NON-NORMED FIT INDEX (NNFI) = 0.90**
PARSIMONY NORMED FIT INDEX (PNFI) = 0.67
**COMPARATIVE FIT INDEX (CFI) = 0.93**
INCREMENTAL FIT INDEX (IFI) = 0.93
RELATIVE FIT INDEX (RFI) = 0.85
CRITICAL N (CN) = 99.27

**LARGEST NEGATIVE STANDARDIZED RESIDUALS**
RESIDUAL FOR     wfcs4 AND     wfc5      -3.81
RESIDUAL FOR     fwcs1 AND     fwc1      -2.59
RESIDUAL FOR     fwcs1 AND     fwc8      -2.93

**LARGEST POSITIVE STANDARDIZED RESIDUALS**
RESIDUAL FOR     wfc6 AND      wfc5       4.21
RESIDUAL FOR     wfcs4 AND     wfct4      2.84
RESIDUAL FOR     fwcs1 AND     wfcs4      2.80
RESIDUAL FOR     fwcs1 AND     fwc6       4.31

**MODIFICATION INDICES FOR LAMBDA-X**

|        | KSI 1 | KSI 2 |
| ------ | ----- | ----- |
| wfc4   | - -   | 3.81  |
| wfc5   | - -   | 0.22  |

```
wfc6        - -           1.29
wfct4       - -           1.56
wfcs4       - -           0.47
fwc1       0.96           - -
fwc6       0.93           - -
fwc8       1.37           - -
fwct4      0.09           - -
fwcs1      1.85           - -
```

**COMPLETELY STANDARDIZED EXPECTED CHANGE FOR LAMBDA-X**

```
            KSI 1        KSI 2
          --------     --------
wfc4        - -         -0.11
wfc5        - -         -0.03
wfc6        - -          0.08
wfct4       - -          0.08
wfcs4       - -          0.04
fwc1       0.08          - -
fwc6      -0.07          - -
fwc8      -0.09          - -
fwct4      0.02          - -
fwcs1      0.11          - -
```

**MODIFICATION INDICES FOR THETA-DELTA**

|        | wfc4 | wfc5  | wfc6 | wfct4 | wfcs4 | fwc1 |
|--------|------|-------|------|-------|-------|------|
| wfc4   | - -  |       |      |       |       |      |
| wfc5   | 0.91 | - -   |      |       |       |      |
| wfc6   | 0.98 | 17.73 | - -  |       |       |      |
| wfct4  | 3.85 | 0.30  | 0.47 | - -   |       |      |
| wfcs4  | 6.48 | 14.50 | 6.27 | 8.06  | - -   |      |
| fwc1   | 0.06 | 1.48  | 0.71 | 1.62  | 3.75  | - -  |
| fwc6   | 0.04 | 0.46  | 0.00 | 0.00  | 0.11  | 0.01 |
| fwc8   | 0.76 | 0.28  | 0.14 | 0.38  | 0.10  | 2.14 |
| fwct4  | 0.88 | 0.72  | 1.48 | 0.21  | 0.01  | 0.02 |
| fwcs1  | 0.01 | 2.57  | 0.70 | 0.03  | 9.95  | 6.69 |

**MODIFICATION INDICES FOR THETA-DELTA**

|        | fwc6  | fwc8 | fwct4 | fwcs1 |
|--------|-------|------|-------|-------|
| fwc6   | - -   |      |       |       |
| fwc8   | 0.67  | - -  |       |       |
| fwct4  | 5.81  | 5.16 | - -   |       |
| fwcs1  | 18.59 | 8.58 | 0.00  | - -   |

**COMPLETELY STANDARDIZED SOLUTION LAMBDA-X**

```
            KSI 1        KSI 2
          --------     --------
```

```
wfc4      0.87        - -
wfc5      0.77        - -
wfc6      0.70        - -
wfct4     0.79        - -
wfcs4     0.80        - -
fwc1      - -         0.65
fwc6      - -         0.77
fwc8      - -         0.70
fwct4     - -         0.75
fwcs1     - -         0.58
```

**PHI**

|         | KSI 1 | KSI 2 |
|---------|-------|-------|
| KSI 1   | 1.00  |       |
| KSI 2   | 0.33  | 1.00  |

**THETA-DELTA**

| wfc4 | wfc5 | wfc6 | wfct4 | wfcs4 | fwc1 |
|------|------|------|-------|-------|------|
| .24  | .40  | .51  | .37   | .36   | .57  |

**THETA-DELTA**

| fwc6 | fwc8 | fwct4 | fwcs1 |
|------|------|-------|-------|
| .41  | .51  | .43   | .66   |

# LISREL Output for Real Estate Salespeople Sample

**LISREL ESTIMATES (MAXIMUM LIKELIHOOD): LAMBDA-X**

|        | KSI 1  | KSI 2  |
|--------|--------|--------|
| wfc4   | 1.39   | - -    |
|        | (0.11) |        |
|        | 12.97  |        |
| wfc5   | 1.42   | - -    |
|        | (0.12) |        |
|        | 12.10  |        |
| wfc6   | 1.40   | - -    |
|        | (0.11) |        |
|        | 12.59  |        |
| wfct4  | 1.04   | - -    |
|        | (0.11) |        |
|        | 9.54   |        |
| wfcs4  | 1.25   | - -    |
|        | (0.11) |        |
|        | 11.36  |        |
| fwc1   | - -    | 1.18   |
|        |        | (0.11) |
|        |        | 11.08  |
| fwc6   | - -    | 1.40   |
|        |        | (0.09) |
|        |        | 14.96  |
| fwc8   | - -    | 1.52   |
|        |        | (0.11) |
|        |        | 13.45  |
| fwct4  | - -    | 1.33   |
|        |        | (0.10) |
|        |        | 13.33  |
| fwcs1  | - -    | 1.15   |
|        |        | (0.10) |
|        |        | 11.57  |

**PHI**

|        | KSI 1  | KSI 2  |
|--------|--------|--------|
| KSI 1  | 1.00   |        |
| KSI 2  | 0.42   | 1.00   |
|        | (0.07) |        |
|        | 6.01   |        |

**THETA-DELTA**

| wfc4 | wfc5 | wfc6 | wfct4 | wfcs4 | fwc1 |
|------|------|------|-------|-------|------|
| 0.91 | 1.24 | 1.03 | 1.40  | 1.19  | 1.22 |

|   (0.13)  |   (0.17)  |   (0.14)  |   (0.16)  |   (0.15)  |   (0.14)  |
|    6.84   |    7.48   |    7.15   |    8.54   |    7.88   |    8.48   |

**THETA-DELTA**

| fwc6   | fwc8   | fwct4  | fwcs1  |
| ------ | ------ | ------ | ------ |
| 0.50   | 1.01   | 0.80   | 1.00   |
| (0.08) | (0.14) | (0.11) | (0.12) |
| 5.99   | 7.43   | 7.51   | 8.33   |

NOTE: For each parameter estimate, three numbers are given:
(a) the unstandardized parameter estimate, (b) a standard error
estimate (in parentheses), and (c) a z/t-value.

## GOODNESS OF FIT STATISTICS

CHI-SQUARE WITH 34 DEGREES OF
FREEDOM = 69.32 (P = 0.00033)
ESTIMATED NON-CENTRALITY PARAMETER (NCP) = 35.32
90 PERCENT CONFIDENCE INTERVAL FOR NCP = (15.32 ; 63.10)
MINIMUM FIT FUNCTION VALUE = 0.39
POPULATION DISCREPANCY FUNCTION VALUE (F0) = 0.20
90 PERCENT CONFIDENCE INTERVAL FOR F0 = (0.085 ; 0.35)
**ROOT MEAN SQUARE ERROR OF APPROXIMATION (RMSEA) = 0.076**
90 PERCENT CONFIDENCE INTERVAL FOR RMSEA = (0.050 ; 0.10)
P-VALUE FOR TEST OF CLOSE FIT (RMSEA < 0.05) = 0.050
EXPECTED CROSS-VALIDATION INDEX (ECVI) = 0.62
90 PERCENT CONFIDENCE INTERVAL FOR ECVI = (0.51 ; 0.77)
ECVI FOR SATURATED MODEL = 0.61
ECVI FOR INDEPENDENCE MODEL = 6.15
CHI-SQUARE FOR INDEPENDENCE MODEL WITH 45 DEGREES OF
FREEDOM = 1086.32
INDEPENDENCE AIC = 1106.32
MODEL AIC = 111.32
SATURATED AIC = 110.00
INDEPENDENCE CAIC = 1148.31
MODEL CAIC = 199.49
SATURATED CAIC = 340.92
ROOT MEAN SQUARE RESIDUAL (RMR) = 0.15
STANDARDIZED RMR = 0.056
GOODNESS OF FIT INDEX (GFI) = 0.93
ADJUSTED GOODNESS OF FIT INDEX (AGFI) = 0.88
PARSIMONY GOODNESS OF FIT INDEX (PGFI) = 0.57
NORMED FIT INDEX (NFI) = 0.94
**NON-NORMED FIT INDEX (NNFI) = 0.96**
PARSIMONY NORMED FIT INDEX (PNFI) = 0.71
**COMPARATIVE FIT INDEX (CFI) = 0.97**
INCREMENTAL FIT INDEX (IFI) = 0.97
RELATIVE FIT INDEX (RFI) = 0.92
CRITICAL N (CN) = 146.57

**LARGEST NEGATIVE STANDARDIZED RESIDUALS**
RESIDUAL FOR      wfct4 AND      wfc6      -2.96

**LARGEST POSITIVE STANDARDIZED RESIDUALS**
RESIDUAL FOR      wfc6 AND      wfc5      2.84
RESIDUAL FOR      fwc6 AND      wfct4      2.80
RESIDUAL FOR      fwcs1 AND      wfct4      2.72
RESIDUAL FOR      fwcs1 AND      wfcs4      2.80
RESIDUAL FOR      fwcs1 AND      fwct4      2.80

**MODIFICATION INDICES FOR LAMBDA-X**

|        | KSI 1 | KSI 2 |
|--------|-------|-------|
| wfc4   | - -   | 2.00  |
| wfc5   | - -   | 4.15  |
| wfc6   | - -   | 0.04  |
| wfct4  | - -   | 7.38  |
| wfcs4  | - -   | 2.19  |
| fwc1   | 0.85  | - -   |
| fwc6   | 0.71  | - -   |
| fwc8   | 1.66  | - -   |
| fwct4  | 0.77  | - -   |
| fwcs1  | 0.35  | - -   |

**COMPLETELY STANDARDIZED EXPECTED CHANGE FOR LAMBDA-X**

|        | KSI 1  | KSI 2  |
|--------|--------|--------|
| wfc4   | - -    | −0.08  |
| wfc5   | - -    | −0.12  |
| wfc6   | - -    | 0.01   |
| wfct4  | - -    | 0.19   |
| wfcs4  | - -    | 0.09   |
| fwc1   | 0.06   | - -    |
| fwc6   | 0.04   | - -    |
| fwc8   | −0.07  | - -    |
| fwct4  | −0.05  | - -    |
| fwcs1  | 0.04   | - -    |

**MODIFICATION INDICES FOR THETA-DELTA**

|        | wfc4 | wfc5 | wfc6 | wfct4 | wfcs4 | fwc1 |
|--------|------|------|------|-------|-------|------|
| wfc4   | - -  |      |      |       |       |      |
| wfc5   | 0.76 | - -  |      |       |       |      |
| wfc6   | 0.84 | 8.06 | - -  |       |       |      |
| wfct4  | 0.94 | 0.60 | 8.76 | - -   |       |      |
| wfcs4  | 0.01 | 5.94 | 0.20 | 3.45  | - -   |      |
| fwc1   | 0.02 | 0.89 | 0.66 | 0.06  | 2.12  | - -  |
| fwc6   | 1.56 | 0.47 | 0.13 | 1.29  | 0.22  | 0.54 |
| fwc8   | 0.18 | 0.04 | 1.58 | 3.08  | 2.38  | 0.20 |
| fwct4  | 5.44 | 0.11 | 0.70 | 1.14  | 3.02  | 1.63 |
| fwcs1  | 0.89 | 3.60 | 0.34 | 2.30  | 10.45 | 0.50 |

**MODIFICATION INDICES FOR THETA-DELTA**

|        | fwc6 | fwc8 | fwct4 | fwcs1 |
|--------|------|------|-------|-------|
| fwc6   | - -  |      |       |       |
| fwc8   | 3.52 | - -  |       |       |

```
fwct4   1.91    0.16      - -
fwcs1   2.66    3.02      7.86      - -
```

## COMPLETELY STANDARDIZED SOLUTION LAMBDA-X

|        | KSI 1 | KSI 2 |
|--------|-------|-------|
| wfc4   | 0.83  | - -   |
| wfc5   | 0.79  | - -   |
| wfc6   | 0.81  | - -   |
| wfct4  | 0.66  | - -   |
| wfcs4  | 0.75  | - -   |
| fwc1   | - -   | 0.73  |
| fwc6   | - -   | 0.89  |
| fwc8   | - -   | 0.83  |
| fwct4  | - -   | 0.83  |
| fwcs1  | - -   | 0.75  |

## PHI

|       | KSI 1 | KSI 2 |
|-------|-------|-------|
| KSI 1 | 1.00  |       |
| KSI 2 | 0.42  | 1.00  |

## THETA-DELTA

| wfc4 | wfc5 | wfc6 | wfct4 | wfcs4 | fwc1 |
|------|------|------|-------|-------|------|
| .32  | .38  | .35  | .56   | .43   | .47  |

## THETA-DELTA

| fwc6 | fwc8 | fwct4 | fwcs1 |
|------|------|-------|-------|
| 0.20 | 0.30 | 0.31  | 0.43  |

SOURCE: Data are adapted from "Development and Validation of Work-Family Conflict and Family-Work Conflict Scales," *Journal of Applied Psychology*, 81(4), Netemeyer, Boles, and McMurrian, copyright 1996 by the American Psychological Association. Adapted with permission from the American Psychological Association.

# Appendix 7B

———•—

## LISREL INPUT FOR MULTIGROUP ANALYSES: FULL
## MEASUREMENT INVARIANCE MODEL

```
title 'WFC-FWC multi-group'
  DA NI=43 NO=151 MA=cm ng=2
  cm fu file=a:\wfc2book.dat fo=5
  (8f10.6/8f10.6/8f10.6/8f10.6/8f10.6/3f10.6)
La
  wfc1 wfc2 wfc3 wfc4 wfc5 wfc6 wfc7
  wfct1 wfct2 wfct3 wfct4 wfct5 wfct6 wfct7 wfct8
  wfcs1 wfcs2 wfcs3 wfcs4 wfcs5 wfcs6 wfcs7
  fwc1 fwc2 fwc3 fwc4 fwc5 fwc6 fwc7 fwc8
  fwct1 fwct2 fwct3 fwct4 fwct5 fwct6 fwct7
  fwcs1 fwcs2 fwcs3 fwcs4 fwcs5 fwcs6 /
se
  wfc4 wfc5 wfc6 wfct4 wfcs4
  fwc1 fwc6 fwc8 fwct4 fwcs1/
  mo nx=10 nk=2
  fr lx(2,1) lx(3,1) lx(4,1) lx(5,1)
  fr lx(7,2) lx(8,2) lx(9,2) lx(10,2)
  va 1.00 lx(1,1) lx(6,2)
  st .5 all
  path diagram
  OU sc rs mi ss tv it=800 tm=10000 AD=OFF
  title 'WFC-FWC measurement model Study One'
  DA NI=43 NO=181 MA=cm
  cm fu file=a:\wfc3book.dat fo=5
  (8f10.6/8f10.6/8f10.6/8f10.6/8f10.6/3f10.6)
La
  wfc1 wfc2 wfc3 wfc4 wfc5 wfc6 wfc7
  wfct1 wfct2 wfct3 wfct4 wfct5 wfct6 wfct7 wfct8
  wfcs1 wfcs2 wfcs3 wfcs4 wfcs5 wfcs6 wfcs7
  fwc1 fwc2 fwc3 fwc4 fwc5 fwc6 fwc7 fwc8
```

```
  fwct1  fwct2  fwct3  fwct4  fwct5  fwct6  fwct7
  fwcs1  fwcs2  fwcs3  fwcs4  fwcs5  fwcs6  /
se
  wfc4  wfc5  wfc6  wfct4  wfcs4
  fwc1  fwc6  fwc8  fwct4  fwcs1/
  mo  lx=in  ph=in  td=in
  st  .5  all
  path diagram
  OU  sc  rs  mi  ss  tv  it=800  tm=1000
```

SOURCE: Data adapted from "Development and Validation of Work-Family Conflict and Family-Work Conflict Scales," *Journal of Applied Psychology*, 81(4), Netemeyer, Boles, and McMurrian, copyright 1996 by the American Psychological Association. Adapted with permission from the American Psychological Association.

# ⊰ EIGHT ⊱

# CONCLUDING REMARKS

————•◦•————

This text has focused on the development and validation of multi-item self-administered measures of unobservable, latent constructs. Effective measurement is a cornerstone of scientific research and is required in the process of testing theoretical relationships among unobservable constructs. The assessment of these constructs is often assumed to be indirect via the use of self-report, paper-and-pencil measures on which multiple reflective items or indicators are used to operationalize constructs. Throughout the book, we have tried to emphasize the importance of theoretical aspects of scale development. As reiterated below, these guiding conceptual issues include construct definition, domain specification, dimensionality, and the nomological network in which constructs are embedded. We cannot overemphasize the importance of a priori theory to the beginning of item development and subsequent empirical aspects of the scale development process.

Following individual chapters regarding scale dimensionality (Chapter 2), reliability (Chapter 3), and validity (Chapter 4), our present effort was organized around the four-step scale development sequence depicted in Figure 1.1 and covered in Chapters 5, 6, and 7. This recommended approach is generally consistent with much of the extant scale development literature (e.g., Churchill, 1979; Clark & Watson, 1995; DeVellis, 1991; Haynes et al., 1999; Nunnally & Bernstein, 1994; Spector, 1992). We are certainly indebted to the many authors who have proposed appropriate scale development procedures and/or described quality scale development endeavors. As the readers of this book undoubtedly realize, the recommended stages, as well as the overlapping activities assumed to constitute each stage, are offered as a logical, sequential process. The process of scale development, however, may well be an iterative and ongoing procedure in which restarts are required as researchers learn from their efforts and mistakes and as revisions are needed in such areas as conceptual definition, item generation, and revisions of construct dimensionality.

Researchers are again encouraged to begin with a theoretically grounded construct definition that specifies clearly the domain of the construct and considers the nomological network surrounding the construct. The hypothesized dimensionality underlying the construct will be driven by this theoretical understanding and conceptualization. Second, researchers are faced with many issues associated with item generation and judging. A substantial number of items composing the original pool (and distributed across the various dimensions for multidimensional constructs) must be generated. Following the deletion and/or revision of ambiguous items, double-barreled statements, and statements of fact, external judging procedures are needed to evaluate the items. These judgmental processes should include both "lay" and "expert" judges used in efforts to enhance both content and face validity. In particular, the domain representativeness of the remaining set of items regarding the overall construct and any multiple dimensions composing the concept should be considered.

Our general third step in the scale development process involves the design and conduct of studies to actually develop and refine the scale. The number of studies required will depend on the specificity of the concept being measured, the dimensionality of the construct, the size and quality of the item pool remaining after judgmental procedures, and, frankly, the ability of the items to load effectively as hypothesized. Some initial pilot testing may be employed to reduce the number of items following judgmental evaluations; however, substantive multiple samples drawn from relevant populations will be required. These data can be used in both exploratory factor analyses (typically employed early in the scale development process to make item deletion decisions) or subsequent confirmatory factor analyses to verify hypothesized structure. Additional variables should be included in these studies to help in subsequent evaluation of validity, as focal measures being developed are refined toward final form. These other concepts (i.e., additional variables) can be used to estimate convergent and discriminant validity, as well concurrent validity. If multiple phases of data collections are involved, test-retest reliability estimates and predictive validity evidence might be obtained from opportunities provided from multiple administrations to a sample over time.

Given the establishment of dimensionality, these initial studies also provide the opportunity to delete and/or revise items based on analysis of corrected item-to-total correlations, average interitem correlations, and internal consistency reliability estimates. These initial studies then are instrumental in establishing the scale's final configuration, as well as the scale's psychometric properties.

The concluding aspects of our scale development process include activities and procedures designed to "finalize" the scale. These procedures likely will involve the collection of additional data to demonstrate the usefulness of the scale, for example, as a moderator of important theoretical relationships or as a predictor of previously unexplained phenomena. Such tests provide evidence that the measure is applicable for use by other researchers, as well as providing evidence of nomological validity. Prior to any hypothesis tests or investigations of theoretical relationships, the data from these last studies will be analyzed using confirmatory factor analyses in further tests of dimensionality, item reliability, construct validity, and shared variance, in addition to providing evidence of discriminant validity between dimensions of multidimensional scales. Estimates of coefficient alpha, as well as correlations among factors for multidimensional scales, also should be reported. In addition, if alternative measures exist (i.e., preexisting or competing scales), then one objective of the scale developer will be to demonstrate that the focal measure predicts some important external criterion or explains some theoretically insightful relationship better than previously developed and/or published competing scales.

Norm scores should be described to assist subsequent researchers in the interpretation of the interval values generated by applications of the new measures being proposed. Mean scores and standard deviations for total samples and important subgroups within representative samples should be reported. Finally, the collection and administration of new measures across a series of samples and contexts provides the opportunity for researchers involved in formal scale development to apply generalizability theory.

# REFERENCES

———•——

Allen, S. J., & Hubbard, R. (1986). Regression equations of the latent roots of random data correlation matrices with unities on the diagonal. *Multivariate Behavioral Research, 21,* 393-398.

Anastasi, A., & Urbina, S. (1998). *Psychological testing.* Englewood Cliffs, NJ: Prentice-Hall.

Anderson, J. C., & Gerbing, D. W. (1988). Structural equation modeling in practice: A review and recommended two-step approach. *Psychological Bulletin, 103,* 411-423.

Bagozzi, R. P. (1993). Assessing construct validity in personality research: Application to measures of self-esteem. *Journal of Research in Personality, 27,* 49-87.

Bagozzi, R. P., & Edwards, J. R. (1998). A general approach for representing constructs in organizational research. *Organizational Research Methods, 1,* 45-87.

Bagozzi, R. P., & Heatherton, T. F. (1994). A general approach to representing multi-faceted personality constructs: Application to state self-esteem. *Structural Equation Modeling, 1*(1), 35-67.

Bagozzi, R. P., & Yi, Y. (1988). On the evaluation of structural equation models. *Journal of the Academy of Marketing Science, 16*(1), 74-94.

Bagozzi, R. P., Yi, Y., & Phillips, L. W. (1991). Assessing construct validity in organizational research. *Administrative Science Quarterly, 36*(3), 421-458.

Bearden, W. O., Hardesty, D., & Rose, R. (2001). Consumer self-confidence: Refinements in conceptualization and measurement. *Journal of Consumer Research, 28*(June), 121-134.

Bearden, W. O., & Netemeyer, R. G. (1998). *Handbook of marketing scales: Multi-item measures for marketing and consumer behavior research.* Thousand Oaks, CA: Sage.

Bearden, W. O., Netemeyer, R. G., & Teel, J. E. (1989). Measurement of consumer susceptibility to interpersonal influence. *Journal of Consumer Research, 15*(March), 473-481.

Bearden, W. O., & Rose, R. L. (1990). Attention to social comparison information: An individual difference factor affecting conformity. *Journal of Consumer Research, 16*(March), 461-471.

Bearden, W. O., Sharma, S., & Teel, J. E. (1982). Sample size effects on chi-square and other statistics used in evaluating causal models. *Journal of Marketing Research, 19*(November), 425-430.

Bentler, P. M. (1990). Comparative fit indices in structural equation models. *Psychological Bulletin, 107,* 238-246.

Bentler, P. M., & Chou, C. (1987). Practical issues in structural modeling. *Sociological Methods & Research, 16*(1), 78-117.

Bollen, K. A. (1989). *Structural equations with latent variables.* New York: John Wiley & Sons.

Bollen, K. A., & Lennox, R. (1991). Conventional wisdom on measurement: A structural equations perspective. *Psychological Bulletin, 110,* 305-314.

Boyle, G. J. (1991). Does item homogeneity indicate internal consistency or item redundancy in psychometric scales? *Personality and Individual Differences, 3,* 291-294.

Browne, M. W. (1990). *MUTMUM PC: A program for fitting the direct product models for multitrait-multimethod Data.* Pretoria: University of South Africa.

Browne, M. W., & Cudeck, R. (1993). Alternative ways of assessing model fit. In K. A. Bollen & J. S. Long (Eds.), *Testing structural equation models* (pp. 136-162). Newbury Park, CA: Sage.

Bruner, G., & Hensel, P. (1997). *Marketing scales handbook: A compilation of multi-item measures* (2nd ed.). Chicago: American Marketing Association.

Byrne, B. M. (2001). *Structural equation modeling with AMOS: Basic concepts, applications, and programming.* Mahwah, NJ: Erlbaum Associates.

Byrne, B., Shavelson, R. J., & Muthen, B. (1989). Testing the equivalence of factor covariance and mean structures: The issue of partial measurement invariance. *Psychological Bulletin, 105,* 456-466.

Cacciopo, J. T., & Petty, R. E. (1982). The need for cognition. *Journal of Personality and Social Psychology, 42,* 116-131.

Calder, B. J., Phillips, L. W., & Tybout, A. M. (1982). The concept of external validity. *Journal of Consumer Research, 9*(December), 240-244.

Campbell, D. T. (1960). Recommendations for APA test standards regarding construct, trait, or discriminant validity. *American Psychologist, 15,* 546-553.

Campbell, D. T., & Fiske, D. W. (1959). Convergent and discriminant validity by the multitrait-multimethod matrix. *Psychological Bulletin, 56,* 81-105.

Carver, C. S. (1989). How should multi-faceted personality constructs be tested? Issues illustrated by self-monitoring, attributional style, and hardiness. *Journal of Personality and Social Psychology, 56*(4), 577-585.

Cattell, R. B. (1966). The meaning and strategic use of factor analysis. In R. B. Cattell (Ed.), *Handbook of multivariate experimental psychology* (pp. 174-243). Chicago: Rand McNally.

Churchill, G. A. (1979). A paradigm for developing better measures of marketing constructs. *Journal of Marketing Research, 16*(February), 64-73.

Churchill, G. A., & Iacobucci, D. (2002). *Marketing research methodological foundations* (8th ed.). Fort Worth, TX: Harcourt College Publishers.

Churchill, G. A., & Peter, J. P. (1984). Research design effects on the reliability of rating scales: A meta-analysis. *Journal of Marketing Research, 21*(November), 360-375.

Clark, L. A., & Watson, D. (1995). Constructing validity: Basic issues in scale development. *Psychological Assessment, 7*(3), 309-319.

Cliff, N. (1988). The eigenvalue-greater-than-one rules and reliability of components. *Psychological Bulletin, 103*(2), 276-279.

Comrey, A. L. (1988). Factor-analytic methods of scale development in personality and clinical psychology. *Journal of Consulting and Clinical Psychology, 56,* 754-761.

Cook, T. D., & Campbell, D. T. (1979). *Quasi-experimentation: Design and analysis issues for field settings.* Boston: Houghton Mifflin.

Cortina, J. M. (1993). What is coefficient alpha? An examination of theory and application. *Journal of Applied Psychology, 78,* 98-104.

Crocker, L., & Algina, J. (1986). *Introduction to classical and modern test theory.* Orlando, FL: Holt, Rinehart, & Winston.

Cronbach, L. J. (1951). Coefficient alpha and the internal structure of tests. *Psychometrika, 31,* 93-96.

Cronbach, L. J., & Meehl, P. E. (1955). Construct validity in psychological tests. *Psychological Bulletin, 52,* 281-302.

Crowne, D. P., & Marlowe, D. (1960). A new scale for social desirability independent of psychopathology. *Journal of Consulting Psychology, 24*(4), 349-354.

DeVellis, R. F. (1991). *Scale development: Theory and applications.* Newbury Park, CA: Sage.

Diamantopoulos, A., & Winklhofer, H. M. (2001). Index construction with formative indicators: An alternative to scale development. *Journal of Marketing Research, 36,* 269-277.

Fan, X., Thompson, B., & Wang, L. (1999). Effects of sample size, estimation methods, and model specification on structural equation modeling fit indices. *Structural Equation Modeling, 6*(1), 56-83.

Finn, A., & Kayande, U. (1997). Reliability assessment and optimization of marketing measurement. *Journal of Marketing Research, 34*(May), 262-275.

Fisher, R. J. (1993). Social desirability bias and the validity of indirect questioning. *Journal of Consumer Research, 20*(September), 303-315.

Floyd, F. J., & Widaman, K. (1995). Factor analysis in the development and refinement of clinical assessment instruments. *Psychological Assessment, 7*(3), 286-299.

Fornell, C., & Larcker, D. F. (1981). Evaluating structural equation models with unobservable variables and measurement error. *Journal of Marketing Research, 18*(February), 39-50.

Friestad, M., & Wright, P. (2001). *Pre-adult education on marketplace persuasion tactics: Integrating marketplace literacy and media literacy.* Unpublished faculty working paper, University of Oregon, Eugene.

Ganster, D. C., Hennessey, H. W., & Luthans, F. (1983). Social desirability response effects: Three alternative models. *Academy of Management Journal, 26*(June), 321-331.

Gardner, H. (1993). *Frames of mind: The theory of multiple intelligences.* New York: Basic Books.

Gerbing, D. W., & Anderson, J. C. (1984). On the meaning of within-factor correlated measurement errors. *Journal of Consumer Research, 11*(June), 572-580.

Gerbing, D. W., & Anderson, J. C. (1988). An updated paradigm for scale development incorporating unidimensionality and its assessment. *Journal of Marketing Research, 25*(May), 186-192.

Green, D. P., Goldman, S. L., & Salovey, P. (1993). Measurement error masks bipolarity in affect ratings. *Journal of Personality and Social Psychology, 64,* 1029-1041.

Hair, J. F., Anderson, R. E., Tatham, R. L., & Black, W. C. (1998). *Multivariate data analysis* (5th ed.). Englewood Cliffs, NJ: Prentice Hall.

Hambleton, R. K., Swaminathin, H., & Rogers, H. J. (1991). *Fundamentals of item response theory.* Newbury Park, CA: Sage.

Hartley, H. O., Rao, J. N. K., & LaMotte, L. (1978). A simple synthesis-based method of variance component estimation. *Biometrics, 34,* 233-242.

Hattie, J. (1985). Methodology review: Assessing unidimensionality of tests and items. *Applied Psychological Measurement, 9*(June), 139-164.

Hayduk, L. A. (1996). *LISREL: Issues, debates, and strategies.* Baltimore, MD: Johns Hopkins University Press.

Haynes, S., Nelson, N. K., & Blaine, D. (1999). Psychometric issues in assessment research. In P. C. Kendall, J. N. Butcher, & G. Holmbeck (Eds.), *Handbook of research methods in clinical psychology* (pp. 125-154). New York: John Wiley & Sons.

Haynes, S., Richard, D. C., & Kubany, E. S. (1995). Content validity in psychological assessment: A functional approach to concepts and methods. *Psychological Assessment, 7,* 238-247.

Herche, J., & Engellend, B. (1996). Reversed polarity items and scale dimensionality. *Journal of the Academy of Marketing Science, 24*(4), 366-374.

Horn, J. L. (1965). A rationale and test for the number of factors in factor analysis. *Psychometrika, 30,* 179-186.

Hoyle, R. (1995). *Structural equation modeling: Issues and applications.* Newbury Park, CA: Sage.

Hu, L., & Bentler, P. M. (1999). Cutoff criteria for fit indices in covariance structure analysis: Conventional criteria versus new alternatives. *Structural Equation Modeling, 6*(1), 1-55.

Hull, J. G., Lehn, D. A., & Tedlie, J. (1991). A general approach to testing multifacted personality constructs. *Journal of Personality and Social Psychology, 61*(6), 932-945.

Iacobucci, D., Ostrom, A., & Grayson, K. (1995). Distinguishing service quality and customer satisfaction: The voice of the consumer. *Journal of Consumer Psychology, 4*(3), 277-303.

Jarvis, W. B. G., & Petty, R. E. (1996). The need to evaluate. *Journal of Personality and Social Psychology, 70*(1), 172-194.

Jöreskog, K., & Sörbom, D. (1989). *LISREL7: A guide to the program and applications* (2nd ed.). Chicago: SPSS.

Kaplan, R. M., & Saccuzzo, D. P. (1997). *Psychological testing: Principles, applications, and issues* (4th ed.). Pacific Grove, CA: Brooks/Cole.

Kelley, J. R., & McGrath, J. E. (1988). *On time and method.* Beverly Hills, CA: Sage.

Kenny, D. A., & Kashy, D. A. (1992). Analysis of the multitrait-multimethod matrix by confirmatory factor analysis. *Psychological Bulletin, 122,* 165-172.

Kishton, J. M., & Widaman, K. F. (1994). Unidimensional versus domain representative parcelling of questionnaire items: An empirical example. *Educational and Psychological Measurement, 54,* 565-575.

Kumar, A., & Dillon, W. R. (1987). Some further remarks on measurement-structure interaction and the unidimensionality of constructs. *Journal of Marketing Research, 24*(November), 438-444.

Lastovicka, J. L., Bettencourt, L. A., Hughner, R. S., & Kuntze, R. J. (1999). Lifestyle of the tight and frugal: Theory and measurement. *Journal of Consumer Research, 26*(June), 85-98.

Lastovicka, J. L., Murry, J. P., Jr., & Joachimsthaler, E. (1990). Evaluating measurement validity of lifestyle typologies with qualitative measures and multiplicative factoring. *Journal of Marketing Research, 27*(February), 11-23.

Lennox, R. D., & Wolfe, R. N. (1984). Revision of the Self-Monitoring Scale. *Journal of Personality and Social Psychology, 46*(6), 1349-1364.

Levine, R. A., & Campbell, D. T. (1972). *Ethnocentrism: Theories of conflict, ethnic attitudes, and group behavior.* New York: John Wiley & Sons.

Lichtenstein, D. R., Ridgway, N. M., & Netemeyer, R. G. (1993). Price perceptions and consumer shopping behavior: A field study. *Journal of Marketing Research, 30*(May), 234-245.

Loevinger, J. (1957). Objective tests as instruments of psychological theory. *Psychological Reports, 3,* 635-694.

MacCallum, R. C., & Browne, M. W. (1993). The use of causal indicators in covariance structure models: Some practical issues. *Psychological Bulletin, 114,* 533-541.

MacCallum, R. C., Roznowski, M., & Necowitz, L. B. (1992). Model modification in covariance structure analysis: The problem of capitalization on chance. *Psychological Bulletin, 114,* 185-199.

Marcoulides, G. A. (1998). Applied generalizability theory models. In G. A. Marcoulides (Ed.), *Modern methods for business research* (pp. 1-28). Mahwah, NJ: Lawrence Erlbaum.

Marsh, H. (1995). Confirmatory factor analysis models of factorial invariance: A multi-faceted approach. *Structural Equation Modeling, 1,* 5-34.

McDonald, R. P. (1981). The dimensionality of tests and items. *British Journal of Mathematical and Statistical Psychology, 34,* 100-117.

McDonald, R. P. (1999). *Test theory: A unified treatment.* Mahwah, NJ: Lawrence Erlbaum Associates.

McDonald, R. P., & Marsh, H. W. (1990). Choosing a multivariate model: Noncentrality and goodness of fit. *Psychological Bulletin, 105,* 430-445.

Messick, S. (1993). Validity. In R. L. Linn (Ed.), *Educational measurement* (2nd ed., pp. 105-146). Phoenix, AZ: American Council on Education and the Oryx Press.

Mick, D. G. (1996). Are studies of dark side variables confounded by socially desirable responding? The case of materialism. *Journal of Consumer Research, 23*(September), 106-119.

Nederhof, A. (1985). Methods of coping with social desirability bias: A review. *European Journal of Social Psychology, 15*(July-September), 263-280.

Netemeyer, R. G., Boles, J. S., & McMurrian, R. C. (1996). Development and validation of Work-Family Conflict and Family-Work Conflict scales. *Journal of Applied Psychology, 81*(4), 400-410.

Netemeyer, R. G., Durvasula, S., & Lichtenstein, D. R. (1991). A cross-national assessment of the reliability and validity of the CETSCALE. *Journal of Marketing Research, 28*(August), 320-327.

Netemeyer, R. G., Pullig, C., & Bearden, W. O. (2002). Observations on some key psychometric properties of paper-and-pencil measures. In A. G. Woodside & E. M. Moore (Eds.), *Essays by distinguished marketing scholars of the Society for Marketing Advances* (pp. 115-138). Amsterdam: JAI.

Neuberg, S. L., West, S. G., Thompson, M. M., & Judice, T. N. (1997). On dimensionality, discriminant validity, and the role of psychometric analyses in personality theory and measurement: Reply to Kruglanski et al.'s (1997) defense of the Need for Closure Scale. *Journal of Personality and Social Psychology, 73,* 1017-1029.

Nevo, B. (1985). Face validity revisited. *Journal of Educational Measurement, 22,* 287-293.

Nunnally, J., & Bernstein, I. H. (1994). *Psychometric theory* (3rd ed.). New York: McGraw-Hill.

Obermiller, C., & Spangenberg, E. R. (1998). Development of a scale to measure consumer skepticism toward advertising. *Journal of Consumer Psychology, 7*(2), 159-186.

Osgood, C. E., & Tannenbaum, P. H. (1955). The principle of congruence in the prediction of attitude change. *Psychological Bulletin, 62,* 42-55.

Park, C. W., Mothersbaugh, D. L., & Feick, L. (1994). Consumer knowledge assessment. *Journal of Consumer Research, 21*(June), 71-82.

Paulhus, D. L. (1984). Two-component models of socially desirable responding. *Journal of Personality and Social Psychology, 46*(3), 598-609.

Paulhus, D. L. (1991). Measurement and control of response bias. In J. P. Robinson, P. R. Shaver, & L. S. Wrightsman (Eds.), *Measures of personality and social psychological attitudes* (pp. 17-59). New York: Academic Press.

Paulhus, D. L. (1993). *The Balanced Inventory of Desirable Responding: Reference manual for BIDR Version 6.* Toronto: Multi-Health Systems.

Perreault, W. D., Jr., & Leigh, L. E. (1989). Reliability of nominal data based on qualitative judgments. *Journal of Marketing Research, 26*(May), 135-148.

Peter, J. P. (1979). Reliability: A review of psychometric basics and recent marketing practices. *Journal of Marketing Research, 16*(February), 6-17.

Peter, J. P. (1981). Construct validity: A review of basic issues and marketing practices. *Journal of Marketing Research, 18*(May), 133-145.

Peterson, R. A. (1994). A meta-analysis of Cronbach's coefficient alpha. *Journal of Consumer Research, 21*(September), 381-391.

Price, J. P., & Mueller, C. W. (1986). *Handbook of organizational measurement.* Marshfield, MA: Pittman.

Raykov, T., & Widaman, K. F. (1995). Issues in applied structural equation modeling research. *Structural Equation Modeling, 2*(4), 289-318.

Richins, M. L. (1983). An analysis of consumer interaction styles in the marketplace. *Journal of Consumer Research, 10*(June), 73-82.

Richins, M. L., & Dawson, S. (1992). A consumer values orientation for materialism and its measurement: Scale development and validation. *Journal of Consumer Research, 19*(December), 303-316.

Robinson, J. P., Shaver, P. R., & Wrightsman, L. S. (1991). Criteria for scale selection and evaluation. In J. P. Robinson, P. R. Shaver, & L. S. Wrightsman (Eds.), *Measures of personality and social psychological attitudes* (pp. 1-15). San Diego: Academic Press.

Rosenberg, M. (1965). *Society and the adolescent self-image.* Princeton, NJ: Princeton University Press.

Rossiter, J. R. (2001). *The C-OAR-SE procedure for scale development in marketing.* Faculty working paper, University of Wollongong, Australia.

Ruekert, R. W., & Churchill, G. A., Jr. (1984). Reliability and validity of alternative measures of channel member satisfaction. *Journal of Marketing Research, 21*(May), 226-233.

Saxe, R., & Weitz, B. A. (1982). The SOCO scale: A measure of the customer orientation of salespeople. *Journal of Marketing Research, 19*(August), 343-351.

Schmitt, N. (1996). Uses and abuses of coefficient alpha. *Psychological Assessment, 8,* 350-353.

Schumacker, R. E., & Lomax, R. G. (1996). *A beginner's guide to structural equation modeling.* Mahwah, NJ: Lawrence Erlbaum Associates.

Sharma, S. (1996). *Applied multivariate techniques.* New York: John Wiley & Sons.

Sharma, S., Shimp, T. A., & Shin, J. (1995). Consumer ethnocentrism: A test of antecedents and moderators. *Journal of the Academy of Marketing Science, 23*(Winter), 26-37.

Sharma, S., & Weathers, D. (2002). *Assessing generalizability of scales used in cross-national research.* Faculty working paper, University of South Carolina, Columbia.

Shavelson, R., & Webb, N. M. (1991). *Generalizability theory: A primer.* Newbury Park, CA: Sage.

Shimp, T. A., & Sharma, S. (1987). Consumer ethnocentrism: Construction and validation of the CETSCALE. *Journal of Marketing Research, 24*(August), 280-289.

Smith, G. T., & McCarthy, D. M. (1995). Methodological considerations in the refinement of clinical assessment instruments. *Psychological Assessment, 7,* 300-308.

Spector, P. E. (1992). *Summated rating scale construction: An introduction.* Newbury Park, CA: Sage.

Steenkamp, J. E. M., & Baumgartner, H. (1992). The role of optimum stimulation level in exploratory consumer behavior. *Journal of Consumer Research, 19*(December), 434-448.

Steenkamp, J. E. M., & Baumgartner, H. (1998). Assessing measurement invariance in cross-national consumer research. *Journal of Consumer Research, 25*(June), 78-90.

Steiger, J. H., & Lind, J. C. (1980, May). *Statistically-based tests for the number of common factors.* Paper presented at the meeting of the Psychometric Society, Iowa City, IA.

Sumner, G. A. (1906). *Folkways.* New York: Ginn Custom Publishing.

Tett, R. P., & Meyer, J. P. (1993). Job satisfaction, organizational commitment, turnover intention, and turnover: Path analyses based on meta-analytic findings. *Personnel Psychology, 46,* 259-293.

Tian, K. T., Bearden, W. O., & Hunter, G. L. (2001). Consumers' Need for Uniqueness: Scale development and validation. *Journal of Consumer Research, 28*(June), 50-66.

Tian, K. T., Bearden, W. O., & Manning, K. C. (2002). *Agents' socially desirable responding: Scale development and validation.* Faculty working paper, University of South Carolina, Columbia.

Trochim, A. (2002). *Construct validity.* Retrieved November 19, 2002, from http:// trochim.human.cornell.edu/kb/constval.htm

Widaman, K. F. (1985). Hierarchically nested covariance structure models for multitrait-multimethod data. *Applied Psychological Measurement, 9,* 1-26.

Wright, P. L. (1975). Factors affecting cognitive resistance to advertising. *Journal of Consumer Research, 2*(June), 1-9.

Zaichkowsky, J. L. (1985). Measuring the involvement construct. *Journal of Consumer Research, 12*(December), 341-352.

Zerbe, W., & Paulhus, D. (1987). Socially desirable responding in organizational behavior: A reconception. *Academy of Management Review, 12*(April), 250-264.

# AUTHOR INDEX

# SUBJECT INDEX

# ABOUT THE AUTHORS

**Richard G. Netemeyer** is a Professor of Commerce at the McIntire School of Commerce at the University of Virginia. He received his PhD in business administration with a specialization in marketing from the University of South Carolina in 1986. He was a member of the marketing faculty at Louisiana State University for 15 years before joining the McIntire faculty in the fall of 2001. He currently teaches quantitative analysis and marketing research at McIntire and conducts research on consumer and organizational behavior topics with a focus on measurement and survey-based techniques. His research has appeared in the *Journal of Consumer Research, Journal of Marketing Research, Journal of Marketing, Journal of Applied Psychology, Organizational Behavior & Human Decision Processes,* and other publications. He is a coauthor of two books pertaining to measurement and is a member of the editorial review boards of the *Journal of Consumer Research, Journal of the Academy of Marketing Science,* and *Journal of Public Policy and Marketing.*

**William O. Bearden,** the Bank of America Chaired Professor of Marketing at the University of South Carolina, received his PhD from the University of South Carolina in 1975 and served on the faculty of the University of Alabama from 1976 to 1978. He has published frequently in the *Journal of Marketing Research* and the *Journal of Consumer Research,* as well as having a number of publications in other marketing and consumer research journals. He coauthored *Marketing Principles and Perspectives* (with Thomas N. Ingram and Raymond W. LaForge, 3rd ed., 2001) and the *Handbook of Marketing Scales: Multi-Item Measures for Marketing and Consumer Behavior Research* (with Richard Netemeyer, 2nd ed., 1999). He is currently on the editorial review boards of the *Journal of Consumer Research,* the *Journal of Marketing,* the *Journal of Consumer Psychology,* the *Journal of Retailing,* and the *Marketing*

*Education Review.* He was an associate editor for the *Journal of Consumer Research* (1999-2002). His awards for teaching included the University of South Carolina Amoco Teaching Award, presented annually to one faculty member; the Outstanding MBA Teacher Award; and the Alfred G. Smith Darla Moore School of Business Teacher of the Year Award. His teaching and research interests include consumer behavior, marketing research, and the evaluation of marketing promotions. He was faculty codirector for the University Lilly Teaching Fellows from 1992 to 1995.

**Subhash Sharma** received his PhD from the University of Texas at Austin in 1978. He is a Professor of Marketing and Charles W. Coker Sr. Distinguished Foundation Fellow in the Moore School of Business at the University of South Carolina. His research interests include research methods, structural equation modeling, pricing, customer relationship management, and e-commerce. He has published numerous articles in leading academic journals such as the *Journal of Marketing, Journal of Marketing Research, Marketing Science, Management Science,* and *Journal of Retailing.* He has also authored *Applied Multivariate Techniques* (1996). He reviews for a number of journals and is on the editorial reviews boards of the *Journal of Marketing, Journal of Marketing Research,* and *Journal of Retailing.*